The Labyrinth of
Narcissism

The Labyrinth of Narcissism

"Journey Through a Toxic Kaleidoscope"

By

Gary Woods

Publisher: Vanguard Publishing House

The Labyrinth of Narcissism

"Journey Through a Toxic Kaleidoscope"

By
Gary Woods
PsychPositivity.Com

ISBN: 978-1-0683446-1-9

Publisher: **Vanguard Publishing House**

Publication Date: April 2025

For permissions requests or inquiries, please contact:

info@vanguardpublishinghouse.com

Disclaimer

This book is based on personal experiences and research. It is only intended for informational purposes and does not replace any professional advice. The names, characters, and events described may have been changed to protect the privacy of individuals. Any resemblance to actual persons, living or dead, is purely coincidental.

The opinions expressed are those of the author and do not reflect the views of any institution or organisation. Readers are encouraged to consult a qualified professional for individual specific advice or support.

To my beloved parents,

Jim and Sybil,

whose love, wisdom, and support shaped me into who I am today. Your presence in my life will always be cherished, and your memory will live on in everything I do.

To my children, grandchildren, and our dog.

Carl, Sasha, Freya, Sienna, and my trusted Siddy Boy

who inspire me every day to continue on this journey providing growth and healing. Your strength, love and support keep me moving forward, and I dedicate this work to you all with all my heart.

To my brother,

Jim,

for his unwavering love and support. Your strength has been a constant source of comfort, and I am forever grateful for everything you do, and have done for me.

To my wonderful friends,

Martin and Sam,

for standing by me through both the light and the dark times. Your friendship and support have helped guide me through some of my toughest moments, and I am forever thankful for you

This book is for you all

Author's Note

As you make your way through *The Labyrinth of Narcissism*, you'll notice recurring patterns and behaviours appearing in various chapters.

Each chapter dives into specific aspects of narcissism and its impact, but they're designed to stand alone. This way, you can explore them in any order you prefer, gaining new perspectives on the same traits.

Traits like grandiosity, lack of empathy, arrogance, manipulation, emotional detachment, and more, will pop up here and there — this is intentional. It's all about helping you see the bigger picture and understanding how narcissistic tendencies play out across different types of narcissism and areas of life, from relationships to the workplace, and everything in between.

Table of Contents

1: Entering the Labyrinth   23 - 28

Introduction to Narcissism and the Complex Journey Ahead

An Introduction to narcissism as both a personality trait and a disorder, including its historical context and the idea of the labyrinth as a symbol.

2: Transcending the Psyche   29 - 40

Clinical Diagnostic Criteria for Narcissistic Personality Disorder (NPD)

A focus on the diagnostic criteria, assessment tools, and distinctions between narcissism and healthy self-esteem.

3: Unravelling the Core   41 - 48

Narcissistic Personality Disorder (NPD): Symptoms and Emotional Development

A detailed examination of NPD, including symptoms and the emotional development of narcissists.

4: The Neural Labyrinth of the Mind   49 - 58

Neuroscientific Insights into Narcissism

How Narcissists see themselves and other people in terms of self-image and superiority. Cognitive processes behind narcissism and the potential for neuroplasticity in treatment.

5: Mapping the Labyrinth's Pathways   59 - 74

Indexing Various Forms of Narcissism and Their Manifestations in Brief

A short comparison of the various types of narcissism with real life case examples.

6: The Grand Façade   75 - 86

Grandiose Narcissism and the Illusion of Superiority

A deeper exploration of the inflated self-image, entitlement, and charm that defines grandiose narcissism.

7: The Spotlight Seeker   87 - 96

Overt Narcissism and the Need for Constant Validation

Examining the outward arrogance and unrelenting demand for admiration that define overt narcissism.

8: The Hidden Corridor   97 - 108

Covert Narcissism and Subtler Manipulations

A deep dive into the manipulative tactics of covert narcissists and how to manage them.

9: The Selfless Mask   109 - 120

Communal Narcissism and the Hidden Desire for Recognition

Examining the complex blend of altruism and self-interest that defines communal narcissism.

10: The Glorified Mirror 121 - 130

Somatic Narcissism and the Obsession with Appearance

Examining somatic narcissism, where physical appearance and validation through beauty dominate self-worth.

11: The Realm of the Mind 131 - 140

Cerebral Narcissism and Intellectual Superiority

An exploration of cerebral narcissism and how intellectual superiority shape's identity and relationships.

12: The Shadowed Pathway 141 - 152

Malignant Narcissism's Dark and Dangerous Traits

Exploring malignant narcissism and its destructive traits, including aggression, paranoia and sadism.

13: The Dark Mask 153 - 164

Psychopathic Narcissism and Calculated Deception

Investigating the manipulative, remorseless traits of psychopathic narcissism and their real-world impact.

14: Distorted Reflections 165 - 178

Narcissism and Co-occurring Disorders

Examining the relationship between narcissism and other mental health disorders.

15: Lost in the Labyrinth   179 - 186

Denial and Ego After Narcissistic Abuse

An exploration of how survivors of narcissistic abuse navigate denial, self-deception, and the complex interplay of ego as they process their trauma.

16: The Labyrinth of Lost Souls   187 - 200

Narcissistic Personality Disorder: Perception of Victimhood and Despair

Exploring narcissists' self-perception as victims, their emotional turmoil, and the impact on relationships.

17: Tangled Intersections   201 - 214

Narcissism in Romantic, Familial, and Friendly Relationships

How narcissism distorts romantic, familial, and friendship dynamics, leaving emotional scars and shattered connections.

18: The Puppet and the Master   215 - 232

Who's Who in the Narcissist's Labyrinth

Unravelling the complex roles in the labyrinth of narcissistic relationships

19: The Veiled Strategies   233 - 258

Manipulative Tactics of the Narcissist

A look at various manipulative tactics used by narcissists.

20: The Narcissistic Cycle 259 - 272

Twists and Turns of Idealisation, Devaluation, and Discard

An overview of the cycle of abuse in narcissistic relationships and its psychological impact.

21: The Unseen Traps 273 - 282

Co-dependency and Empathy in Narcissistic Relationship

Understanding co-dependency dynamics and strategies for building emotional independence.

22: Inheriting the Labyrinth 283 - 296

Children of Narcissists and the Generational Cycle

Exploring the generational impact of narcissism and pathways to healing.

23: The Psychological Pitfalls 297 - 308

Narcissism's Impact on Mental Health

Mental health effects for both narcissists and their victims.

24: Shifting Walls of the Labyrinth 309 - 316

Echoes of the Digital Abyss: Narcissism in the Digital Age

The influence of social media on narcissistic behaviour and self-protection.

25: Finding the Way Out   317 - 328

Treatment and Management of NPD: Therapeutic Interventions

Overview of therapeutic interventions for narcissism.

26: Guarding the Entrance   329 - 342

Red Flags, Prevention, and Awareness of Narcissistic Traits

Raising awareness to foster healthy relationships.

27: Escaping the Labyrinth   343 - 350

Recovery, Healing, and Self-Care after Narcissistic Abuse

Strategies for overcoming narcissistic abuse and rebuilding self-esteem.

28: Journeys Through the Labyrinth   351 - 358

Case Studies of Narcissistic Behaviour

Case studies highlighting the complexities of narcissistic behaviour and recovery.

29: Reflections from the Labyrinth   359 - 372

Personal Reflections from My Own Journey Through the Abyss

Final personal reflections on narcissism's complexities, its impact, and my personal journey toward understanding and healing.

"The wound is where the light enters you"

– Rumi

Preface

Navigating the Labyrinth:

Writing *The Labyrinth of Narcissism* has been both a deeply personal journey and a labour of love. My own experiences of navigating the emotional traps laid by a narcissist inspired me to create this book — not just as a means of understanding my own journey, but as a way to help other people find their way out of the labyrinth.

This book isn't just about exposing the dark corners of narcissistic abuse; it's about reclaiming your voice and your freedom. It's about shedding light on the manipulation, deceit, and control that can leave even the strongest people questioning their reality. Most importantly, it's about finding the courage to step out of the labyrinth and into the light of healing and self-discovery.

I'd like to thank you all for trusting me to guide you on this journey. Whether you're trying to understand what's happened to you, break free, or support someone else, I hope these pages give you clarity, incentive, and hope.

Gary Woods

Introduction

Welcome to the Labyrinth:

What makes narcissistic abuse so insidious is its invisibility. Unlike physical abuse, it leaves no outward visible scars — only the deep wounds of confusion, self-doubt, and despair. *The Labyrinth of Narcissism* is a book about understanding, surviving, and ultimately escaping the mental and emotional labyrinth created by a narcissist.

This book is divided into two main parts. The first focuses on recognising the labyrinth: the patterns, tactics, and behaviours of a narcissist, and understanding the ways they manipulate and control. The second part is about finding your way out, offering practical tools for healing and rebuilding your life after narcissistic abuse.

Throughout these pages, you'll find insights, personal reflections, and strategies for reclaiming your sense of self. Whether you're just beginning to recognise the dynamics of narcissistic abuse or are well into your healing journey; my hope is that this book becomes both a guide and a source of solace, empowering you to take the first steps towards freedom.

Gary Woods.

Chapter 1

Entering the Labyrinth

Introduction to Narcissism and the Complex Journey Ahead

An introduction to narcissism as both a personality trait and a disorder, including its historical context and the idea of the labyrinth as a symbol

The labyrinth of narcissism isn't just a labyrinth of twisted hallways — it's a journey through the complex intersections of personality, behaviour, and control. Narcissism has captured the attention of many, but it's more than a trendy label for difficult people. It's a deeply rooted psychological concept that shapes the understanding of personality and behaviour.

In my own journey, I've come across people who at first glance seemed charming, confident, even magnetic. It took years — and a lot of painful lessons — to recognise these traits as part of something far more sinister: narcissistic manipulation.

Personal Reflection:

Looking back, I didn't know I was entering a labyrinth when I first met the woman, I thought I'd spend the rest of my life with. She was confident, alluring, and knew how to make me feel like the most important person in the world. I didn't realise that beneath the surface, her need for control and admiration was setting me up for an emotional trap that'd take years to escape.

For a lot of people, the initial allure of charm and confidence quickly spirals into a darker reality, as seen in experiences like this. Throughout this book I'll navigate the winding paths of narcissistic behaviour.

You'll learn how narcissism manifests in various forms, how to recognise its signs, and most importantly, how to protect yourself from falling into its traps.

In this chapter, I'll lay the groundwork for understanding narcissism by exploring its historical origins, how our perception has evolved, the key traits that define it, and the implications it holds for everyday life.

Understanding this progression is essential. It highlights how something that starts as a natural part of development can spiral into behaviour that's harmful, not just to the individual but to the people around them.

So, buckle up! Understanding narcissism isn't just an academic exercise; it's crucial for recognising its impact on relationships, workplaces, and communities.

As you journey through *The Labyrinth of Narcissism*, you'll notice it's divided into sections, each shedding light on a unique aspect of narcissism. This structure will help you unravel the complexities of narcissism and its impact on our lives.

I'll start by setting the stage and looking at where narcissism comes from and how people's views on it have changed over time. Then, I'll dive into the different ways narcissism shows up, from obvious behaviours to more subtle ones, and explore what really drives narcissistic behaviour.

As we move forward, I'll explore how narcissism shows up in relationships — whether romantic, family-based, or friendships — and share practical tips on how to handle these challenges.

I'll also look at how narcissism impacts mental health, explore ways to treat it, and discuss strategies to protect yourself from narcissistic influence.

In the final sections, I'll focus on recovery, providing tools and strategies to help you rebuild your self-esteem, and take back control after dealing with narcissistic abuse.

Each chapter is created to give you clear insights, practical advice, and a better understanding of narcissism, so you can navigate this complex topic with confidence and clarity.

The idea of narcissism traces back to Greek mythology, where Narcissus was so captivated by his own reflection that he couldn't tear himself away. But today, we're looking beyond just vanity; we're exploring a phenomenon that impacts various aspects of our lives.

Imagine walking through a labyrinth with confusing twists and turns, shifting walls, and every step leading deeper into a labyrinth of uncertainty. Narcissistic abuse feels just like this labyrinth; it's unpredictable, disorienting, and full of dead ends.

Understanding Narcissism

Understanding narcissism is a journey where each turn offers deeper insight into its true nature. Some paths seem familiar, while others lead to darker corners of manipulation, grandiosity, and emotional detachment.

To guard against narcissism effectively, we need to understand what it entails.

Narcissism is viewed on a spectrum, with healthy self-esteem at one end and narcissistic personality disorder (NPD) at the other. While not everyone displaying narcissistic traits has NPD, these traits can still significantly impact relationships.

Key Characteristics of Narcissism Include

- **Grandiosity:**

A tendency to overestimate your own importance and abilities.

- **Need for Admiration:**

A constant craving for attention and validation from other people.

- **Lack of Empathy:**

Difficulty in recognising or caring about the feelings and needs of other people.

- **Entitlement:**

The belief that you're worthy of special treatment or consideration.

- **Exploitation of Other People:**

Exploiting other people for selfish benefit, with little or no consideration for their emotions.

- **Envy and Arrogance:**

Feeling envious of other people's successes while believing that you're superior.

By understanding these traits, we can identify potential red flags in our interactions, which is crucial for protecting ourselves from emotional manipulation.

The Wounds That Never Heal

One key aspect in understanding narcissistic behaviour is the idea that a narcissist's wounds rarely if ever heal. Unlike other people who confront their pain and grow, a narcissist avoids healing by numbing their emotions, dismissing their vulnerabilities, and perpetually looking for external validation. They become experts in masking their pain, but the wound festers just beneath the surface.

This perpetual cycle of emotional avoidance means their need for admiration is unrelenting.

They might seem untouchable, but their dependence on validation is what keeps them trapped. They're literally addicted to praise, admiration, and attention, looking for sources of external affirmation to fill the void left by their unresolved pain.

When they fail to receive this admiration, or worse, face criticism or rejection, the wound reopens, sparking a rage that's disproportionate to the situation.

Narcissism has come a long way in psychology. It's no longer just about being self-absorbed; it now includes a range of traits and behaviours that can deeply affect people and society.

Let's start unravelling the nuances of narcissism, how it manifests in today's world, and its impact on our lives.

Remember: "Knowledge is power."

Chapter 2

Transcending the Psyche

Clinical Diagnostic Criteria for Narcissistic Personality Disorder (NPD)

A focus on the diagnostic criteria, assessment tools, and distinctions between narcissism and healthy self-esteem

Understanding Narcissistic Personality Disorder (NPD) can be overwhelming, but breaking it down makes it easier to understand. Recognising the signs of NPD is crucial, whether you're identifying it in yourself, someone else, or searching for help because of its effects.

Guidelines like those in the DSM-5 (Diagnostic and Statistical Manual of Mental Disorders, Fifth Edition) and the ICD-11 (International Classification of Diseases, 11th Edition) are used to diagnose NPD. These guidelines focus on a pattern of long-term behaviours that typically show up in early adulthood and can have a major impact on relationships, work, and self-perception.

Personal Reflection:

When I first fell for her, everything felt like a dream. She had a way of making me feel loved and adored; it was intoxicating. But as the relationship progressed, I began to realise that love, for her, was more about possession than connection. Her affection was conditional, tied to my compliance with her needs and expectations.

What Makes Narcissistic Personality Disorder Different?

NPD is more than just being self-centred or overly confident — it's a personality disorder that impacts how a person interacts with the world. At its core, NPD revolves around three key traits — grandiosity (believing they are superior to other people), a constant need for admiration, and a lack of empathy for other people's feelings. Let's look at how professionals define this condition using the two main diagnostic tools: the DSM-5 and ICD-11.

DSM-5 Criteria for NPD in Plain Terms:

The DSM-5 is widely used in the U.S. and lists specific traits to identify NPD. To be diagnosed, someone has to consistently show at least five of the following traits over a long period across different areas of their life:

1.   Inflated Self-Importance:

They might brag about their achievements or expect to be treated as special even when they haven't done anything remarkable. As an example, they might expect other people to defer to their opinions or give them preferential treatment in every situation.

2.   Obsessed with Fantasies of Success and Power:

Their daydreams might revolve around being the best in their field, having unlimited wealth, or achieving "perfect" love. They might constantly talk about how they're destined for greatness.

3.   Believing They are Special and Unique:

They see themselves as being better than other people and think only certain high-status people can understand or relate to them. For instance, they might insist that only the "best" doctor or therapist is good enough for them.

4.   Constantly Needing Praise:

They crave admiration and validation from other people, fishing for compliments or putting other people down to make themselves look better. Their self-esteem depends heavily on external approval.

5.   Feeling Entitled:

They expect special treatment, whether at work, in social situations, or at home. If they don't get what they feel they deserve, they can react with anger or frustration.

6.   Using Other People for Personal Gain:

They exploit people to achieve their goals, disregarding the harm it causes them. For example, they might use a friend's connections to get ahead at work without any concern for how their actions impact that friend.

7.   Lacking Empathy:

A defining trait of NPD is a lack of empathy. Narcissists struggle to recognise or understand the feelings and needs of other people. When someone close to them is upset, they often dismiss their emotions or accuse them of being "too sensitive.

8.   Envying Other People or Believing Other People Envy Them:

They often resent someone else's success or happiness or assume people are jealous of them without any evidence to support it.

9.   Arrogant or Condescending behaviour:

They come across as smug or superior, belittling other people and acting as if they're always right.

To meet the criteria for NPD, these behaviours have to be consistent, widespread, and cause significant problems in the person's life, particularly in relationships or work.

ICD-11's Take on NPD

The ICD-11 is used more internationally and takes a broader approach. It focuses less on listing specific traits and more on how a person's behaviours and sense of self affect their daily life. According to the ICD-11, a narcissist's inflated sense of self-worth and need for validation often lead to difficulties in forming healthy relationships, functioning at work, or handling everyday challenges.

This system highlights "maladaptive behaviour," which means the narcissist's actions don't just cause harm to other people — they also prevent the narcissist from living a balanced, fulfilling life. For example, their constant need to feel superior can make it impossible for them to form genuine connections with other people or handle setbacks appropriately.

How the DSM-5 and ICD-11 Differ

Both systems agree on the key traits of NPD — grandiosity, entitlement, and lack of empathy — but they approach diagnosis differently. The DSM-5 breaks things down into specific observable behaviours, making it easier to identify patterns. The ICD-11 on the other hand, focuses more on how these behaviours affect the person's overall functioning. While the DSM-5 looks at behaviours in isolation, the ICD-11 emphasises the broader impact of these behaviours on the person's life and relationships.

The Role of Diagnosis in Understanding NPD

While a clinical diagnosis of NPD can be helpful for both personal insight and therapeutic intervention, it's important to note that not everyone exhibiting narcissistic traits has NPD.

A lot of people display some narcissistic tendencies without meeting the full criteria for a personality disorder. Understanding the criteria is crucial for distinguishing between someone who might be temporarily exhibiting self-centred behaviour, and someone whose behaviours are consistent, ingrained, and damaging to themselves, and other people.

NPD is a complex, multifaceted disorder that requires a complex understanding. Its traits can sometimes be subtle or masked by the person's outward charm or high-functioning persona, making it hard to spot. However, when the criteria are met, and the behaviours are disruptive, it's essential to acknowledge the disorder for what it is, so that appropriate steps — whether through therapy or self-care strategies — can be taken.

Psychological Assessments and Tools Used to Diagnose NPD

Diagnosing Narcissistic Personality Disorder (NPD) is a complex and delicate process, requiring a deep dive into a person's behavioural patterns, emotional responses, and personal interactions. Unlike more straightforward mental health conditions, NPD is hidden beneath these layers of grandiosity, self-importance, and denial. It's essential to look beyond the narcissist's defensive posturing and assess their psychological state using reliable and well-established diagnostic tools.

The Role of Clinical Interviews

One of the most effective ways to diagnose NPD is through a clinical interview. This is typically conducted by a trained mental health professional, like a psychologist or psychiatrist, who can ask probing questions that help uncover the underlying thought patterns and behaviours that characterise narcissism. These interviews focus on understanding a person's self-perception, interactions with other people, and their emotional responses to various situations.

During the interview, the professional will try to identify the hallmark traits of NPD, like an excessive need for admiration, a lack of empathy, a sense of entitlement, and the tendency to exploit other people for personal gain.

It's not just about asking direct questions, but about reading between the lines, observing the narcissist's reactions, and noticing subtle contradictions in how they present themselves, versus their underlying feelings.

The challenge is that most narcissists are very skilled at presenting a carefully polished image of themselves — one that possibly doesn't fully align with the reality of their internal struggles and masks the extent of their disorder. As such, this diagnostic tool is normally combined with other methods for an even clearer picture.

Self-Report Questionnaires and Personality Inventories

In addition to clinical interviews, there's a number of self-report questionnaires and personality assessments that can help screen for NPD. These are designed to identify someone's self-reported behaviours, attitudes, and emotional experiences.

One tool used is called the Narcissistic Personality Inventory (NPI). The NPI is a series of statements about narcissistic traits, and people are asked to agree or disagree with each statement. This provides an insight into their self-perception, their need for admiration, and their interactions with other people.

While these assessments are valuable, they do have limitations.
For instance, narcissists are highly skilled at self-presentation, allowing them to downplay or deny their more destructive tendencies in self-report questionnaires. This is why these questionnaires are seldom used on their own and are generally paired with a more thorough clinical assessment.

Projective Tests: Exploring the Subconscious

Projective tests are another way of figuring out if someone has narcissistic personality disorder. These tests work by digging into the unconscious parts of their mind, using things like pictures or abstract images. They're asked to interpret what they see, and their response provides a window into how they process emotions, relationships, and internal conflicts.

One of the most famous projective tests is the Rorschach Inkblot Test, where someone looks at a series of inkblot images and explains what they see. Their interpretations can reveal a lot about their emotional state and personality traits, including any narcissistic tendencies. For instance, narcissists can try to project their feelings of grandiosity or superiority onto the inkblots, showing how they view themselves and the world around them.

While these kinds of tests provide useful insights into someone's subconscious, they need to be handled carefully. They're only a small part of a bigger picture, so it's best to use them alongside other forms of assessment to get a clearer understanding of the person.

The Role of Family and Relationship Dynamics

Another key factor in diagnosing NPD is examining family and relationship patterns. Narcissism fundamentally affects relationships and understanding the way someone interacts with close family members, friends, and romantic partners can shed light on the extent of their narcissistic traits. Sometimes, the people closest to the narcissist can identify behaviours that align with NPD — like manipulation, exploitation, and a lack of empathy — but these are only fully understood when looked at in accordance with the person's overall relationship patterns.

A family history, especially from early childhood, can provide critical clues.

Was the person raised in an environment where love and attention were conditional?

Were they frequently compared to other people or held to impossibly high standards?

Did they grow up in an environment where they were neglected with a failed sense of security and self-worth?

These kinds of experiences can shape how someone sees themselves and their place in the world.

If a child learns that they need to "earn" love through success or perfection, they can grow into an adult who seeks admiration and validation as a way to fill that emotional void.

The Challenges of Diagnosing Narcissistic Personality Disorder

Diagnosing NPD is no easy task. Narcissists rarely see themselves as having a problem and actively resist the idea that something might be wrong. They normally react with anger, denial, or defensiveness if someone suggests or implies that their behaviour isn't normal. This makes it tough for professionals to get a complete and honest assessment.

What's more, narcissism often doesn't exist in isolation. A lot of people with NPD also struggle with other issues like depression, anxiety, or substance abuse. These additional problems can mask or complicate the signs of narcissism. For example, a narcissist who's also dealing with depression might come across as withdrawn or moody, making their grandiosity and entitlement less obvious at first glance.

The Defence Mechanism: The Inner Struggles Behind the Mask

One of the most important things to understand about narcissists is that their outward behaviour often hides deeper insecurities.

What looks like confidence or arrogance on the surface is usually a way of protecting themselves from feelings of vulnerability or inadequacy.

- **Grandiosity: A Shield Against Shame:**

Grandiosity serves as the first line of defence against the vulnerability that they constantly feel. This inflated self-image is like an armour, designed to shield them from the underlying shame and fear of being unworthy.

When a narcissist projects this larger-than-life persona, they're not just looking for attention; they're trying to convince themselves that they're valuable and deserving of admiration.

But the armour comes at a price. In order to maintain the illusion of superiority, narcissists engage in constant self-promotion, manipulation, and the devaluation of other people.

They have to perpetually be seen as more than they are, because their sense of self is fragile, unstable, and easily shattered.

Beneath the manufactured exterior is someone who's terrified of being seen as ordinary, or worse, insignificant, which drives much of their behaviour.

The Fragile Nature of Narcissistic Self-Esteem

The relationship between narcissism and self-esteem is complex, revealing deeper insecurities.

Not all narcissists are the same. Some display an outward confidence that masks their inner struggles, while others have a more fragile self-esteem that makes them highly sensitive to criticism. Regardless of the type, most narcissists rely heavily on external validation to maintain their self-image.

- **Inflated Self-Esteem:**

Grandiose narcissists display an exaggerated sense of self-worth. They project confidence, but this is a facade masking feelings of inadequacy. Their inflated self-esteem serves as a shield against the inner doubts that they're trying to escape, presenting a confident front to the world while struggling internally.

- **Fragile Self-Esteem:**

On the other hand, vulnerable narcissists have a much more fragile sense of self. They're highly sensitive to criticism and often experience self-doubt.

Their narcissistic behaviours act as a defence, helping them protect their self-image from external threats. Inside, they're constantly fighting to maintain a positive view of themselves, even when it's built on shaky ground.

- **The Constant Struggle for Validation:**

Ever wonder how narcissists maintain their sense of self-esteem? It's a bit of a balancing act. They rely on external sources — looking for approval from other people, showcasing their achievements, or minimising their shortcomings.

These behaviours heavily influence how they relate to people, making their relationships complex. When self-esteem is built on other people's opinions, it traps them in a loop of needing constant validation, which can be exhausting for them, and everyone around them.

This creates a vicious cycle: they seek constant approval from other people to feel good about themselves, but no amount of praise is ever enough to fill the emptiness they feel inside.

Over time, this need for validation strains their relationships and leaves them feeling isolated and unfulfilled.

Conclusion: Piecing Together the Puzzle

Understanding and diagnosing narcissistic personality disorder is like putting together a puzzle. No single test or tool can give you the full picture.

Instead, it requires a combination of methods — questionnaires, projective tests, clinical interviews, and an in-depth look at family and relationship dynamics.

Even then, diagnosing NPD can be tricky. The narcissist's resistance to self-awareness, combined with the complexity of their inner struggles, makes it a challenging process. But by taking a comprehensive approach and considering both their outward behaviours and deeper insecurities, it's possible to uncover the truth about their personality.

For people dealing with narcissists — whether as friends, family members, or professionals — this understanding is invaluable. Recognising the patterns of NPD not only helps explain the narcissist's behaviour but also empowers other people to make informed decisions about how to navigate these relationships in a healthy way.

Chapter 3

Unravelling the Core

Narcissistic Personality Disorder (NPD): Symptoms and Emotional Development

A detailed examination of NPD, including symptoms and the emotional development of narcissists

Narcissistic Personality Disorder, (NPD), is often misunderstood or misdiagnosed, but its impact on relationships and mental health is profound. Understanding the symptoms and diagnostic criteria is key to recognising narcissism in the people around us.

Personal Reflection:

When I first began training in psychology and researching narcissism, I couldn't quite believe that the person I had loved fit the clinical definition of comorbid personality disorders. It seemed too extreme, too clinical. But the more I read about the symptoms the more I began to see that I wasn't just dealing with difficult behaviour. I'd been entangled with someone whose entire identity was built around multiple traits.

This personal journey shows just how complex narcissistic traits can be, hiding in plain sight before fully revealing their impact.

In this chapter I'll break down the clinical aspects of NPD, helping you to identify its signs and to better understand the diagnostic process, both in formal assessments and everyday encounters.

The Core Characteristics of Narcissism

Narcissism is a term used casually in everyday conversation, but it's not just a label that we throw around. It's actually a complex psychological concept encompassing a range of traits and behaviours that vary in intensity.

When it comes to mental health, there's a significant difference between normal narcissistic traits, and narcissistic personality disorder. While some level of self-importance and confidence is natural, these traits become concerning when they disrupt relationships, social functioning, or overall well-being.

Narcissistic personality disorder is a misunderstood mental health condition. It's characterised by persistent grandiosity, a need for excessive admiration, and a lack of empathy. People with NPD see themselves as superior and believe they're entitled to special treatment. These traits can affect multiple areas of their lives, causing significant distress or impairments in their ability to function.

NPD Versus Normal Narcissistic Traits

It's important to understand that not all narcissistic traits indicate NPD. Normal narcissism is a natural part of human development and an essential part of self-esteem. For example, feeling pride in achievements or looking for validation is common, and to some degree, beneficial for personal growth and motivation.

However, these traits become problematic when they intensify and disrupt someone's ability to maintain healthy relationships, function effectively in social settings, or lead a fulfilling life.

This distinction is key to identifying whether someone's behaviour reflects normal narcissistic tendencies or something more severe.

The Spectrum of Narcissism

Narcissism exists on a spectrum — it's not a black-and-white issue. At one end are traits like confidence and assertiveness, which can be positive and even helpful in achieving personal and professional success. On the other end, these same traits can escalate into behaviours that disrupt daily life and relationships.

Understanding this spectrum helps distinguish between normal tendencies and the behaviours associated with narcissistic personality disorder. Recognising where someone falls on this range allows for greater self-awareness and provides a framework for identifying when support or intervention might be necessary.

Defining Key Differences Between Normal Narcissism and NPD

- **Entitlement:**

One of the primary and prominent characteristics of narcissism is an exaggerated sense of entitlement. People with narcissistic traits in "everyday life" might feel like they deserve special treatment in certain situations, but this doesn't usually lead to exploitative behaviour.

However, when it comes to NPD, this sense of entitlement is on a whole other level. These people tend to harbour an unreasonable belief that they deserve special treatment, and that other people should automatically meet their expectations and needs without question. This creates an environment where they believe rules simply don't apply to them.

This entitlement shows up in demands for special treatment, whether at work, in social situations, or within personal relationships, and it leads to frustration when their lofty expectations aren't met. Narcissists can become furious or deeply disappointed when things don't go the way they expect. It's common for them to lash out and become overly demanding because they're convinced that they deserve more than anyone else.

Whether it's demanding emotional support, expecting financial help, or simply trying to maintain their image, narcissists view other people as tools to be used for their own gain — whether that's personal goals, or boosting their self-image. They don't see other people as individuals with their own needs and feelings. They'll manipulate situations or people to push their agenda, ignoring the emotional, practical, and personal costs to the people they're using.

Understanding this sense of entitlement is crucial because it sheds light on how these unrealistic expectations shape their behaviour and affect their relationships. This not only diminishes their own satisfaction but also creates a toxic atmosphere for people in their vicinity.

- **Grandiosity:**

Let's talk about grandiosity, one of the key traits of narcissism. It's not just about having a big ego — it's about how narcissists view themselves. They see themselves as more important than other people and believe they deserve special attention.

Grandiosity can show up in two main ways. Some narcissists are very obvious about it — they brag about their achievements, constantly fish for compliments, and make sure everyone knows how great they think they are. These people need to be admired and will go out of their way to stay in the spotlight.

Then, there's a more subtle side to grandiosity. While they might not openly brag, their actions still reveal their belief in their superiority. They manipulate people or situations to serve their own needs, without saying it directly.

Grandiosity explains much of a narcissist's behaviour and how their inflated self-view harms relationships. It's a key reason why they struggle to connect meaningfully with other people.

- **Grandiosity and Self-Perception:**

In normal narcissism, people might feel proud of their achievements or unique qualities but don't necessarily believe they're superior to other people.

They can have healthy self-esteem and confidence without needing to belittle other people to feel validated.

In contrast, people with NPD have a constant need to feel superior, belittling other people to maintain their sense of grandiosity.

- **Need for Admiration:**

Now let's explore the need for admiration. One of the most prominent red flags of NPD is an overwhelming need for constant attention and validation. Narcissists don't just feel special — they rely on praise and acknowledgment to sustain their self-worth. This is a significant driving force for these people.

Their self-esteem is closely tied to how other people see them, prompting them to seek affirmation and recognition relentlessly. They go to great lengths to be the centre of attention in any situation, sometimes resorting to manipulative behaviours to regain the admiration they crave.

Unlike normal narcissism, where occasional validation-seeking behaviours are balanced by other aspects of life, NPD makes this pursuit central to the detriment of relationships and personal well-being because this need becomes excessive and insatiable.

Being in the spotlight temporarily boosts their confidence, but when the expected admiration isn't received, frustration sets in.

This can lead to defensive reactions, manipulative tactics, and even hostility as they attempt to reclaim the validation, they believe they deserve.

Understanding this need is essential, as it highlights the lengths narcissists will go to for the admiration, they rely on to maintain their fragile sense of self-worth.

- **Exploitation of Other People:**

Exploitation of other people is a behaviour regularly engaged in by narcissists.

Their self-centred perspective leads them to engage in manipulation, looking for ways to fulfil their wants without considering the consequences for other people. This relentless focus on their own desires blinds them to the needs of the people around them.

This self-centred focus means that they have no compunction about walking all over other people to get what they want. This exploitation results in broken trust, once again contributing to damaged relationships, as other people start to feel exploited.

When people are consistently manipulated or used for personal gain, they begin to feel unappreciated, disrespected, and left questioning their own worth and feelings.

- **Envy and Arrogance:**

Envy and arrogance are two intertwined traits characteristic of narcissistic behaviour. Narcissists feel the need to undermine other people to elevate themselves. They tend to experience intense envy towards people who possess qualities or achievements that they crave.

Instead of celebrating other people's successes, they view them as threats. This envy then typically manifests as arrogance. They belittle other people in an attempt to reinforce their own inflated sense of superiority.

This toxic combination of envy and arrogance creates a cycle where they continually undermine the people around them to maintain their fragile self-esteem, making genuine connections almost impossible.

- **Superiority Complex:**

Narcissists tend to have a deep-seated belief that they're better than everyone else. They really think they're more capable, smarter, and better than everyone around them. This sense of superiority can lead them to dismiss or belittle other people, especially if they feel insecure or overlooked. When talking to people they see as inferior to them, they sometimes talk in a condescending way or with contempt.

They can't seem to accept that anyone else might be equally or more capable than they are. This inflated sense of self-importance results in them disregarding other people's opinions, feelings, or contributions. Criticism is hard for them to take — they're quick to dismiss it, firmly believing that their perspective is the only one that matters.

- **Manipulative Behaviour:**

Manipulation is a key tactic narcissists use to control the people around them. They can twist facts, distort reality, or use guilt to make other people comply with their demands. Manipulative behaviour can also include playing on someone's emotions or making them feel responsible for the narcissist's happiness or well-being. This can lead to feelings of confusion and self-doubt in the person being manipulated.

- **Emotional Outbursts and Anger:**

Narcissists tend to have low tolerance for criticism or any situation where their self-image is challenged. When this happens, they can respond with rage, arrogance, or passive-aggressive behaviour. These emotional outbursts can be disproportionate to the situation, and they can direct their anger towards other people, blaming them for their perceived failures.

If someone reacts with intense anger or hostility when confronted with minor issues, it's a warning sign. Narcissists have fragile egos, and even the smallest threat to their self-esteem can trigger an explosive reaction.

Why It Matters

Differentiating between normal narcissistic traits and NPD is crucial for both understanding and managing the disorder. Recognising that someone's behaviour goes beyond typical narcissism can help in securing the appropriate intervention. For people struggling with NPD or who find themselves affected by someone with these traits, understanding the distinction can be liberating — it offers a clearer path toward healing and self-protection.

Conclusion

While everyone can display a degree of narcissism, it's the intensity and prevalent nature of these traits that define narcissistic personality disorder.

NPD isn't merely about being self-centred or occasionally looking for admiration — it's a deeply ingrained pattern that affects how someone interacts with the world and the people around them. By understanding the differences between normal narcissism and pathological narcissism, we can better navigate the challenges that arise from both personal relationships and social aspects.

Chapter 4

The Neural Labyrinth of the Mind

Neuroscientific Insights into Narcissism

How narcissists see themselves and other people in terms of self-image and superiority. Cognitive processes behind narcissism and the potential for neuroplasticity in treatment

Narcissism isn't just a quirky personality trait; it's far more complex. It's not just a simple flaw in character or an overblown ego, but a deeply ingrained pattern of thoughts, feelings, and behaviours that are tied to the way the brain functions. Research shows that narcissism has its roots in brain structure, chemistry, and function, with certain neural processes that drive narcissistic tendencies.

The Narcissist's Self-Image

Perception of Other People and Over Inflated Ego

At the heart of narcissism is a distorted self-image. Narcissists view themselves as superior beings, entitled to admiration and special treatment. This inflated self-image goes beyond surface-level attitudes; it's deeply rooted in how their brains work. They see the world through a lens that enhances their own grandiosity, while downplaying the achievements and worth of other people. This twisted perspective makes it difficult for them to connect with those around them in a genuine way.

Narcissists show a bias in how they think about themselves and other people, inflating their sense of entitlement and importance. This distorted view of self isn't just psychological — it's shaped by specific neural pathways that focus on the self, often at the expense of other people.

Neuroscience suggests that narcissism is more than a personality quirk or learned behaviour — it's also linked to specific brain chemistry and development. It's rooted in biology.

Personal Reflection:

When I started studying psychology and digging into the science behind narcissism, it was a real eye opener. It wasn't just that she didn't want to empathise; I realised that her brain was actually wired up differently. The realisation hit home hard, but it made me see that no matter how hard I'd been trying, I was never going to change her. I could finally start letting go of the guilt she'd been trying to project onto me.

In this chapter, I'll explore the neuroscience of narcissism, explaining how the brain's structure and function contribute to narcissistic behaviours and emotional responses. I'll dive into the narcissistic mind, looking at how the brain shapes this personality and what new research tells us about brain patterns in people with narcissistic traits.

Cognitive Biases: The Filters of Narcissism

Cognitive biases are the shortcuts our brains use to make sense of the world. For narcissists, these biases can become extreme. They see themselves as grand and entitled, often dismissing any criticism as a personal attack, while accepting praise as proof of their superiority.

Emotional Regulation and Empathy: A Neurological Challenge

Imagine a narcissist being confronted with the consequences of their actions — perhaps they've hurt someone they care about. Instead of feeling remorse, they focus on how the situation affects them, unable to grasp the pain they've caused. This lack of empathy isn't necessarily a choice — it can be a product of how their brain works, prioritising self-preservation over emotional connection.

Understanding Narcissism Through a Neuroscientific Lens

When a healthy person receives feedback, they might reflect, learn, and grow. A narcissist, however, is more likely to reject criticism, blaming other people or external factors for any flaws. This inability to accept constructive feedback can prevent growth and harm relationships, creating a cycle that reinforces their self-centred beliefs.

Personal Reflection:

I always wondered why she never understood or cared about the pain she caused. It was as if her brain operated on a different wavelength when it came to emotions. The more I researched narcissism, the more I realised that her inability to empathise wasn't necessarily just a choice — it was ingrained. The neurological studies I've come across have helped me make sense of the sheer disconnect I experienced with her.

This personal reflection mirrors the experiences of many who have dealt with narcissists. It's easy to assume their behaviour is deliberate or cruel but understanding the neuroscience behind it reveals something much more complex. Their actions might not just be shaped by their environment but also by biological factors.

By learning about these brain differences, we can begin to understand the confusing behaviour of narcissists.

To truly grasp this phenomenon, we need to look deeper into how narcissism shapes perception, affects behaviour, and interacts with the brain's structure.

Let's dive into the key cognitive processes and neural factors that influence how narcissists view themselves, other people, and the world around them.

Neuroscientific Perspectives:

Thanks to advances in brain imaging techniques like fMRI and PET scans, we now have the ability to observe how certain parts of the brain function in people with narcissistic traits.

This new insight helps us understand that narcissism isn't just about personality — it's about brain chemistry and structure. These findings explain why narcissists struggle with empathy, emotional regulation, and self-awareness. Their brains are wired to focus on themselves, making it hard for them to form meaningful connections with other people.

The Anterior Insula, Posterior Cingulate Cortex, and Empathy:

The anterior insula and posterior cingulate cortex are areas of the brain involved in empathy and emotional awareness.

In narcissists, these areas often show reduced activity, which might explain why they have difficulty empathising with other people. Their brains don't register the emotional states of other people the way non-narcissists do, contributing to their manipulative, self-centred behaviour.

Narcissists tend to have an overactive insula when it comes to their own emotions, but the part of the insula responsible for empathising with other people is underactive. This makes it challenging for them to connect emotionally with other people, creating a barrier in relationships.

The Amygdala and Fear Responses:

The amygdala is responsible for emotional regulation, particularly in how we respond to fear and threats. In narcissists, the amygdala is often hyper-reactive, which explains why they tend to view even small criticisms as serious threats to their ego. Narcissists can react with anger or withdrawal when their self-image is challenged, as their amygdala triggers a stress response to protect their fragile self-esteem.

This heightened reactivity can lead to narcissistic rage — an intense and sudden emotional outburst caused by perceived threats to their self-worth. This is not just a temper flare-up; it's a neurological response that amplifies their emotional distress.

The Hippocampus and Memory Distortion:

The hippocampus, which is responsible for memory and emotional regulation, plays a unique role in narcissistic behaviour. Research suggests that narcissists may have differences in the hippocampus, leading them to prioritise memories that support their inflated self-image while dismissing or distorting negative feedback. This selective memory helps explain why narcissists exaggerate their accomplishments and downplay their failures.

This pattern of remembering only positive experiences — or rewriting their personal history — can make relationships difficult. It also explains why narcissists seem so focused on their own achievements and unaware of their shortcomings.

The Prefrontal Cortex and Emotional Regulation:

The prefrontal cortex helps us make decisions, control impulses, and regulate emotions. In narcissists, this area often functions less effectively, which could explain why they struggle with emotional control, especially when their sense of superiority is threatened. Narcissists often react impulsively instead of pausing to consider the broader context, making decisions based on emotion rather than reason.

Default Mode Network (DMN):

The Default Mode Network is active when we think about ourselves or daydream. In narcissists, this network is hyperactive, which makes them focus excessively on themselves. This overactivity reinforces their self-centred worldview, making it difficult for them to consider other peoples' perspectives or build meaningful relationships.

Superior Temporal Sulcus (STS): Social Perception and Understanding:

The superior temporal sulcus is important for interpreting social cues, such as facial expressions and tone of voice. In narcissists, dysfunction in the STS may impair their ability to read other peoples' emotions.

This dysfunction could contribute to their distorted view of relationships. Narcissists may see people more as tools to achieve their goals, rather than as individuals with their own needs and feelings.

Anterior Cingulate Cortex (ACC):

The ACC helps regulate emotions, monitor conflicts, and make decisions. Dysfunction in this area can cause narcissists to misinterpret feedback and struggle with emotional regulation, leading to behaviours like overestimating their achievements and deflecting criticism.

The Nucleus Accumbens (NAc): The Brain's Reward System:

The Nucleus Accumbens plays a crucial role in processing rewards and reinforcing pleasurable behaviours. For narcissists, this area is highly sensitive to social validation. Compliments and admiration trigger a pleasurable response, reinforcing their need for external approval. However, this dependence on validation can make them vulnerable to emotional distress when they don't receive the praise they expect.

A Complex Portrait of the Narcissistic Brain

Understanding narcissism as a product of brain chemistry and cognitive biases helps us view it in a more compassionate light. These neurological factors provide insight into why narcissists behave the way they do, and why their behaviour can feel so rigid and unchangeable.

It's important to recognise that narcissism isn't a reflection of your worth. The emotional disconnect you feel with a narcissist is often the result of their brain structure, not your value as a person.

So, what does this really mean?

It suggests that biological factors might be driving some of the behaviours we see in narcissists.

When these brain areas don't function as they should, it can warp how a person sees themselves and their ability to relate to other people. It indicates that narcissism isn't solely about personality traits; biological elements also play a crucial role.

Recognising this link is key to developing effective approaches for managing narcissistic behaviour and its effects on personal relationships and society at large.

Neuroplasticity and the Potential for Change

The big question for those affected by narcissistic abuse is, "Can narcissists change?" The answer lies in neuroplasticity — the brain's ability to reorganise itself and form new neural connections. While narcissistic traits can be deeply ingrained, there is hope. With the right therapy and effort, people with narcissistic traits can modify their behaviours and improve their emotional intelligence.

However, change is difficult. A core feature of narcissism is the belief that they don't need to change. To overcome this, narcissists have to first recognise their behaviour as a problem and be willing to work on it.

What Neuroscience Means for the Future of Narcissism

New therapies based on our understanding of the brain could offer hope for people with narcissistic traits.

Techniques that stimulate certain brain regions, like the prefrontal cortex, could improve emotional regulation and empathy, offering a path toward change.

As neuroscience advances, we could see more targeted treatments that address the structural differences in the brains of narcissists. These therapies could make a real difference for both narcissists and the people they affect.

Final Thoughts

Understanding the Neural Labyrinth:

This chapter makes it clear that narcissism is far more complex than just a personality trait — it's deeply rooted in how the brain is structured and how it functions. Understanding the neurological side of narcissistic behaviour helps explain why narcissists act the way they do and why changing that behaviour is so difficult. Their inability to emotionally connect with other people isn't simply a character flaw — it could be down to how their brain is wired.

Change is hard, but it's not impossible. The brain has the ability to adapt and reorganise itself — a process known as neuroplasticity — which means there's hope for change. But the biggest obstacle is recognising the need to change in the first place, and that's something narcissists struggle with because of their inflated sense of superiority. For people dealing with narcissistic abuse, understanding the neurological roots of this behaviour can bring a sense of clarity.

It helps make sense of the confusion and emotional pain caused by their actions and offers a more compassionate view without excusing the harm.

As research into narcissism and brain function continues, new therapies may develop to help narcissists break free from the rigid patterns of behaviour that hold them back.

But until those solutions are available, it's crucial for people affected by narcissism to prioritise their own emotional well-being. Seeking support, setting boundaries, and protecting themselves are essential when navigating these complicated and damaging relationships.

In the end, understanding narcissism is about balancing compassion with self-preservation. When we understand the brain behind the behaviour, we're in a stronger position to protect ourselves and build healthier, more meaningful relationships — free from the toxicity that comes with narcissistic abuse.

Chapter 5

Mapping the Labyrinth's Pathways

Indexing Various Forms of Narcissism and Their Manifestations in Brief

A short comparison of the various types of narcissism with real life case examples

In this chapter, I'll provide a brief overview of the different types of narcissism and their patterns — whether glaringly obvious or deceptively hidden.

This short breakdown will help you identify the type of narcissist in your life so you can jump straight to the in-depth chapter that's most relevant to your situation.

Understanding the Complexity of Narcissism

Narcissism manifests in various ways, from the obvious grandiosity of overt narcissism to the more subtle and insidious manipulation of covert narcissism.

Personal Reflection:

I always thought that narcissists were all about being loud and needing everyone's attention. It wasn't until I encountered a more covert narcissist that I realised how subtle and dangerous their manipulation could be. She never openly demanded admiration, but I always felt like I was walking on eggshells. The quiet criticisms and passive-aggressive behaviour left me feeling small, confused, and constantly looking for her approval.

Narcissism is far from a straightforward topic — it's a complex issue with a lot of layers and variations. It's not just a simple label we can place on someone; it manifests differently in everyone.

In this chapter, I'm going to explore the various types of narcissism you might encounter in everyday life. I'll dig into their psychological roots, the behaviours that emerge in social settings, and how these traits can be perceived in different cultures. By examining these various aspects of narcissism, we can better understand how they shape people's lives and their interactions with other people.

So, join me as I uncover how narcissism operates in our daily lives. Recognising these nuances is the first step in identifying and addressing its influence on our relationships. After all, knowledge is power; when you understand what you're dealing with, navigating the complexities of these interactions becomes much more manageable.

Types of Narcissism in Brief

Exploration of the Different Types of Narcissism

If we take a look at narcissism, we can see that it manifests itself in multiple forms. It's essential to recognise that it can be categorised into different types, each with its own unique traits, characteristics, and behavioural patterns.

While most people associate narcissism with an inflated ego and grandiosity, the manifestations can be far more complex.

In some cases, narcissistic traits can even blend with other troubling behaviours, such as sadism, or psychopathy, creating even more dangerous and difficult-to-recognise dynamics.

Broadly, narcissism can be classified into various types and subtypes like, grandiose, overt, covert, communal, somatic, cerebral, malignant, and psychopathic.

Understanding these distinctions is essential for recognising how narcissistic traits influence behaviour in different contexts and the people around them.

Grandiose and Overt Narcissism

Grandiose and overt narcissism are very similar and are often used interchangeably because both describe the more openly self-centred, confident, and attention-seeking type of narcissism.

While both terms describe similar characteristics, some psychologists use grandiose to emphasise the "magnitude" of the self-importance and superiority these individuals feel, whereas overt highlights the "visibility" of narcissistic traits. Overall, however, they refer to almost the same core personality type.

Grandiose Narcissism

First up is grandiose narcissism, the type most commonly associated with the term "narcissist." This form is characterised by an inflated sense of self-worth and an unquenchable need for admiration.

Key Traits of Grandiose Narcissism

- **Exaggerated Self-Importance:**

Grandiose narcissists have a tendency to centre everything around themselves. They boast about their achievements and expect other people to recognise their superiority without question. It's as if they want to shout: "Look at me! — I'm the best!"

- **Preoccupation with Fantasies of Success:**

These individuals lose themselves in grand visions of success, power, or brilliance. They pursue high-status goals with a relentless drive that can overwhelm the people around them. They thrive on validation from other people to sustain these ambitions.

- **Constant Need for Admiration:**

Grandiose narcissists can never seem to get enough attention.

They actively seek out admiration through ostentatious displays of wealth, status, or achievements. If they don't receive the accolades, they believe they deserve, they can become defensive or agitated.

- **Lack of Empathy:**

One of the most troubling aspects of grandiose narcissism is a significant deficit in empathy. This lack can lead to exploitative behaviours and a disregard for the feelings and needs of the people around them.

Case Example:

John, a successful entrepreneur, prides himself on being the "visionary" of his industry. At social gatherings, he regularly boasts about his business empire and tells elaborate stories about his achievements, often exaggerating details to make himself seem larger-than-life. John actively seeks admiration, surrounding himself with people who praise him, and becomes visibly agitated if someone challenges his claims or outshines him. For John, the focus has to always be on his brilliance, and he dismisses other peoples' successes as insignificant compared to his own.

Overt Narcissism

Overt narcissism is the most visible and recognisable form. People with overt narcissism display grandiosity, entitlement, and an obvious need for admiration. They crave attention, boast about their achievements, dominate conversations, and expect other people to acknowledge their superiority. Lacking empathy, they dismiss or belittle opposing opinions and believe they deserve special treatment. Though often extroverted and charismatic, their interactions are self-serving, and they exaggerate accomplishments to remain the centre of attention.

Key Traits of Overt Narcissism

- ### Grandiosity:

They have an inflated sense of self-importance, often exaggerating their achievements. They believe they deserve admiration and recognition, and any challenge to their superiority frustrates them.

- ### Attention-seeking:

They constantly crave attention and validation, dominating conversations. They feel empty without praise and can become upset if they don't remain the centre of attention.

- ### Entitlement:

They expect special treatment and believe they deserve privileges other people don't. If things don't go their way, they can become demanding or angry.

- ### Arrogance:

They act with superiority and dismiss other people's opinions, belittling those around them. Their arrogance isolates them and reinforces their inflated sense of self-importance.

Case Example:

Sarah presents herself as humble, frequently talking about how unfair life's been to her. She subtly criticises other people's achievements, often implying they had it easier or were more fortunate. While she constantly seeks reassurance from friends about her worth, she rarely reciprocates emotional support.

Covert (or Vulnerable / Hypersensitive) Narcissism

The Hidden, Introverted, and Vulnerable Forms of Narcissism

Now, let's shift our focus to covert narcissism, also known as vulnerable narcissism, or hypersensitive narcissism, which shares some traits with grandiose narcissism, but seems less visible. This type presents a different set of challenges:

Unlike overt narcissists, covert narcissists are more introverted and can appear insecure or self-effacing. However, they still possess the same underlying sense of entitlement and grandiosity, but it's expressed in subtler ways.

Key Traits of Covert Narcissism:

- ### Subtle Manipulation:

Covert narcissists excel in subtlety, using passive-aggressive tactics to manipulate situations without overt displays of grandiosity. This indirect approach allows them to seek attention or admiration without drawing too much notice.

- ### Victim Mentality:

They often present themselves as perpetual victims, leveraging their perceived suffering to elicit sympathy and attention. This strategy helps them connect with other people while masking their narcissistic tendencies.

- ### Self-Doubt and Insecurity:

Despite harbouring a sense of grandiosity, covert narcissists struggle with significant self-doubt and insecurity. This internal conflict shapes their behaviour, making them highly sensitive to external validation.

- **Fragile Self-Esteem:**

People with vulnerable narcissism typically battle with low self-esteem. Their narcissistic traits act as a defence mechanism against deep-seated insecurities. They're not merely putting on a brave front; they're trying to shield themselves from emotional harm.

- **Hypersensitivity to Criticism:**

Vulnerable narcissists react intensely to criticism or rejection. When their self-image is threatened, they can experience a range of emotions from shame to anger, which can be disproportionate to the situation.

- **Internalised Grandiosity:**

Unlike their grandiose counterparts, vulnerable narcissists don't openly display their sense of superiority. Instead, they might express their entitlement through self-pity, or a constant sense of victimisation, which reflects a complicated internal struggle.

- **Challenges in Relationships:**

Their hypersensitivity and need for constant reassurance complicate their relationships. They might feel misunderstood or invalidated, making interpersonal interactions especially challenging.

- **Passive-aggression:**

Covert narcissists regularly use passive-aggressive behaviours as a means of expressing their frustrations indirectly. Rather than openly confronting issues, they might sulk, or engage in subtle sabotage to show their dissatisfaction, without engaging in direct conflict.

- **Envy and Resentment:**

These people can harbour envy toward other people's success or happiness, this fuels their resentment. Their hidden bitterness can motivate their interactions while they struggle constantly with a sense of being overlooked or undervalued compared to other people.

Case Example:

James often portrays himself as shy and humble, rarely seeking attention. However, he frequently drops hints about his struggles, saying things like, "No one really understands what I go through." When other people achieve success, he becomes withdrawn, subtly undermining their accomplishments by saying, "It's easy for them; they have everything handed to them." If someone criticizes him, he reacts with hurt feelings and passive-aggressive remarks, leaving other people unsure of what went wrong.

Communal Narcissism

A Virtuous Facade with Hidden Self-Interest

Communal narcissists present themselves as kind-hearted people, but their selflessness is motivated by a need for validation and admiration. They engage in charitable work or community efforts, not for the benefit of other people, but to be seen as moral and virtuous. Their grandiosity comes from the belief that they're better, or more giving than other people.

Key Traits of Communal Narcissism

- **Grandiosity in Altruism:**

Communal narcissists perform good deeds, but their motivation is to be seen as morally superior. They believe that their charitable acts elevate them above other people in a moral or spiritual sense.

- **Exploitation of Good Deeds:**

Charitable actions or acts of kindness are seen as a means to gain admiration and validation. Their true motive isn't selflessness but rather self-glorification.

- **Entitlement:**

Despite their outwardly altruistic behaviour, they expect recognition and rewards for their good deeds. They may feel unappreciated or resentful if other people don't acknowledge their "generosity."

- **Lack of True Empathy:**

Their focus on how their actions reflect on themselves means they're often unable to fully empathise with the people they help. Their concern isn't really for the welfare of other people but for how they're seen by these other people.

Case Example:

Lisa frequently volunteers and posts about her charitable work on social media, expecting admiration for her generosity. While she promotes herself as selfless, she becomes upset when her efforts aren't praised, and she competes with other people for recognition in the community.

Somatic Narcissism

Obsession with Physical Appearance as a Source of Validation

Somatic narcissists focus on their physical appearance, using their body and attractiveness as a means to garner attention and admiration. They're obsessed with their looks, fitness, or health, and measure their worth based on external beauty.

Key Traits of Somatic Narcissism

- **Obsession with Physical Appearance:**

Somatic narcissists place excessive importance on their looks or physical strength. They constantly seek validation based on how they appear to other people and believe their attractiveness enhances their value.

- **Superficiality:**

They evaluate themselves and other people, primarily based on external attributes, like physical beauty or fitness. This leads them to prioritise appearance over deeper qualities such as personality or intellect.

- **Objectification of Other People:**

They may compare their own appearance to other people, treating them as either competitors or sources of admiration based on how they measure up physically.

- **Validation-Seeking:**

Somatic narcissists are preoccupied with receiving compliments and validation for their physical appearance. They may constantly check their reflection or post photos online to receive affirmation from other people.

Case Example:

Chris spends hours at the gym and posts shirtless photos on social media, fishing for compliments about his physique. He constantly compares his looks to other people and becomes envious or hostile when someone else is deemed more attractive.

Cerebral Narcissism

Pride in Intellectual Superiority and Dismissing Other People's Ideas

Cerebral narcissists pride themselves on their intellectual abilities and believe that their intelligence makes them superior. They look down on people they perceive as less educated or less intelligent, engaging in condescending behaviour or intellectual one-upmanship.

Key Traits of Cerebral Narcissism

- **Intellectual Superiority:**

Cerebral narcissists believe their intellect makes them inherently superior to other people. They seek admiration for their knowledge and look down on other people for lacking the same intellectual abilities.

- **Dismissive of Other People's Ideas:**

They often dismiss or belittle other people's ideas or opinions, viewing them as inferior. They try to assert dominance by undermining other people's contributions in discussions.

- **Condescending Attitude:**

Their conversations often take on a condescending tone, as they use their intellect to assert control in interactions, believing they're always right.

- **Lack of Emotional Awareness:**

Cerebral narcissists tend to prioritise intellectual pursuits over emotional connections. This leads to a lack of understanding of the emotional needs of other people, as they see emotions as inferior to logic and reason.

Case Example:

Mark loves to dominate conversations by discussing complex topics to highlight his intelligence. He frequently belittles other people for not understanding or keeping up with his intellect. When other people present their views, he dismisses them as uninformed or simplistic.

Malignant Narcissism

A Dangerous Combination of NPD, Antisocial Behaviour, and Aggression:

At the most severe end of the spectrum, you find malignant narcissism.

Malignant narcissism is an extreme and dangerous form that combines traits of narcissism with elements of antisocial personality disorder (ASPD), sadism, and paranoia.

This form of narcissism is characterised by a combination of grandiosity, entitlement, and antisocial behaviours.

However, people with malignant narcissism aren't only grandiose and manipulative, but also exhibit aggressive, hostile, and often sadistic tendencies. They enjoy inflicting pain or harm, whether emotional or physical, and have little to no remorse for their actions.

Malignant narcissists aren't only preoccupied with their own needs but are also cruel and exploitative toward other people. They actively enjoy seeing other people suffer and can use manipulation, and even cruelty to maintain control.

Key Traits of Malignant Narcissism

- **Antisocial Tendencies:**

Malignant narcissists engage in deceitful or harmful behaviours with little to no regard for the consequences. Their actions are driven by a need to dominate and control other people.

- **Paranoia:**

They exhibit extreme suspicion and distrust, often assuming that other people have ulterior motives. This paranoia can lead to pre-emptive attacks on perceived enemies.

- **Aggression and Sadism:**

Malignant narcissists take pleasure in causing harm to other people, whether emotionally, mentally, or physically. Their actions are often sadistic, and they enjoy manipulating or belittling other people for their own amusement.

- **Lack of Remorse:**

They rarely feel guilt or regret for their harmful actions, viewing themselves as justified in their behaviour. Their lack of remorse further enables their malicious actions.

Case Example:

Tom thrives on dominating other people, both at work and in his personal life. He takes pleasure in belittling employees and driving his colleagues into fear or submission.

When confronted about his behaviour, Tom becomes aggressive and deflects blame, retaliating with malicious intent to destroy the other person's reputation.

Psychopathic Narcissism

A Fusion of NPD and Psychopathy

Psychopathic narcissism is a chilling blend of narcissistic personality disorder (NPD) and psychopathy, combining traits of grandiosity and entitlement with a complete lack of empathy and conscience.

This form of narcissism is marked by a dangerous mix of charm, manipulation, and a ruthless disregard for other people. Psychopathic narcissists are calculated and cold, driven by self-interest and power, rather than emotional needs or connections. Unlike malignant narcissists, they might not overtly display aggression or sadism, but they're just as harmful, using manipulation and deception as primary tools to achieve their goals.

These people exhibit superficial charm, using their charisma to exploit and control other people. Beneath the surface is a predatory nature that prioritises personal gain over any ethical considerations. Their relationships are transactional, and they view people as tools to be used and discarded.

Key Traits of Psychopathic Narcissism

- ### Superficial Charm:

Psychopathic narcissists use their charisma and charm to manipulate other people for personal gain, often deceiving people into trusting them.

- ### Cold Calculation:

They're highly strategic and calculating, carefully exploiting people for this personal gain, without any concern for the damage they cause.

- ### Lack of Empathy:

Like other narcissists, psychopathic narcissists lack the ability to understand or care about the feelings of other people. Their indifference to other peoples' suffering makes them more dangerous.

- ### Impulsivity:

Their behaviour can be reckless and impulsive, often acting without regard for the consequences, driven by self-interest and a desire for immediate gratification.

Case Example:

Lisa, a successful executive, is known for her charm and persuasive skills. She effortlessly wins over clients and colleagues, but behind closed doors, she manipulates and undermines anyone who threatens her ambitions. When her assistant challenges her unethical practices, Lisa retaliates by spreading false rumours, ensuring the assistant's professional reputation is irreparably damaged.

Her actions are calculated and devoid of remorse, focused solely on maintaining her own status and control.

Different Manifestations

Narcissism doesn't show up the same way in everyone. It takes on different forms, shaped by the person, their environment, and their deepest insecurities.

Each form brings its own set of challenges — not just for the narcissist but for the people caught in their web. Recognising how narcissism manifests across different behaviours and personalities makes it easier to spot and address in everyday life.

This brief look at the different types of narcissism shows how these traits can surface in subtle, often deceptive ways. By understanding how these behaviours unfold, we can better navigate the complex and often hidden world of narcissism.

Bringing It All Together

In this chapter, I've briefly explored the many faces of narcissism: grandiose, overt, covert, communal, somatic, cerebral, malignant, and psychopathic. Each type brings its own behaviours and problems, affecting both the narcissist and the people around them.

By understanding these different forms, you can start to recognise them in your own life. This awareness is the first step towards setting healthy boundaries and protecting yourself. Whether it's a narcissist in your personal life, at work, or anywhere else, recognising the signs gives you the power to respond in a way that protects your well-being.

The more you understand how narcissism works, the better prepared you'll be to handle it.

Now that I've outlined the different types of narcissism, it's time to dig deeper into each one — to uncover their complexities and learn how to deal with them head-on.

Chapter 6

The Grand Facade

Grandiose Narcissism and the Illusion of Superiority

A deeper exploration of the inflated self-image, entitlement, and charm that defines grandiose narcissism

Before I dive into grandiose narcissism:

Yes, there is a difference between grandiose narcissism, and overt narcissism, although the terms are often used interchangeably. This confusion is understandable because the two share so many similarities that it's easy to mistake them for the same thing.

Before exploring grandiose narcissism, it's important to understand how it differs from overt narcissism.

Both involve a deep need for admiration and feeling superior to other people, but they show up in different ways.

Grandiose narcissism is how a person sees themselves at their core — these people genuinely believe they're better than everyone else; More talented, more deserving, and more special. This inflated sense of self-worth isn't just a fleeting thought; it's an ingrained belief that shapes their worldview and interactions with everyone else. They construct a mental image of themselves as exceptional, and they fiercely protect this image at all costs.

Overt narcissism, on the other hand, is how their inner grandiosity manifests outwardly. It's the visible behaviour that stems from their exaggerated self-perception — being loud, boastful, attention-seeking, and often arrogant.

This behaviour isn't random or accidental; it's a deliberate effort to reinforce their self-image by demanding admiration and approval from other people.

In Summary:

Knowing this difference helps us understand not just what they do, but why they do it.

In simple terms, think of grandiose narcissism as what's going on in their minds, (the belief that they're amazing) — and overt narcissism as how they act, (showing off and demanding attention).

Recognising this distinction helps you see beyond the surface charm or arrogance and understand the underlying psychological mechanisms driving their actions.

Now that I've clarified that, let's dive deep!

Grandiose Narcissism:

The Need for Admiration and the Fragile Ego

People with this trait often seem confident and charming, but underneath, they're deeply insecure. What looks like unshakable confidence is really a mask hiding a fragile ego that needs constant praise to stay intact. Any kind of criticism or failure can feel like a personal attack, leading them to react defensively or even lash out.

They need other people to constantly reaffirm their superiority, and this dependency makes them vulnerable to anything that threatens their inflated self-image. Criticism, perceived failure, or even being ignored, can feel like an attack on their very identity.

These moments of insecurity often provoke extreme defensiveness, denial, or anger, as they scramble to protect the illusion of perfection they've constructed. Their behaviour is striking. They project an aura of charm and charisma, captivating everyone in the room.

Initially, their energy might seem genuine, even magnetic. But over time, their compulsion for constant attention becomes evident. It's not just a desire; it's a need. Their self-worth is like a car that needs to be constantly refuelled with admiration. The more they receive, the more they need, like an insatiable thirst that can never be quenched.

Their self-worth isn't something they can refill on their own; it relies on other people to stay intact. Without it, they feel exposed and vulnerable, so they constantly search for more, trying to refill what continually drains away. For everyone around them, this creates an unpredictable and exhausting atmosphere.

Personal Reflection

At first, her confidence was magnetic. She seemed unstoppable, full of energy and ambition. But as time went by, I realised her world revolved entirely around her need to be admired. Every compliment fed her, but the slightest criticism felt like an attack. If I dared to question her, she would lash out or completely dismiss me.

I started to see the cracks in the facade. Everything she did revolved around her need to be admired. Compliments weren't just nice; they were fuel to her. It became clear that she thrived on being the centre of attention, and she didn't handle it well when the spotlight shifted away. The moment she faced any criticism, no matter how gentle, or well-intentioned, it was like I'd flipped a switch and I was a problem.

It felt like I'd threatened the perfect fantasy world she'd built for herself, and she couldn't allow that to happen. Slowly, I realised that her confidence wasn't as unshakable as it seemed. It was like a house of cards — impressive from the outside, but critically balanced, ready to collapse with the slightest nudge.

This story might feel familiar to people who've encountered a grandiose narcissist. Their charm and confidence can be dazzling at first, but their deep need for admiration and intolerance for criticism can create chaos in the long run. Let's look closer at what drives their behaviour and how it affects everyday life.

The Core of Grandiose Narcissism

Grandiose narcissism is all about seeing yourself as more important than anyone else. These people honestly believe they're smarter, better, and more deserving than everyone around them.

This isn't a quiet or humble belief; they declare it boldly and unapologetically, making it the centrepiece of their identity.

In any setting — whether social, professional, or personal — they position themselves as the star of the show. They dominate conversations, crave the spotlight, and expect other people to support them without question. They're not just confident; they're overconfident to the point of arrogance, dismissing other people's opinions and perspectives as inferior.

To maintain their self-esteem, they build an image of perfection and success that they're desperate to uphold. This isn't just about looking good; it's about protecting their fragile sense of self-worth. Any threat to this carefully crafted image — whether it's criticism, failure, or even perceived indifference — can feel catastrophic to them. They might react with anger, denial, or attempts to discredit the person who challenged them.

For a grandiose narcissist, life's like a performance, and they're the lead actor. But they're not just performing, they actually demand applause. Anyone who doesn't applaud risks being pushed aside or labelled as an enemy.

How Grandiose Narcissism Manifests

Once you learn to recognise the signs it becomes easier to spot. Key traits include overwhelming confidence and a constant need for admiration.

These individuals often seem self-assured and authoritative at first, but this confidence can quickly become oppressive. They dominate conversations, dismiss differing viewpoints, and expect constant attention, all in an effort to reinforce their inflated sense of self-importance.

Here's how these traits often show up in everyday life:

- **Overwhelming Confidence:**

Grandiose narcissists exude self-assurance that can be intoxicating at first. They seem to have all the answers and carry themselves with authority. Over time, however, their confidence can feel oppressive. They often dismiss other peoples' ideas, refuse to acknowledge different perspectives, and dominate conversations to keep the spotlight on themselves.

- **Exaggerated Achievements:**

They love to highlight their accomplishments, but their stories are often exaggerated or outright fabricated. Taking credit for other people's work or inflating their contributions isn't uncommon — all in an effort to appear superior. Their need to be admired overrides any commitment to honesty or fairness.

- **Lack of Empathy:**

Grandiose narcissists struggle to consider other peoples' feelings or needs. Their intense focus on themselves makes it difficult — or impossible — for them to step into someone else's shoes. This leaves the people around them feeling overlooked, unheard, and undervalued.

- **Sensitivity to Criticism:**

Despite their bold exterior, grandiose narcissists are incredibly sensitive to even the smallest hint of criticism. They can react with aggression, denial, or by attacking the person who criticised them. Their need to protect their image overrides everything else, including relationships.

- **Exploiting People for Personal Gain:**

Relationships are transactional to them. They see people as tools to boost their ego — whether for admiration, status, or resources. Once someone is no longer useful, they're discarded without hesitation or remorse.

Grandiose Narcissism in Relationships

Being in a relationship with a grandiose narcissist can feel like being caught in a storm — mesmerising at first but ultimately leaving you battered and drained.

Their initial charm and intensity can sweep you off your feet, creating the illusion of a perfect connection. However, as time passes, the cracks begin to show, exposing a relationship dynamic that's far from healthy. Recognising and understanding these patterns can help you make sense of the chaos they bring into your life.

The Cycle of Love-Bombing and Devaluation

Grandiose narcissists are masters of love-bombing, a tactic where they shower you with affection, compliments, attention, and sometimes extravagant gifts. In the early stages of a relationship, this can feel exhilarating. They might tell you how special and unique you are, making you feel like the most important person in their world. This phase can be so intoxicating that you overlook red flags, convinced you've found someone extraordinary.

However, this initial high is unsustainable. Once they feel secure in the relationship — or if you start asserting your own needs — their behaviour changes. They begin to devalue you. What once felt like adoration, now turns into criticism, dismissiveness, or even outright hostility. They might nitpick your flaws, undermine your confidence, or accuse you of being ungrateful. This shift is often subtle at first, leaving you confused and questioning what you did wrong.

The cycle of love-bombing and devaluation is designed to keep you off balance. You might find yourself chasing the early days of the relationship, trying to regain their approval and affection.

Unfortunately, this is exactly what they want — to maintain control by making you doubt yourself and focus on pleasing them.

Always Competing

For a grandiose narcissist, relationships are not about mutual support or partnership.

They view them as arenas for competition. They must be the best, whether it's the smartest, the most talented, or the most successful. This constant need to outshine other people extends to their partners, creating an environment where your achievements are seen as threats, rather than reasons to celebrate.

For example, if you receive a promotion at work, they downplay your success or find a way to shift the focus back to themselves. They'll say something like, "Well, it's no surprise — you only got it because I've been supporting you." This behaviour ensures that they remain the centre of attention, even when the moment should be about you.

This competitive mindset can be exhausting. Instead of feeling supported, you might find yourself in a constant struggle to prove your worth or avoid their subtle, (or not-so-subtle) attempts to diminish you.

Ignoring Emotional Needs

Because grandiose narcissists view relationships primarily as a source of admiration and validation, they often neglect the emotional needs of their partners. Genuine empathy is not their strong suit, and they struggle to see beyond their own desires.

If you express feelings of hurt, frustration, or sadness, they might dismiss them outright or accuse you of being too sensitive.

Over time, this emotional neglect can leave you feeling invisible. You may stop voicing your needs altogether, fearing that doing so will only lead to further rejection or conflict.

The relationship becomes one-sided, centred entirely on maintaining their ego, while your own emotional well-being is left by the wayside.

The Long-Term Effects of Grandiose Narcissism

Spending time around a grandiose narcissist — whether as a partner, friend, or colleague — can be incredibly draining. Their relentless need for validation, coupled with their dismissiveness and manipulative behaviour, leaves those around them feeling emotionally battered. Even after the relationship ends, the effects of their behaviour can linger, impacting your sense of self and your ability to trust other people.

- **Eroded Self-Worth:**

One of the most damaging impacts of being close to a grandiose narcissist is the gradual erosion of your self-esteem. Their constant criticisms, whether overt, or subtle, can make you question your value. You may start to internalise their negative comments, believing that you're not good enough or capable enough. This self-doubt can seep into other areas of your life, affecting your confidence in your abilities and decisions.

For example, if a grandiose narcissist regularly belittles your achievements, you might begin to downplay them yourself, even when other people recognise your success. Over time, this can lead to a distorted sense of self-worth, making it difficult to see your own strengths and accomplishments.

- **Emotional Burnout:**

Trying to navigate the demands of a grandiose narcissist is emotionally exhausting. Their need for constant attention and their unpredictable reactions to criticism or perceived slights can leave you feeling like you're walking on eggshells.

You may spend an inordinate amount of time and energy trying to keep the peace, anticipate their needs, or avoid triggering their anger.

This level of emotional labour can lead to burnout, leaving you drained and unable to focus on your own well-being.

You might find yourself neglecting your own needs and desires, simply because you're too tired to address them.

- **Fear of Trusting Again:**

The manipulative and self-centred nature of grandiose narcissists can make it difficult to trust other people after the relationship ends. You may find yourself second-guessing people's intentions, wondering if they also have hidden agendas. This hypervigilance, while understandable, can make it challenging to form new healthy relationships.

It's important to recognise that this fear is a natural response to the emotional wounds caused by a grandiose narcissist. With time, support, and self-reflection, it's possible to rebuild your ability to trust and connect with other people.

Recognising Grandiose Narcissism

Although grandiose narcissists can be incredibly charismatic, their true nature often reveals itself through consistent patterns of behaviour. Learning to recognise these signs can help you protect yourself from being drawn into their influence.

- **Exaggerated Speech:**

They frequently talk about themselves in ways that seem too good to be true. They might embellish their successes or take credit for accomplishments that aren't theirs.

- **Dismissive Behaviour:**

They show little interest in other people's ideas or opinions, often dismissing them without consideration.

- **Constant Demand for Praise:**

Their need for validation is insatiable, and they can become irritable, defensive, or even hostile if they feel they aren't receiving enough attention.

By paying attention to these behaviours, you can spot grandiose narcissists early and take steps to protect your emotional well-being.

Coping with Grandiose Narcissists

If you must interact with a grandiose narcissist, whether in your personal life or at work, it's essential to prioritise your own mental and emotional health. While you can't change their behaviour, you can take steps to minimise their impact on you.

- ### Do Not Invest Emotionally

Remember, their behaviour is not a reflection of you — it's about their need for validation and control. Avoid taking their actions personally and try not to engage in their attempts to provoke you. Maintaining an emotional distance can help you stay grounded and prevent their manipulative tactics from affecting your self-esteem.

- ### Set Clear Boundaries:

Grandiose narcissists will push as far as you allow. Setting and enforcing boundaries is crucial for maintaining your peace of mind.

Whether it's limiting the time you spend with them or refusing to engage in certain discussions, clear boundaries can help you protect your emotional well-being.

- ### Lean on Support Systems:

Dealing with a narcissist can feel isolating, but you don't have to face it alone. Reach out to trusted friends, family, or a therapist to share your experiences and gain perspective. Having a support system can provide much-needed validation and reassurance, reminding you that you're not alone in this struggle.

Moving Forward

Recognising grandiose narcissism is a powerful step toward reclaiming your sense of self and building healthier relationships. While these individuals can be captivating, their charm often comes at a significant cost.

By understanding their behaviour and focusing on your own well-being, you can navigate these relationships without losing sight of who you are.

Above all, remember that you deserve relationships based on mutual respect, empathy, and genuine connection. By spotting the signs of grandiose narcissism and knowing how to respond, you can protect yourself, rebuild your confidence, and move forward with strength and clarity.

Chapter 7

The Spotlight Seeker

Overt Narcissism and the Need for Constant Validation

Examining the outward arrogance and unrelenting demand for admiration that define overt narcissism

Overt narcissism is the most visible and assertive form of narcissistic personality disorder (NPD). Unlike covert narcissists, who mask their self-centredness behind false humility, overt narcissists wear their arrogance as a badge of honour. Their self-worth is entirely dependent on external validation. They crave the spotlight, viewing attention, admiration, and adoration as essential to their existence. They believe the world should revolve around them and act with an overwhelming sense of entitlement, as if they're inherently deserving of special treatment.

Where covert narcissists cloak their inflated sense of self in an illusion of humility, overt narcissists are open in their self-absorption, demanding attention without any attempt to disguise it. They make no effort to hide the toll their behaviour takes on other people, and their boisterous nature amplifies their need for admiration. This craving is so powerful that it disrupts the harmony of any environment they enter—especially in relationships. It becomes evident to everyone around them that their focus is on satisfying their unrelenting hunger for validation.

Relationships with them are marked by conflict and emotional exhaustion, as the narcissist's needs overshadow any consideration for other people. They leave behind a wake of emotional turmoil, often leaving those closest to them feeling drained, ignored, and insignificant.

These people live in a world where they're the main character, and everyone else exists to either praise them or support them.

Their interactions are dominated by a deep-seated belief that they're exceptional, deserving of special treatment, and above the rules that apply to other people. Their unrelenting pursuit of admiration and validation isn't just a need—it's a compulsion—and it drives almost every aspect of their lives.

In relationships, they can be charismatic at first, drawing people in with their confidence and larger-than-life personalities. But this initial charm quickly fades as their overwhelming self-centredness becomes more obvious. They rarely, if ever, consider the needs, feelings, or desires of other people, and this imbalance creates significant emotional strain for the people around them.

In this chapter, I'll unpick overt narcissism, delving into the traits and behaviours that define this personality type. By shedding light on their relentless pursuit of validation, I hope to equip you with the tools to recognise and navigate interactions with these people. This is especially important because, despite their brashness, a lot of people still find it difficult to distance themselves from the narcissist's magnetic allure.

Personal Reflection:

At first, it was easy to be swept up in her charisma and confidence. But as time went on, it became clear that it wasn't enough for her to simply be seen — it was as if she actually needed to be worshipped. Any attention that wasn't directed at her was quickly dismissed, and any challenge to her perceived greatness was met with rage. She just wanted a one-sided relationship where her needs could come first.

I started to feel like I was invisible. My own emotions and needs started fading into the background as she continued her quest for admiration. Despite my best efforts to show her love and support, I was continually left feeling unimportant and emotionally drained.

The Core of Overt Narcissism:

At the core of overt narcissism lies an insatiable need for external validation. This need isn't a simple craving; it's an integral part of their sense of identity.

Unlike covert narcissists who manipulate other people subtly to gain admiration, overt narcissists seek validation in the most obvious and direct ways.

Without constant reinforcement, their self-worth is fragile, and the absence of recognition can trigger feelings of inadequacy, insecurity, and anger.

A defining trait is their profound sense of superiority and entitlement. They don't just want admiration; they actually expect it as their birthright.

This belief that they're inherently special, superior, and above the norms of society drives them to seek attention and status with unmatched determination.

Their view of themselves as superior to other people forms the very basis of their self-esteem and is what propels them forward in life to the detriment of anyone in their path.

However, this relentless pursuit blinds them to the needs or feelings of other people, leaving a trail of damaged relationships, emotional turmoil, and personal conflict.

How Overt Narcissism Manifests:

Overt narcissism is marked by bold and unapologetic behaviour. These people demand attention at every opportunity, and their actions reflect a profound sense of entitlement.

Their need for admiration leads to exaggerated displays of superiority and boastful stories. Not only do they believe that they're inherently special and deserving of admiration, but they also expect other people to recognise and acknowledge it without exception.

In conversation, they rarely allow other people to speak for long. Seeing every interaction as an opportunity to reinforce their own image, they dominate discussions, steering every topic back to themselves.

This chapter is designed to uncover the core of overt narcissism, offering insights to help you identify the key traits of this personality type and understand how to manage interactions. These people can often appear charming and affable at first but understanding the patterns of behaviour that follow can help you spot the signs early on.

The truth is, while overt narcissists are often easy to identify, their impact on your emotional well-being can be more insidious than it seems. Recognising these traits and behaviours will provide you with the awareness you need to protect yourself and navigate these difficult relationships more effectively.

Here's a closer look at how their narcissism plays out:

- **Bold Arrogance:**

They exude confidence, often to the point of arrogance, believing that they're inherently superior to everyone around them.

This exaggerated sense of self-importance can be incredibly off-putting to other people. However, this arrogance is a crucial part of their effort to maintain their image as someone special. In their mind, showing any vulnerability or weakness would tarnish their carefully constructed persona. They expect other people to recognise their worth without question, and they'll react defensively when faced with criticism or even constructive feedback.

- **Constant Need for Attention:**

For overt narcissists, being in the spotlight isn't a choice — it's a necessity. They thrive on admiration and recognition, whether it's at a social gathering, in the workplace, or within their personal relationships. If the attention shifts away from them for even a moment, they can resort to dramatic gestures, interrupt conversations, or create conflict just to reassert their presence. In their minds, their value is only validated by constant external acknowledgement. The longer they go without it, the more desperate their attempts become to reclaim the attention.

- **Self-Absorbed Conversations:**

They struggle to let other people have the floor. They dominate discussions, steering every topic back to themselves. Even when they appear to listen, it's just a ploy to shift the focus back to their own experiences or achievements. Their conversations rarely allow for meaningful exchanges of ideas or emotions. It's all about showcasing their success, their importance, or their struggles. As a result, other people in the conversation are left feeling unheard or dismissed.

- **Sense of Entitlement:**

Overt narcissists believe they deserve special treatment and will react vehemently to any perceived slight. Whether it's being overlooked for a promotion, not receiving the praise they believe they deserve, or simply being ignored in a social setting, they take any form of neglect personally. They respond with irritation, anger, or even hostility. This sense of entitlement can extend to a variety of situations, from expecting other people to accommodate their needs, to demanding that other people praise, or worship them at every turn.

- **Exploitation of Other People:**

While overt narcissists might not be as subtle or manipulative as some other narcissistic types, they'll still use other people to get what they want. Whether it's through leveraging people for their own gain, dismissing people's needs in favour of their own, or taking credit for someone else's work, they rarely think about the well-being of those around them. Other people often feel used, drained, and unappreciated in relationships with them. It's not about connection; it's about what other people can do to serve their needs.

Overt Narcissism in Relationships

Relationships with overt narcissists are emotionally taxing and unbalanced. These individuals centre every interaction on their own needs and desires, leaving little room for mutual care or understanding.

They expect constant admiration and validation, viewing their partner as an extension of their ego rather than as an equal participant in the relationship. Partners are expected to constantly provide praise and attention. Any failure to meet these expectations is met with frustration or even hostility.

- **Everything Revolves Around Them:**

Whether it's their achievements, emotions, or desires, the partner of an overt narcissist is expected to cater to them without question. The partner's own emotions or desires often go unacknowledged, and their needs are rarely prioritised.

In fact, the narcissist can view any expression of their partner's needs or concerns as a threat to their own emotional security and can react with defensiveness or contempt.

- **Expectations of Constant Praise:**

They expect their partner to act as a cheerleader, providing constant admiration, praise, and attention. If their partner fails to meet these expectations, they can react with irritation, anger, or even passive-aggressive behaviour.

It's as though the narcissist feels betrayed when they don't receive the constant validation they demand. Even small lapses in attention can lead to resentment and retaliation.

- **Emotional Neglect:**

Overt narcissists struggle to empathise with their partner's emotional needs because they're too consumed by their own hunger for praise. This emotional neglect can lead to feelings of isolation, frustration, and loneliness in the relationship. Narcissists are incapable of offering the emotional support that their partner needs, and as a result, their partner can feel emotionally starved or unseen.

The Long-Term Effects of Overt Narcissism

The emotional toll of interacting with these people can be profound and far-reaching, often leaving lasting scars that persist long after the relationship ends. The constant demands for attention, emotional manipulation, and neglect can damage a person's mental health, leading to feelings of inadequacy, emotional exhaustion, and even long-term trauma.

Survivors of Relationships with Overt Narcissists Often Experience:

• Diminished Self-Esteem:

Living in the shadow of an overt narcissist can erode self-worth, leaving the person feeling unworthy or inadequate. The overt narcissist's relentless focus on themselves, without regard for the other person's emotional needs, can make the survivor feel invisible or insignificant. Over time, this can have a devastating impact on their self-esteem and their ability to trust in their own value.

• Emotional Exhaustion:

Trying to keep up with an overt narcissist's ever-changing demands for attention and admiration is draining. Survivors often describe feeling physically and mentally depleted, as if all their energy was consumed by the relationship. The emotional exhaustion can become so overwhelming that it affects their ability to function in other areas of their life, from work to personal relationships.

• Difficulty Trusting Other People:

Being manipulated, used, and dismissed by an overt narcissist can cause survivors to question their own judgment and struggle to trust other people.

The betrayal they've experienced makes it difficult to believe that other people are genuinely interested in them for who they are, rather than for what they can provide.

As a result, they can have difficulty forming healthy relationships in the future, always fearing that they'll be used or exploited again.

Recognising Overt Narcissism

While overt narcissists are easy to spot because of their bold behaviour and extreme need for attention, recognising the subtle ways in which they manipulate their environment can be equally helpful.

Here are some warning signs to keep an eye out for:

• **Unabashed Self-Promotion:**

They frequently boast about their accomplishments, status, and importance. They can regularly brag about their skills, achievements, or possessions, often exaggerating their success in an attempt to appear more impressive or superior.

• **Lack of Concern for Other People:**

They rarely show concern for anyone's needs unless it benefits them directly. If other people's emotions or needs don't serve the narcissist's agenda, they're dismissed or ignored.

• **Entitlement and Irritability:**

They react explosively to perceived disrespect. Their fragile ego is masked by a confident exterior, but when they don't get what they want, they become irritable, frustrated, and prone to emotional outbursts.

Coping Strategies for Dealing with Overt Narcissists

Dealing with an overt narcissist requires setting firm boundaries and being prepared to manage their demands.

Here are some effective strategies for coping:

- **Set Rigid Boundaries:**

Clearly communicate what behaviour you won't tolerate. Make it abundantly clear when their behaviour becomes unacceptable and stick to your limits. Enforce these boundaries with consistency and assertiveness to prevent their behaviour from taking over your life.

- **Don't Take Their Behaviour Personally:**

An overt narcissist's need for admiration and their critique of you is a reflection of their own insecurities, not a reflection of your worth. Don't internalise their reactions or criticisms and don't allow them to manipulate you into providing constant validation.

- **Seek Support:**

Leaning on friends, family, or a therapist can help you manage your feelings and keep perspective when dealing with an overt narcissist. Having a support system will remind you that you're not alone and can provide much-needed emotional nourishment when dealing with an overt narcissist's emotional drain.

Moving Forward

Overt narcissism may present itself in bold and brash ways, but understanding it is key to protecting yourself from its emotional toll. While their behaviour can be extremely difficult to tolerate, recognising the insecurity at its core can help you detach from its emotional weight.

By maintaining firm boundaries, prioritising your own needs, and seeking support, when necessary, you can navigate relationships with them while preserving your own mental health and well-being.

By enforcing boundaries and focusing on relationships built on mutual respect and care, you can free yourself from their draining influence.

It's important to recognise that their need for validation actually stems from deep insecurity, rather than strength.

You deserve to be in relationships that are balanced, nurturing, and based on mutual respect — not relationships that revolve around someone else's ego.

Take the first step by reclaiming your sense of self and surrounding yourself with people who uplift and support you. Recognising overt narcissism is a key step in reclaiming your emotional health and building relationships grounded in empathy and understanding.

Chapter 8

The Hidden Corridor

Covert Narcissism and Subtler Manipulations

A deep dive into the manipulative tactics of covert narcissists and how to manage them.

Covert narcissism demands a much more in-depth look due to its complexity, it operates in the shadows, hiding beneath a facade of sensitivity or introversion, which sets it apart from other forms of narcissism.

It's harder to recognise, but no less damaging. It presents a unique and insidious challenge in relationships, leaving victims confused by a manipulation that's as subtle as it is destructive, and causing them to question their reality.

This quieter form of narcissism can leave deeper emotional scars because it's difficult to detect. Its hidden nature makes it particularly damaging, as it can go unnoticed for long periods, quietly eroding the victim's self-worth.

In this chapter, I'll take a deeper dive into the destructive world of covert narcissism, exploring its traits and impact. I'll also provide insights into recognising and addressing it.

Understanding this hidden corridor of narcissism is a vital step towards reclaiming self-worth.

It's toxic nature allows it to mask the hallmark traits of NPD, making it particularly harmful — and, at times, even sinister.

Personal Reflection:

I didn't even realise at the time that I was being manipulated. Her criticisms were always veiled in concern, and her insults disguised as naivety or vulnerability — the way she always tried to make me feel guilty for my own emotions. I found myself constantly apologising, even when I hadn't done anything wrong. It wasn't the screaming or blatant demands that wore me down. It was the constant feeling that I could never do enough.

The condemnation I faced whenever I made a decision she didn't like. I looked in the mirror one day and barely recognised myself. It was a slow erosion of my confidence; I just didn't see it coming until I had nothing left to give.

Looking back, I now see how I was entangled in the web of a narcissist. Her weapon wasn't her booming voice or aggressive demeanour; it was her constant attempts to make me feel like I was always falling short. Every moment was carefully calibrated to undermine my confidence, but it was done so subtly that I didn't notice the damage until it was too late.

The power of covert narcissism lies in its stealth. It creeps into your life under the guise of care, humility, or vulnerability, making you feel like a bad person for even suspecting their motives.

This chapter is my way of shedding light on this hidden form of abuse, so other people don't have to stumble blindly as I did. It will focus on the aspects of covert narcissism, giving you the tools to spot it and protect yourself from its slow, insidious effects.

The Quiet Manipulators: Understanding Covert Narcissism

When we think of narcissists, most of us picture loud, self-centred people who love to be the centre of attention.

But covert narcissism is different — quieter, yet just as damaging. It can be tougher to spot because it doesn't come with the grand gestures and flashy behaviour we associate with narcissism, but its effects on relationships can be profound, leaving those affected confused and emotionally exhausted.

Covert narcissists can easily be described as wolves in sheep's clothing. They lack the brashness and bravado of their overt counterparts, but their underlying motivations remain the same: to dominate, control, and feed their insatiable need for validation. However, their methods are far more subtle.

Covert narcissism, often referred to as "vulnerable narcissism," is the less obvious but equally destructive counterpart to overt narcissism. Unlike overt narcissists, who are outwardly grandiose and attention-seeking, covert narcissists appear introverted, insecure, or even humble. However, beneath this seemingly modest exterior lies the same core of entitlement, self-importance, and a need for admiration.

Even though covert narcissists don't openly demand attention, they still crave validation. They manipulate through subtle means, often positioning themselves as victims or martyrs to garner sympathy. They might come across as shy, reserved, or sensitive, which helps disguise their deeper need for control. This facade disarms their victims, making it difficult to recognise the narcissistic behaviour beneath the surface.

For example, a covert narcissist might say, "I know I'm not as smart as you, but I was just trying to help," after sabotaging a project. On the surface, this appears self-effacing, but it's a manipulative attempt to shift guilt onto the victim.

The Deep Dive

Covert narcissists don't exhibit the same overt arrogance as their counterparts, but their manipulations are no less damaging.

Their ultimate goal remains the same: to satisfy their need for superiority and control. They don't demand admiration openly, but they do feel wronged or overlooked when they don't receive the validation, they believe they deserve.

In the following sections, I'll delve deeper into how covert narcissism manifests in different types of relationships, how to spot its more subtle signs, and practical strategies for protecting yourself from its harmful effects.

Signs You're Dealing with a Covert Narcissist

Recognising covert narcissism can be deceptively difficult. Covert narcissists tend to operate under the radar, using subtle and insidious tactics that might not be immediately obvious. Their behaviours can feel confusing, draining, or even destabilising, but understanding the signs can empower you to take back control.

Key traits to keep an eye out for:

- **Constant Need for Reassurance:**

Covert narcissists often express their need for validation in indirect ways. They can downplay their achievements or magnify their flaws to elicit reassurance, frequently fishing for compliments.

They might make self-deprecating remarks like, "I'm probably not good enough for this," or "I don't look as good as I used to," hoping you'll jump in to offer praise or reassurance.

This need for validation is continuous, and when they don't receive it, they can begin to feel worthless or neglected, placing the burden of their self-esteem squarely on your shoulders. This becomes a never-ending cycle where their confidence hinges on your approval, leaving you constantly responsible for their emotional well-being.

This need for reassurance becomes so overwhelming that it can drain your own energy and sense of self-worth, while you're left trying to manage their insecurities and neglecting your own needs.

- **Emotional Blackmail:**

One of the most common tools in the covert narcissist's emotional manipulation arsenal is guilt. Rather than openly demanding your attention or affection, they use subtle guilt-tripping statements that place the blame on you. For instance, they might say, "I'll just stay home while you go out with your friends," creating a situation where you feel selfish for wanting to enjoy your own time.

Over time, these guilt-laden statements can begin to erode your own sense of self, making you second-guess your own decisions and actions. You may find yourself prioritising their needs over your own, only to feel emotionally drained and manipulated, even as you try to meet their ever-changing demands.

- **Feigning Vulnerability:**

Covert narcissists often manipulate other people by presenting themselves as weak, fragile, or misunderstood. They might play the victim to evoke sympathy, carefully curating a persona of someone who's always been wronged or who's perpetually suffering from an unfair world.

This portrayal of vulnerability can make them seem more approachable and worthy of care, but it's ultimately a tactic to garner attention and support without ever having to face their own shortcomings or take accountability for their actions.

This manipulation of vulnerability not only keeps them in the centre of attention but also creates a toxic dynamic where their emotional needs are always put ahead of yours, further entangling you in their web of control.

- **Sabotaging Other People:**

Covert narcissists operate under the guise of being supportive, but beneath the surface, they're secretly trying to undermine everyone in order to maintain control. They make backhanded compliments or offer assistance that can lead to setbacks. These actions might appear innocent or unintentional, but they serve to keep you feeling inferior without catching on to their manipulation.

In relationships, this makes you feel constantly on edge and wondering whether the support is genuine or part of a masterplan to keep you dependent and under control.

- **Silent Treatment and Passive-Aggression:**

When a covert narcissist is upset, they rarely address the issue directly. Instead, they engage in passive-aggressive behaviour or withdraw emotionally, leaving you to guess what went wrong. The silent treatment is a particularly powerful weapon, as it creates a profound sense of rejection and isolates you, leaving you emotionally drained and responsible for keeping the peace.

Instead of communicating their feelings or frustrations, they shut you out, punishing you for perceived slights. Over time, this can create a cycle where you're always walking on eggshells, afraid of upsetting them and triggering their silent treatment.

Recognising Covert Narcissism in Different Contexts

Covert narcissism doesn't only affect romantic relationships — it can manifest in families, friendships, and workplaces as well. In each of these settings, covert narcissists employ similar tactics of manipulation and control, but the dynamics can differ slightly.

- **In Families:**

A covert narcissist within a family may position themselves as the perpetual victim. They often foster competition or rivalry between siblings, pitting them against each other to maintain control. The narcissist's primary goal is to receive attention and validation, and they will manipulate family members into prioritising their emotional needs over other people.

- **In Friendships:**

Friendships with covert narcissists can feel one-sided. They often dominate conversations, subtly shifting the focus to themselves, and can guilt-trip friends into providing emotional support without reciprocating. These relationships can leave you feeling emotionally drained, as the narcissist continually seeks validation while offering little in return.

- **In the Workplace:**

Covert narcissists in the workplace often operate under the guise of being hardworking, helpful colleagues.

However, behind the scenes, they may spread rumours, undermine other peoples' efforts, or take credit for work they didn't do. They are experts at presenting a false persona of collaboration while covertly sabotaging the success of the people around them to maintain their sense of superiority.

Understanding the Hidden Agenda of Covert Narcissists

Covert narcissists are masters of masking their true motives. Unlike overt narcissists, who loudly demand admiration, covert narcissists are much subtler. They rarely make explicit demands or requests; instead, they manipulate through passive-aggressive means or veiled suggestions. Their manipulations are disguised as vulnerability or self-sacrifice, making them hard to detect.

This hidden agenda can often be overlooked or misunderstood, especially when the narcissist seems to be acting out of kindness or humility. However, it's crucial to remember that their actions are driven by the need to control, feed their self-esteem, and gain validation — but they do so without ever openly asking for it.

They might say something like, "I don't want to bother you, but I feel so alone," when what they really want is for you to drop everything and attend to them. The complexity of these statements lies in how they position themselves as needing help while shifting the responsibility for their emotional state onto you.

The Power of Passive-Aggression

One of the hallmark traits of a covert narcissist is passive-aggressive behaviour. Rather than confronting issues directly, they often use subtle, indirect methods to express dissatisfaction or manipulate other people.

This can range from sarcasm to sulking, to a more subtle form of undermining, such as pretending to be helpless or playing the victim.

This is another common passive-aggressive tactic. When a covert narcissist feels slighted or when their unrealistic expectations aren't met, they withdraw emotionally or refuse to communicate. This creates a sense of confusion and discomfort in the victim, as the silence often leaves them wondering what went wrong and what they need to do to repair the situation.

The result is often a toxic cycle where the victim is constantly walking on eggshells, trying to avoid upsetting the covert narcissist, and simultaneously questioning whether they've done something wrong. Over time, this can wear down the victim's confidence, leading to a diminished sense of self-worth.

Gaslighting and Doubt

Gaslighting is a particularly subtle tactic that covert narcissists use to maintain control. This psychological manipulation causes the victim to doubt their memory, perceptions, or even sanity. A covert narcissist might deny things they've said or done, making you question your own reality. They may even twist situations to make you feel at fault, even when it's clear they're the one in the wrong.

For example, a covert narcissist might tell you, "That's not how it happened," or "You're being too sensitive, it wasn't a big deal." This creates an environment where the victim begins to question their own thoughts and feelings, undermining their sense of stability and reality.

As the gaslighting continues, the victim's confidence erodes further, and they become increasingly reliant on the narcissist's version of events.

This makes it even harder to break free from the relationship, as the victim can begin to doubt their own instincts and trust the narcissist instead.

Tactics for Escaping the Covert Narcissist's Web

Since covert narcissists rely on subtlety and manipulation, it can be difficult to escape their control. However, recognising their tactics and learning how to protect yourself is the first step in regaining control over your life.

- **Establish Firm Boundaries:**

One of the most effective ways to protect yourself from a covert narcissist is by setting clear, non-negotiable boundaries. They'll test your limits, pushing you to bend to their needs. Stand firm in your decisions and refuse to be manipulated by their passive-aggressive tactics.

- **Recognise Manipulative Behaviours:**

The more you understand about covert narcissism, the easier it becomes to spot their manipulative behaviours. Whether it's fishing for compliments, playing the victim, or using guilt to control you, recognising these patterns allows you to detach emotionally and take back control of the situation.

- **Seek Support:**

Dealing with a covert narcissist can be isolating, especially when they turn other people against you. It's essential to reach out for support from trusted friends, family members, or a therapist. Having a support system that understands narcissistic abuse can help you maintain perspective and remind you that you're not overreacting.

- **Build Emotional Resilience:**

Strengthening your emotional resilience is key when dealing with covert narcissists. Focus on building your self-worth through self-care, setting time aside for activities that nourish your mental and emotional health. This will help you stay grounded and less susceptible to the narcissist's tactics.

- **Trust Your Intuition:**

If something doesn't feel right, trust your instincts. Narcissists are skilled at creating a false reality, but your intuition is often your first line of defence.

If you feel uneasy or confused in a relationship, take a step back and assess the situation. Your gut can be a powerful tool in protecting your emotional well-being.

Breaking Free from the Narcissist's Grip

Breaking free from a covert narcissist's grip is one of the most challenging parts of the recovery process.

The narcissist's manipulative tactics can make you feel isolated, confused, and drained. However, it's possible to regain your independence and sense of self-worth.

- **No Contact or Low Contact**

One of the most powerful strategies for escaping a covert narcissist is to implement no contact or low contact. This means cutting off communication entirely or limiting interactions to only the essentials. It can be difficult, especially if the narcissist is someone close to you, but this is necessary for your emotional and mental health. Even limited interactions can be toxic, so protecting yourself by disengaging is essential.

- **Gradually Build Your Independence**

Covert narcissists are skilled at fostering dependence on them, whether it's emotional, financial, or social.

Reclaiming your independence means re-establishing your own identity outside of the narcissist's influence.

This might involve rediscovering hobbies, strengthening relationships with supportive friends and family, or seeking professional help to build confidence and self-esteem.

- **Work Through the Trauma of Narcissistic Abuse**

Leaving a covert narcissist can be traumatic. The manipulation, gaslighting, and emotional abuse can leave lasting scars on your sense of self and emotional health. Therapy, especially with someone familiar with narcissistic abuse, can help you process the trauma.

It's important to acknowledge the pain, validate your experience, and work through it in a safe and supportive environment.

- **Healing from the Inside Out**

Healing from narcissistic abuse isn't just about cutting ties with the narcissist; it's also about rebuilding yourself. Start by focusing on your mental and emotional health. Practising mindfulness, journaling, and engaging in self-compassion exercises can help you heal.

Recognising the damage done to your sense of self-worth is a critical step in reclaiming your power and rediscovering who you are outside of the narcissist's influence.

- **Empower Yourself with Knowledge**

The more you learn about covert narcissism and narcissistic abuse, the better equipped you are to protect yourself in the future. Educating yourself about the psychological manipulation tactics used by narcissists helps you develop the tools needed to recognise and avoid such individuals moving forward. Empowerment through knowledge is a key part of reclaiming your life and moving forward.

Moving Forward with Confidence and Self-Worth

Rebuilding your life after being in a relationship with a covert narcissist requires a lot of time, patience, and self-compassion.

The damage to your confidence, trust in other people, and emotional health can feel overwhelming, but healing is possible. By taking small, intentional steps toward recovery, you can emerge from the labyrinth of narcissistic abuse stronger, wiser, and more resilient. While it may seem daunting at first, every step forward is a victory. Trust in your ability to heal and allow yourself the patience to recover fully.

Remember, you are not defined by your experiences with a narcissist. Your worth is inherent, and you have the power to reclaim your life on your terms.

As you move forward, trust that your healing journey will bring you closer to the person you were always meant to be — strong, independent, and free from the toxic grip of narcissistic manipulation.

The journey may not be easy, but it will be worth it.

Chapter 9

The Selfless Mask

Communal Narcissism and the Hidden Desire for Recognition

Examining the complex blend of altruism and self-interest that defines communal narcissism

Communal narcissists often hide their need for admiration behind a facade of kindness. Unlike overt narcissists, who crave attention for personal success or fame, communal narcissists seek validation through their self-proclaimed "good deeds."

They might appear altruistic, deeply involved in helping other people or supporting noble causes, but beneath the exterior lies a manipulative drive for recognition.

They tend to act as if they are morally superior, wanting everyone to see them as the most compassionate, self-sacrificing person in the room. This blend of self-interest with apparent altruism makes them difficult to identify and, in many ways, even harder to confront.

In this chapter, I'll explore communal narcissism, unpacking how these narcissists use their "acts of kindness" to secure admiration, manipulating other people while presenting themselves as paragons of virtue.

The hidden self-interest behind their seemingly charitable behaviour is what makes communal narcissism particularly dangerous — people with this personality type can do significant harm while appearing to do good.

Personal Reflection:

I thought I'd found someone who truly cared, someone who was dedicated to helping other people. But over time, it blew my mind that someone so kind and giving could have such a dark side. She was always offering to help other people and talking about making the world a better place. But the more I got to know her, the more I realised it was all about the recognition she got.

I came to realise that her so-called "acts of kindness" were always about her — about the praise she would receive and the image she could project. If no one praised her or showed appreciation for her "selflessness," she'd sulk or become angry, revealing a side I hadn't seen before. Her "help" wasn't really for other people — it was for her ego.

This experience is just one example of how communal narcissists operate. While they might appear as pillars of selflessness, the underlying motivations are self-serving.

Let's now delve deeper into the traits and behaviours that characterise these people. The aim is to shed light on this type of narcissism, helping you recognise its traits and understand how these people exploit the guise of kindness to manipulate and control the people around them.

The Core of Communal Narcissism

At the heart of communal narcissism is an intense need to be admired for "goodness." These people are driven by a desire to be seen as morally superior, regularly using acts of kindness to elevate their social status.

While their actions might initially seem genuinely altruistic, their true motivation is always self-serving — they're not just helping other people; they're using their "good deeds" to secure admiration and recognition

As I observed this pattern, I began to wonder whether genuine altruism even existed, or if everyone, deep down, was just trying to secure some form of recognition. It's a difficult thing to accept: how can someone's kindness be so self-serving, and yet look so selfless?

How Communal Narcissism Manifests

Communal narcissists don't openly boast about their achievements like overt narcissists. Instead, they boast about their kindness, generosity, or values.

The communal narcissist's "good deeds" make them seem above reproach, leaving their victims unsure of how to address the toxic dynamics. But beneath their helpful exterior, communal narcissists still share the core traits of narcissistic personality disorder: a need for admiration, a sense of entitlement, and a lack of genuine empathy.

Personal Reflection:

She would always talk about how "everyone needed her" and how "no one else could handle the responsibility" she took on. At first, I admired her dedication. But soon, I realised the unspoken truth: if everyone didn't acknowledge how hard she worked or how much she sacrificed, she'd react with passive-aggressive behaviour, or worse, shut down completely.

The Traits of Communal Narcissism

Common traits and manifestations of communal narcissists

- **Virtue Signalling:**

Communal narcissists love using charity or social causes to make themselves look morally superior. They don't care about the cause itself — what they really want is praise and recognition for being "good."

- **Martyrdom:**

They love playing the long-suffering hero. By highlighting their sacrifices, they guilt-trip other people into giving them the attention and sympathy they're desperate for. What looks like frustration or venting is just another manipulative way to make everything about them.

• Control Through 'Kindness':

When a communal narcissist offers to help, it always comes with strings attached. Their so-called kindness is just another way to control people and get their own way. If you don't want their help or don't show enough gratitude, they'll quickly turn passive-aggressive or resentful.

• Competition in Compassion:

Even kindness is a competition for them. They need to be the most giving, the most understanding, or the most selfless in the room. If someone else outshines them, they'll either dismiss the other person's efforts or try to one-up them by saying things like, "I would've done it better."

• Manipulative Altruism:

Their generosity is never genuine. It's always about what they can get in return — admiration, praise, or special treatment. If they don't get the recognition they expect, they'll quickly become bitter, revealing their true motives.

• Need for Public Recognition:

They're obsessed with being noticed for their efforts. Whether it's through social media or dropping hints in conversations, they go out of their way to make sure everyone knows about their "good deeds." If they don't get the public acknowledgment, they're after, they sulk or lash out.

• Exploitation of Vulnerability:

They're master's at spotting other people's weaknesses and using them to their advantage. If they help someone in need, it's only because they know it'll guarantee them admiration. Their so-called generosity is just another form of manipulation.

- **Emotional Coercion:**

If you don't respond to their "kindness" in the way they want, they'll punish you by withdrawing affection, sulking, or being passive aggressive. Their help is never free — it's a transaction, and you'll always end up paying for it.

The Psychological Roots of Communal Narcissism

To understand communal narcissists, we need to examine their deep-seated insecurities. At their core, they share the same emptiness and fragile sense of self-worth that drives all narcissistic behaviours.

For them, presenting as morally superior or altruistic provides a socially acceptable way to fill that void. But genuine selflessness doesn't exist, it's replaced by a strategic attempt to gain validation.

This behaviour could be a reflection of early experiences, where praise or attention might have been tied to helping or pleasing other people. Over time, their identity has become intertwined with being seen as "good."

A communal narcissist's inability to self-validate leads them to rely heavily on external approval, which they achieve through their carefully curated so called "good deeds."

Their narcissistic traits could have developed from a need to prove their worth to other people, this is sometimes linked to childhood experiences where they learned to gain approval through self-sacrifice or appearing morally superior.

These early patterns of behaviour can also be carried into adulthood, where they continue to seek validation through public acts of kindness and social involvement.

Communal Narcissism in Relationships

In relationships, communal narcissists can initially appear unbelievably supportive and loving, but their genuine motivation slowly comes to light over time. Relationships with communal narcissists can be draining and emotionally taxing, as the balance of genuine care is never equal.

- ## Conditional Love:

They might offer love or support, but it's always on the condition that the other person gives them praise, admiration, or recognition. If these conditions aren't met, they can withdraw or become emotionally distant.

- ## Emotional Manipulation:

Communal narcissists guilt-trip other people into recognising their "sacrifices." For instance, they might say, "After everything I've done for you, is this how you repay me?" This is designed to create a scenario where you feel indebted to them, even if their help wasn't asked for. Their emotional manipulation involves twisting situations to make you feel as though you owe them something, even when their actions were never really selfless.

- ## Guilt-Driven Expectations:

They are masters at making other people feel guilty for not acknowledging their "selflessness." If someone fails to show proper appreciation, they react with passive-aggressive behaviour or guilt-trip that person into giving them the recognition they feel they deserve.

- ## Undermining Independence:

Because communal narcissists want to be seen as indispensable, they discourage their partners from being independent. They frame their actions as concern, by saying things like, "I just want to make sure you're okay," while discreetly trying to imply that you can't manage without them. This is a classic manipulation tactic, where their need to be needed becomes central to the relationship. They fabricate a perceived scenario where you depend on them, not just for help, but for validation and emotional support.

The Long-Term Effects of Communal Narcissism

Over time, being involved with a communal narcissist can take a toll on your mental and emotional well-being.

The impact of being manipulated can be subtle, but the emotional toll is real. The constant subtle manipulations and guilt can lead you to experience:

- **Erosion of Self-Worth:**

After consistently giving in to the demands of a communal narcissist, survivors can begin to feel as though they're not worthy of genuine affection or love unless they meet certain expectations.

- **Exhaustion from Emotional Labour:**

The constant need to validate and acknowledge the communal narcissist's "goodness" can leave other people feeling emotionally drained, as their own needs are repeatedly overlooked in favour of the narcissist's desires.

- **Distrust of Other People's Motives:**

Because communal narcissists operate under this guise of altruism, you can end up becoming cynical and suspicious of other people, wondering if everyone's kindness comes with strings attached.

- **Confusion:**

Their outward kindness conflicts with their controlling behaviour, making it hard to understand their true intentions.

- **Feeling Undervalued:**

Their need to dominate in the realm of "goodness" can leave you feeling unappreciated or overshadowed.

- **Isolation:**

They discourage your connections with other people, positioning themselves as your primary source of support.

Recognising Communal Narcissism

Spotting communal narcissism can be challenging because their behaviour often looks positive on the surface.

Here's some key signs to watch for:

- **Excessive "Good Deed" Self-Promotion:**

They constantly remind other people of their good work or sacrifices making sure that their charitable actions are visible to everyone by using social media or even word-of-mouth to highlight their "good deeds."

- **Constant Need for Validation:**

Do they seem upset or resentful if they don't receive enough praise for their actions?

While they might seem selfless, they demand constant praise and recognition for their contributions. If they don't receive it, they can become frustrated or passive aggressive.

- **Conditional Help:**

Their offers of help are rarely unconditional. They expect something in return, whether it's recognition, gratitude, or admiration.

- **Guilt-Tripping:**

Do they make you feel bad for not appreciating them enough or if you set boundaries?

- **Competing in Kindness:**

Do they downplay other people's efforts to make themselves look better?

Coping Strategies for Dealing with Communal Narcissists

Dealing with a communal narcissist requires setting clear boundaries and being aware of their manipulative tendencies.

Here are some strategies:

- **Establish Boundaries:**

Communal narcissists will test your limits under the guise of helping, so it's crucial to establish firm boundaries and avoid allowing them to manipulate you into meeting their needs for constant validation. Don't feel obligated to accept their help if it doesn't feel genuine, and don't let their insistence pressure you into doing so.

- **Avoid Engaging in Guilt:**

When they try to make you feel guilty, remember you're not responsible for their emotions or need for praise. Stand firm and don't let them manipulate you into feeling bad.

- **Limit Praise:**

While it's natural to appreciate someone's efforts, avoid feeding their need for constant validation. Offer sincere appreciation when it's appropriate but avoid praising them excessively for every little action they take.

Keep your praise proportional to the situation and be aware of how much recognition they're seeking.

- **Be Cautious of Emotional Manipulation:**

When the narcissist is using guilt or shame to manipulate you into giving them recognition or affection. Recognise this emotional manipulation and don't internalize it.

- **Recognise the Pattern:**

Understanding that their behaviour is about seeking validation can help you take their actions less personally. Their behaviour is rooted in their own insecurities, not your lack of appreciation, or a reflection of your worth.

- **Practice Self-Care:**

It's important to prioritise your own emotional needs and seek support, when necessary, especially if you feel emotionally drained or exploited by the narcissist.

- **Seek Support:**

Dealing with a communal narcissist can be emotionally taxing. Talk to trusted friends, family, or a therapist about your experiences to gain perspective and support. External viewpoints can help you understand the situation more clearly and offer advice on how to protect your emotional well-being.

Moving Forward

Recognising and dealing with communal narcissism can be challenging, especially when their behaviour is so closely tied to positive actions.

Understanding communal narcissism is essential for protecting yourself from the hidden manipulation and emotional toll it can take.

Understanding their need for validation and the manipulative tactics they use can empower you to set boundaries and protect your emotional well-being.

While communal narcissists might appear selfless on the surface, their actions are ultimately about serving their ego. By recognising this dynamic, you can navigate relationships with them more effectively and you can avoid getting caught in their web of manipulation and focus on building healthier, more authentic connections.

It's possible to build healthier relationships based on mutual respect, where both parties give without expecting constant validation in return.

Remember: you deserve relationships built on genuine care and mutual respect, not manipulation and control disguised as kindness. It's important to acknowledge that while helping other people is noble, when it is done for self-serving purposes, it damages the people around them.

By learning to identify and manage communal narcissism, you can break free from the cycle of manipulation and reclaim your sense of self-worth.

Chapter 10

The Glorified Mirror

Somatic Narcissism and the Obsession with Appearance

Examining somatic narcissism, where physical appearance and validation through beauty dominate self-worth

Somatic narcissism is a form of narcissism that's often overlooked, but it's a more prevalent and impactful personality trait than many realise. Unlike malignant narcissism, which is driven by a desire for control and dominance, somatic narcissism focuses primarily on physical appearance and body image.

People with somatic narcissism place their sense of self-worth almost entirely on external validation, especially related to their looks, sexuality, and physical appeal. This type of narcissist is deeply invested in the idea that their value is determined by how other people see them, and they rely heavily on admiration of their physical form to feel validated.

In this chapter, I'll dive deeper into somatic narcissism and explore how an obsession with physical appearance influences the lives, relationships, and self-image of those affected. I'll explain how somatic narcissists view themselves and the world, and how their external focus shapes the reality of those around them, whether in romantic relationships, friendships, or professional environments.

Ultimately, this chapter will provide you with a comprehensive understanding of somatic narcissism and offer insights into recognising this type of narcissism in other people, as well as strategies for protecting yourself from its damaging effects.

Personal Reflection:

I remember thinking that she strived for her beauty to be showstopping — something that could silence a room, but there was an emptiness to her. Every moment seemed like it was a stage performance, with a need to be seen and adored by everyone.

Whenever admiration faded, a desperate need for attention would set in, and I realised that underneath the surface, she was chasing validation on a level that no praise would ever satisfy. It was like watching someone continuously look in a mirror, searching for worth in their reflection.

As you reflect on these thoughts, it's important to remember that somatic narcissism isn't simply about being vain or self-absorbed. It runs much deeper than that. Somatic narcissists are driven by an insatiable hunger for recognition, admiration, and validation, with their self-worth inextricably tied to how other people view them. When the attention they crave fades, the extent to which they rely on external validation leaves them feeling vulnerable, leading to feelings of inadequacy and insecurity.

The cycle they're trapped in can be exhausting for both them, and the people around them.

The Essence of Somatic Narcissism

At its core, somatic narcissism is a personality trait marked by a profound preoccupation with someone's physical appearance. Unlike narcissists who seek power and control through psychological manipulation or intellectual superiority, somatic narcissists are fixated on how they look, how other people perceive them, and how much admiration they can attract. Their self-esteem is fragile and fluctuates based on the validation they receive about their physical traits — whether it's compliments on their attractiveness, their body, or their style.

This kind of narcissism is particularly challenging because it often involves a facade of beauty and charm that makes it easy for other people to overlook the deeper psychological issues at play.

Somatic narcissists tend to thrive in environments where physical appearance is highly valued, such as in the entertainment industry, social media, or even the fashion world.

Their fixation on looks can lead them to view their bodies as tools to gain attention, which results in an ongoing, almost obsessive effort to maintain or enhance their physical appearance.

However, this fixation on beauty comes at a cost. Somatic narcissists often neglect deeper emotional growth or the cultivation of meaningful fulfilling relationships. Their worldview is shaped by an external focus, leading them to place little value on inner qualities or emotional intimacy. For them, appearances are everything, and they measure their worth by how much they are admired and adored by other people.

How Somatic Narcissism Manifests

Somatic narcissism manifests in a variety of ways, all revolving around an individual's obsession with their looks and the attention they can attract based on their physical appearance. Below are some key traits and behaviours commonly observed in somatic narcissists:

- **Obsession with Appearance:**

Somatic narcissists spend a considerable amount of time, money, and effort on grooming, fitness, and beauty routines. They often invest in expensive clothing, beauty treatments, or even plastic surgery in order to maintain an image of perfection. Their self-esteem is inextricably linked to how they look and how other people perceive them. They're constantly seeking affirmation, whether it's through social media likes, compliments from friends, or admiration from strangers.

Their entire sense of self can be influenced by a fleeting compliment or a moment of attention, leading to a constant cycle of validation-seeking behaviours. When this attention wanes, they can feel empty or worthless, prompting them to seek new sources of admiration. This constant hunger for recognition leads to frustration and a sense of inadequacy, because no amount of attention is ever enough to satisfy their deep need for validation.

- **Superficial Relationships:**

Relationships with somatic narcissists are often shallow, transactional, and based on appearance rather than substance.

They are adept at attracting people with their charm and physical appeal, but they struggle to form deep emotional connections. They try to surround themselves with admirers who praise their looks, but they regularly lack the capacity for genuine empathy or emotional intimacy.

Because somatic narcissists prioritise external validation, they often see relationships as a means to bolster their self-esteem. They look for partners, friends, and colleagues who'll reflect their idealised image back to them, rather than fostering relationships that are built on mutual respect, trust, and shared emotional connection.

- **Need for Constant Admiration:**

The need for constant admiration and positive reinforcement is one of the defining features of somatic narcissism. These individuals thrive on attention, particularly when it relates to their physical appearance. Whether it's compliments about their looks, their clothes, or their body, somatic narcissists live for the adoration and praise they receive from other people.

This constant need for admiration can make them exhausting to be around, as they always go to great lengths to ensure they remain the centre of attention. They monopolise conversations, exaggerate their achievements, or even engage in dramatic behaviour to capture the gaze of other people. When the attention fades, they feel abandoned or unloved, prompting them to seek out new sources of validation.

- **Sexual Validation:**

For many somatic narcissists, sexuality becomes another tool for validation. Their self-worth is closely tied to how sexually desirable they're perceived to be. As a result, somatic narcissists tend to use flirtation, seduction, or promiscuity to maintain their sense of worth. They thrive on sexual attention and regularly engage in risky or inappropriate behaviour to secure admiration and approval.

This fixation on sexual validation can lead to unhealthy and dysfunctional relationships, where emotional intimacy takes a backseat to physical attraction. Partners of somatic narcissists can feel as though they are being used as objects of desire rather than as individuals with their own emotional needs and desires.

Somatic Narcissism in Relationships

Being in a relationship with a somatic narcissist can be extremely draining and emotionally exhausting. These people often demand constant affirmation and admiration, but they struggle to provide the same level of emotional support or intimacy in return. Their relationships are built on superficial qualities rather than true emotional connection, and they prioritise their own image and validation over the needs of their partner.

•   **Jealousy and Competitiveness:**

Somatic narcissists feel envious or threatened if they believe someone else is attracting more attention than they are. This jealousy can spill over into their relationships, where they might try to undermine their partner's confidence or distract attention away from other people in order to regain the spotlight. This competitiveness can create a toxic atmosphere, where both partners are constantly vying for attention, and the relationship becomes more about who can be the most admired rather than about mutual care and support.

•   **Emotional Detachment:**

Somatic narcissists often struggle with emotional intimacy and connection. Their preoccupation with their appearance and the validation they receive from other people make it difficult for them to engage on a deeper emotional level.

Relationships with them can feel empty, as somatic narcissists show little interest in their partner's feelings, struggles, or needs. This emotional detachment can leave the partner feeling unseen and unappreciated, as their worth is often measured solely by how they reflect or enhance the narcissist's image.

- **Emphasis on Public Image:**

For somatic narcissists, public image is everything. They might be affectionate and attentive in public settings, wanting to appear like the perfect couple or the ideal family, but behind closed doors, they can be emotionally distant, abusive and neglectful. The image they project to other people is of utmost importance, and they'll go to great lengths to maintain a picture-perfect appearance, even if it means neglecting the emotional needs of their partner.

The Long-Term Effects of Somatic Narcissism

The relentless pursuit of physical validation takes a toll, not only on somatic narcissists but also on the people who form relationships with them. The need for admiration can create a constant cycle of superficial interactions, leaving emotional damage in its wake.

- **Deterioration of Self-Worth:**

As somatic narcissists age or face physical changes, their self-worth begins to erode. They become anxious about losing their physical appeal and, in turn, feel less worthy. The reliance on external validation means that they struggle to find self-worth from within, and when they can no longer meet their own or other people's standards of beauty, they experience depression, anxiety, and a deep sense of inadequacy.

- **Relational Exhaustion for Partners:**

Partners of somatic narcissists often experience emotional exhaustion from the constant need to reinforce the narcissist's self-image. They can feel as though they're living in the shadow of the narcissist's needs, where their own feelings, needs, and desires are overlooked. The one-sided nature of these relationships can lead to burnout and resentment.

- **Isolation and Superficiality:**

The obsession with appearance can isolate somatic narcissists from forming meaningful connections with other people.

Their relationships tend to be shallow, and they may feel lonely or disconnected, despite the superficial admiration they receive. This emotional emptiness can lead to feelings of isolation, as they struggle to find deeper connections beyond the surface.

Recognising Somatic Narcissism

Recognising the traits of somatic narcissism can help you protect yourself from the damaging effects of this type of narcissist. Here are some warning signs to watch for:

- **Preoccupation with Physical Appearance:**

Somatic narcissists frequently talk about their looks, their body, and their appearance, seeking validation and admiration at every turn. Their conversations almost always revolve around topics such as weight, beauty, clothing, or physical fitness.

- **Attention-Seeking Through Sexuality:**

A strong tendency to flirt or engage in seductive behaviour is another red flag. They will use their sexuality to attract attention and admiration, seeing their desirability as a key part of their identity.

- **Emotionally Shallow Relationships:**

Somatic narcissists struggle to engage in emotionally deep relationships. Their connections with other people are superficial, with little interest in emotional depth or shared experiences beyond looks, status, or fashion.

Coping Strategies for Dealing with Somatic Narcissists

Dealing with somatic narcissists requires setting clear boundaries and prioritising your own emotional wellbeing.

Here are some strategies to help protect yourself:

- **Focus on Your Own Self-Worth:**

Remember that your value isn't based on your appearance or how other people perceive you. Building self-esteem rooted in your inner qualities will help protect you from becoming overly influenced by the somatic narcissist's need for validation.

- **Establish Clear Boundaries:**

Somatic narcissists will constantly test your boundaries, pushing you to continually reinforce their image. It's essential to set limits on behaviour that makes you uncomfortable.

- **Avoid Excessive Compliments or Validation:**

While it may seem harmless to compliment a somatic narcissist, excessive validation only serves to reinforce their behaviour. Strive for balanced interactions that focus on deeper qualities and shared experiences, rather than surface-level praise.

- **Seek Support:**

Engaging in a relationship with a somatic narcissist can be mentally and emotionally exhausting. Seeking support from friends, family, or a therapist can help provide clarity, restore your sense of self-worth, and offer guidance on how to cope with the emotional challenges of dealing with a somatic narcissist.

Moving Forward

Understanding somatic narcissism helps illuminate the cycle of empty validation and the impact it can have on both the narcissist and the people around them. Recognising these traits can empower you to protect your emotional health, ensuring that you aren't drawn into the superficial allure of these relationships. Real value and fulfilment come from relationships built on empathy, mutual respect, and shared growth, rather than an obsession with appearance.

Embrace relationships that encourage authenticity, self-worth, and emotional depth. When you surround yourself with people who value you for who you truly are, beyond just the surface, you can build strong, lasting bonds that support your personal growth and emotional well-being. By prioritising real connections, you can break free from the superficial grip of somatic narcissism and reclaim your life.

Chapter 11

The Realm of the Mind

Cerebral Narcissism and Intellectual Superiority

An exploration of cerebral narcissism and how intellectual superiority shape's identity and relationships

Cerebral narcissism represents a distinctive, less obvious, but deeply impactful form of narcissistic behaviour. It's characterised by an overwhelming obsession with intelligence, wit, and a relentless pursuit of intellectual superiority.

Unlike other forms of narcissism that revolve around physical appearance or charm, cerebral narcissists base their sense of self-worth almost entirely on their mental capabilities.

They see their intellect as their defining feature, it's the thing that sets them apart and elevates them above other people. But this intense focus on intellect comes at a cost to the people around them, leaving them feeling diminished, patronised, or trapped in a constant cycle of competition for respect, acknowledgment, and validation.

In this chapter, I'll take a closer look at cerebral narcissism, exploring the arrogant need for the intellectual validation that defines this particular type of narcissistic behaviour. Together, we'll explore how this mindset manifests in behaviours that can shape, and often, strain relationships.

The aim is to deepen your understanding of how this mindset manifests and affects people involved with cerebral narcissists, help you to identify its tell-tale signs, appreciate its complexities, and the best ways for you to protect yourself from its insidious consequences.

Personal Reflection:

I used to think her knowledge was impressive. She'd bring up random facts, and I'd find myself drawn to how much she seemed to know. But over time, it became clear that it wasn't about sharing knowledge; it was about holding power.

The more I questioned or disagreed, the more she tried to belittle me, as if my thoughts were just inferior shadows of hers. She tried to make me feel small, like my mind wasn't enough to keep up.

This chapter will help you understand cerebral narcissism at a deeper level, so you can recognise the key traits, patterns, and tactics used by cerebral narcissists. It also offers insights into when it might be time to establish boundaries in order to protect your own self-worth and mental peace.

The Essence of Cerebral Narcissism

Cerebral narcissism isn't formally recognised as a clinical diagnosis, but it's a well-known set of narcissistic traits that focus on the intellectual realm rather than physical appearance or charm. People with cerebral narcissism rely heavily on their intellectual abilities to validate their self-worth. They view themselves as intellectually superior to other people, especially in areas such as logic, knowledge, creativity, or even critical thinking. The need to always "be right" or demonstrate superiority in intellectual pursuits becomes a defining aspect of their identity.

This constant need for intellectual validation shapes their interactions with the world and with the people around them. It's not just about having an opinion; it's about making other people feel as though their ideas are inherently inferior.

While physical admiration might fuel other types of narcissists, cerebral narcissists seek respect and adoration based on their intellectual abilities.

This pursuit of intellectual superiority can result in a pattern of condescension, criticism, and competitive intellectual dominance in their relationships.

The cerebral narcissist's need to feel smarter than the people around them can make them dismissive of other people's ideas and contributions, focusing primarily on their own perceived brilliance.

In their interactions, cerebral narcissists may monopolise conversations, constantly steer discussions toward their areas of expertise, and feel threatened if anyone challenges or disagrees with them.

For them, intellectual dominance isn't just about winning debates — it's a way of asserting control and demonstrating superiority over other people. Their conversations lack genuine engagement or mutual respect, instead serving as platforms to assert control and prove their brilliance.

How Cerebral Narcissism Manifests

Cerebral narcissism reveals itself through behaviours that focus on establishing and maintaining intellectual superiority.

Here are some common traits that define this type of narcissist:

- **Intellectual Superiority:**

Cerebral narcissists often seek intellectual dominance in various settings, whether in casual conversations, work environments, or social gatherings. For example, at work, they may take every opportunity to correct colleagues' presentations, belittle other people's Ideas in meetings, or redirect discussions to their areas of expertise. In casual settings, they might constantly drop obscure references or excessively name-drop famous intellectuals to elevate their own status.

Even when their knowledge isn't needed, they subtly remind other people of their intellectual prowess by offering unsolicited advice or critiques, leaving other people feeling inferior. This need for constant validation of their intelligence often results in a strained atmosphere, where collaboration feels more like a competition to prove who's smarter.

- **Dismissive Attitude:**

People with cerebral narcissism have little patience for different perspectives. They actively dismiss other people's ideas with a combination of impatience and disdain as unworthy of serious consideration, scoffing at viewpoints they see as less intelligent or ill-informed and redirecting conversations to focus on their preferred topics.

This habit is designed to marginalise other people's opinions and reinforce the cerebral narcissist's belief in their own intellectual infallibility.

- **Monopolisation of Discussions:**

For a cerebral narcissist, conversations are less about exchange and more about dominance. They dominate discussions by steering them toward topics they know well, and disregarding or invalidating other people's contributions. For them, the goal of a conversation isn't mutual exchange or understanding but instead asserting their intellectual superiority. Their need to be the "smartest person in the room" often means they engage in long monologues, leaving little or no room for other people to express themselves.

- **Logic Over Empathy**

Cerebral narcissists prioritise intellect over emotional connection, often responding to emotional disclosures with cold analysis or attempts to "solve" feelings, rather than offering empathy or understanding. This invalidates emotional experiences, making other people feel as though their emotions are irrational or unimportant.

Over time, this dynamic can lead partners, friends, or family members to suppress their emotional needs to avoid being dismissed or belittled. The cerebral narcissist's inability or unwillingness to engage emotionally creates a void where genuine connection should exist. The imbalance between logic and empathy erodes trust and emotional intimacy, leaving other people feeling isolated and unsupported.

Cerebral Narcissism in Relationships

Being in a relationship with a cerebral narcissist can be mentally and emotionally exhausting. Whether in friendships, romantic partnerships, or family relationships, people who interact with cerebral narcissists tend to feel belittled, unappreciated, and intellectually inadequate, with the cerebral narcissist taking centre stage and their counterpart relegated to the shadows.

Here's how cerebral narcissism can affect relationships:

- **Control Through Critique:**

Cerebral narcissists don't just criticise for the sake of improving someone's thoughts; they use critique as a method to assert dominance. For example, in a relationship, a cerebral narcissist might frequently challenge their partner's decision-making, no matter how trivial, and provide lengthy explanations of why their partner is wrong. One evening, you may decide on a restaurant for dinner, but the cerebral narcissist dismisses your choice and begins to lecture you on the "right" kind of food based on health trends.

This might seem minor, but over time, this undermines the partner's confidence in their own judgment, making them question their ability to make decisions on their own. In extreme cases, this creates a dependency where the partner feels unable to act without the narcissist's approval. This ongoing dynamic diminishes the partner's autonomy and fosters a power imbalance with the cerebral narcissist always positioned as the intellectual authority.

- **Emotional Detachment:**

Intellectual pursuits often take precedence over emotional connection for cerebral narcissists. Their partners might feel emotionally neglected, as their needs for empathy, support, and affection are often ignored in favour of discussions about facts, logic, or intellectual superiority. The narcissist's inability or unwillingness to engage in emotional dialogue can leave their partner feeling isolated, as if their feelings and emotional experiences are unimportant.

- **Validation Through Debate:**

For cerebral narcissists, debate isn't about understanding other people's viewpoints or seeking common ground — it's about "winning." They argue to prove themselves right, not to engage in meaningful conversation.

For their partner, this can feel like a constant battle for intellectual validation, where their thoughts and ideas are dismissed, and they're left feeling intellectually inferior.

Long-Term Effects of Cerebral Narcissism

Living with or being close to a cerebral narcissist can be mentally draining and can have long-lasting effects on your mental well-being, leaving lasting effects on self-esteem. Over time, you might experience the following:

- **Self-Doubt in Intelligence:**

The emotional toll of constantly being belittled by a cerebral narcissist can stretch far beyond the relationship. Partners or friends may start to question their intellectual abilities in other aspects of their lives. They might avoid offering their opinions in meetings at work, hesitate to speak up in social situations, or defer to other people when making decisions, fearing their ideas will be ridiculed.

For instance, after being repeatedly mocked for their presentation at work, someone might begin to second-guess their ideas in future meetings. They might find themselves avoiding new projects or staying silent during brainstorming sessions for fear of being embarrassed.

Over time, this can result in a pervasive sense of self-doubt that extends beyond the relationship with the narcissist, affecting their ability to trust their own judgment and seek out intellectual validation in other contexts.

- **Loss of Confidence in Communication:**

Due to the cerebral narcissist's frequent dismissiveness, over time other people, or their partners can feel uncomfortable voicing their opinions or ideas for fear of ridicule or correction. This can lead to a gradual erosion of self-confidence and a reluctance to speak up in intellectual or social situations.

- **Emotional Disconnection:**

Over time, a relationship with a cerebral narcissist can become emotionally hollow. What begins as subtle distance often turns into a complete lack of emotional presence. Their partner may feel like they're speaking into a void — their feelings met with cold logic or indifference. Even when the narcissist is physically present, there's a growing sense of loneliness, as emotional intimacy fades into silence.

Recognising Cerebral Narcissism

Cerebral narcissists can be hard to spot because their behaviour often appears charming and intellectual at first. However, there are certain signs you can watch for that may help you recognise them:

- **Unsolicited Corrections:**

Cerebral narcissists frequently correct other peoples' grammar, knowledge, or reasoning, often without being asked. They find fault with even the smallest details to assert their intellectual dominance. For example, you might mention an idea you've read about, and before you even finish your sentence, the cerebral narcissist interrupts with, "Actually, that's not quite right." Even if the correction is trivial — like the year a historical event occurred — it leaves you feeling as though they're always waiting for you to make a mistake.

Over time, these minor corrections can build up, reinforcing the narcissist's position as the "authority" in all discussions, while leaving you feeling unsure of your own knowledge.

- ### Disdain for 'Simple' People or Ideas:

Cerebral narcissists have little patience for people they view as intellectually inferior. They tend to show contempt for people who they believe have simpler or less sophisticated ideas, which can create a hierarchy of intelligence in their relationships.

- ### Endless Need to Be Right:

One of the key traits of cerebral narcissism is the refusal to accept when they're wrong. They rarely admit fault, and they'll go to great lengths to justify their position, seeing every conversation as an opportunity to showcase their intellect and prove they're right.

Coping Strategies for Dealing with Cerebral Narcissists

Navigating relationships with cerebral narcissists can be extremely challenging.

Here are some strategies that can help you protect your own emotional and intellectual well-being:

- ### Limit Engagement in Intellectual Showdowns:

Avoid getting caught in the trap of constantly debating or defending your ideas. State your views clearly but calmly, and don't let their dismissive attitude make you question your own worth or intelligence.

- ### Set Boundaries on Critical Behaviour:

If the cerebral narcissist's constant criticism is damaging to your self-esteem, set firm boundaries. Let them know how their behaviour impacts you and make it clear that you won't tolerate being belittled or corrected unnecessarily.

- **Prioritise Your Emotional Needs:**

While intellectual validation might be important to a cerebral narcissist, your emotional needs are just as critical. Seek support from friends, family, or a therapist who can offer empathy, understanding, and validation for your emotional experiences. It's also helpful to engage in self-care routines that prioritise your emotional health, such as regular mindfulness exercises, journaling, or spending time in nature.

For instance, setting aside an hour each week to talk with a trusted friend or journaling about your feelings can help you process the emotional neglect you might feel. This will ensure you're not left emotionally drained while dealing with the cerebral narcissist's constant need for validation.

- **Strengthen Your Self-Worth:**

Cerebral narcissists can chip away at your confidence, so it's important to regularly remind yourself of your own strengths and capabilities. Surround yourself with people who value you for who you are, not just for your intellectual abilities.

Moving Forward

Understanding cerebral narcissism is an important step in protecting your mental and emotional space. While cerebral narcissists can be challenging to deal with, it's possible to navigate these relationships with the right tools and strategies.

Establishing clear boundaries, recognising when you are being intellectually undermined, and seeking out healthy supportive environments can help you maintain a strong sense of self.

Cerebral narcissists often thrive on intellectual dominance, but with self-awareness and support, you can learn to protect yourself from their manipulative tactics.

It's essential to remember that your worth isn't defined by how you compare to other people, especially those who try to diminish you for their own gain.

Over time, as you grow stronger in your self-belief and set firmer boundaries, you'll be able to engage with cerebral narcissists in a way that protects your mental health and well-being, while maintaining respect for your own intelligence and emotional needs. Understanding that your ideas and emotions are valid, regardless of how a cerebral narcissist might attempt to undermine them, is key.

Your thoughts and contributions are valuable, and you deserve to be in relationships where your intellect and emotions are acknowledged and respected.

Chapter 12

The Shadowed Pathway

Malignant Narcissism's Dark and Dangerous Traits

Exploring malignant narcissism and its destructive traits, including aggression, paranoia and sadism

Malignant narcissism is one of the most destructive forms of narcissism. It's more than selfishness or vanity — it's a dangerous mix of toxic traits aimed at undermining, controlling, and dehumanising other people. Fuelled by ambition and entitlement, it combines antisocial tendencies, paranoia, aggression, and a chilling lack of empathy. Malignant narcissism isn't just about coexisting with other people — it's about actively stripping away their identity and dignity, leaving them vulnerable to domination and emotional destruction.

This dangerous amalgamation of traits leaves a trail of profound emotional destruction, plunging victims into a state of confusion, fear, and social isolation. The psychological toll can be overwhelming, as survivors grapple with the weight of manipulation and the loss of their autonomy.

It's an existence likened to walking through a labyrinth where every turn leads to further entrapment rather than escape.

As a survivor of narcissistic abuse, I can attest to the depths of the psychological distress caused by malignant narcissists.

They don't just want to control — they want to break you down to the point where you doubt your very existence. The emotional confusion is deliberate and designed to disorientate. No matter how hard you try to make sense of their behaviour, it remains deliberately blurred, pulling you deeper into a psychological maze of fear, doubt, and subjugation.

In this chapter, I'm going to expose the dangerous, predatory side of malignant narcissism, shedding light on the harmful effects it has on the lives of people who become entangled with it. Drawing from personal reflections and a deeper understanding of its mechanisms, I'll uncover the manipulative tactics malignant narcissists use to destroy the well-being of other people. I aim to equip readers with the tools necessary to recognise, confront, and protect themselves from this insidious force.

Personal Reflection:

I remember constantly questioning whether I'd done something wrong. Perhaps I'd done something to deserve this torment? Every time I tried to figure it out, she intensified her efforts to keep me under her control — swinging between a relentless dance of charm and abuse, leaving me perpetually on edge. Her words could soothe when she wanted something then cut like knives the next.

It wasn't until I felt totally drained, emotionally, physically, and mentally, being lost and manipulated beyond recognition, that I understood just how deep her anger and manipulation could go. Once she had finally overwhelmed me, I saw the true depths of her toxicity. It was like dancing with darkness in a shadow that wanted to consume me.

The purpose of this chapter is to illuminate the traits, behaviours, and long-term consequences associated with malignant narcissism.

I'll look at the traits that define it, how it manifests in relationships, and the long-term psychological effects it can leave in its wake. You'll also learn how to protect yourself from its devastating grip.

The Essence of Malignant Narcissism

Malignant narcissism occupies a grim intersection between narcissistic personality disorder (NPD) and antisocial personality traits.

This hybrid pathology creates a far more sinister and destructive version of narcissism than typically seen in its covert or overt forms

Malignant narcissists exhibit the hallmark features of traditional narcissism, such as an exaggerated sense of self-importance and an insatiable need for validation. However, these traits are coupled with an alarming disregard for the rights, feelings, and autonomy of other people.

Their methods are rooted in manipulation and exploitation, but their ultimate aim is far more destructive. For these people, power isn't a means to an end — it's the end itself.

Malignant narcissists seek control and dominance. They actually derive pleasure from the pain they inflict. The driving force behind their behaviour isn't merely the need for validation or adoration — it's the need to instil fear and maintain psychological control over other people.

Their behaviour is sadistic, marked by a callous indifference to the suffering they cause. Their lack of empathy renders them oblivious to the emotional devastation they leave in their wake, leaving their victims feeling helpless, dehumanised, and trapped in a psychological maze with no clear exit.

How Malignant Narcissism Manifests

Malignant narcissism manifests in ways that are unbelievably difficult to understand, especially for people caught in its web.

It's not a passive or subtle form of narcissism; It's as overt as it is destructive, it's manipulative, and violent in its tactics.

Malignant narcissism relies on passive-aggressive tactics operating with brazen hostility and an unrelenting desire to control. It's an active, predatory force that seeks to undermine, intimidate, and destabilise its targets.

The tactics employed are insidious, leaving their victims second-guessing their actions and questioning their perceptions. It's only when the damage is too deep to ignore that the victim realises, they've been manipulated beyond recognition. The constant psychological warfare is exhausting. Relationships, both intimate and otherwise, become war zones where the narcissist deploys charm and cruelty in equal measure, shifting gears rapidly to keep the victim destabilised.

Defining Traits of Malignant Narcissism

Malignant narcissists rarely bother to disguise their intentions. They can be openly hostile, wielding intimidation, verbal abuse, threats, or even physical violence to maintain their grip and control over other people.

Their aggression isn't born from passion or momentary anger; it's a calculated deliberate strategy to instil fear. Their need for control is so intense that they won't hesitate to use cruelty to consolidate their dominance, ensuring their victims remain in a state of subjugation.

These individuals view aggression as a tool, not an emotional response. It's premeditated, and it serves a very specific purpose — to maintain power and control. The use of violence, whether emotional or physical, is a tactic to destabilise their target, ensuring their victim is in constant fear of retribution.

- **Paranoia and Distrust:**

Malignant narcissists operate under a cloud of paranoia. They believe that everyone is out to get them, or undermine them, which fuels their aggressive behaviour. This "us versus them" mindset makes it easy for them to manipulate people around them into thinking they're part of an exclusive group of besieged people compelled to defend themselves against perceived threats.

These people live in a world where trust is a foreign concept. Paranoia becomes a weapon, used to encourage other people to form alliances based on fear and a shared sense of external danger.

The distrust they instil is contagious, making other people feel as though they need to align themselves with the narcissist in order to survive.

This fuels a cycle of fear and manipulation that ensnares even the most well-intentioned people. Over time, the narcissist isolates their target from anyone who challenges their intentions.

- **Sadistic Pleasure:**

One of the most chilling aspects of malignant narcissism is the sadistic pleasure they derive from inflicting pain.

Their actions aren't reactive; they're actually proactive, driven by a desire to assert their power through making other people suffer — they actively set out to harm other people in order to feel powerful. Whether it's through humiliation, gaslighting, or outright abuse, they revel in their ability to control and destroy.

This sadism is often subtle but profound, leaving the victim in emotional agony. The narcissist might disguise their actions with a thin veil of justification, but the harm they cause is intentional, and it leaves deep scars on their victims.

- **Exploitation and Deceit:**

Malignant narcissists are master manipulators using other people for their own gain. They lie, deceive, and exploit people without a second thought. The well-being of the people around them is irrelevant to them; they only care about achieving their goals, no matter the cost to anyone else.

They don't see relationships as partnerships, but as opportunities for ruthless exploitation. Lying and deceiving come as naturally to them as breathing, and they pursue their goals with an unflinching disregard for the well-being of other people. Victims are simply stepping stones to reach their objective.

Malignant Narcissism in Relationships

Relationships with malignant narcissists are among the most damaging and destructive because of the way these people distort and control every aspect of them, these relationships are some of the most harrowing and destructive human experiences.

The relationships malignant narcissists form are rarely long-lasting, not because of their victims' ability to escape, but due to the irreparable damage they cause. These people are relentless in their pursuit of control and dominance, distorting every aspect of the connection to serve their own insidious goals.

What starts as an intense, often whirlwind bond — fuelled by charm and charisma — rapidly devolves into a psychological battleground where the narcissist wields fear, manipulation, and emotional abuse as weapons.

Whether the relationship is romantic or otherwise, the malignant narcissist's presence leaves their victims scarred, doubting their own self worth and reality. It's no exaggeration to describe these relationships as a serious form of psychological warfare.

- **Control Through Terror:**

The primary weapon of a malignant narcissist is terror. They use intimidation, threats, and violence to maintain control, making it clear that defiance will result in punishment. This terror isn't limited to immediate threats; it extends into the victim's psyche, making them fearful to act, speak, or even think independently.

As the victim becomes isolated from friends, family, and other support systems, they become entirely dependent on the narcissist, trapped in an emotional prison where any attempt at resistance feels futile.

- **Gaslighting and Reality Distortion**

Gaslighting is a hallmark of malignant narcissism. By distorting reality and planting seeds of doubt, these individuals undermine their victims' confidence in their own perceptions and memories. Over time, victims begin to question their sanity, doubting their ability to interpret events accurately. This psychological disorientation weakens the victim's independence, leaving them more vulnerable to further manipulation and control.

- **Emotional Blackmail:**

Malignant narcissists excel at emotional blackmail, employing threats of abandonment, harm, or retaliation to keep their victims under control in order to keep them from leaving.

This keeps them trapped in a constant state of anxiety, unsure whether their relationship will ever be safe or stable. Their tactics can also include dramatic ultimatums and calculated guilt-trips.

This emotional manipulation makes it almost impossible for the victim to break free, because they're left paralysed by the terror of the narcissist's unpredictable and retaliatory behaviour.

- **Past Life Triangulation:**

Malignant narcissists love to involve a third party to create conflict and stir up jealousy, insecurity, and competition. They sometimes use a former partner to manipulate the victim into feeling threatened or inferior. By comparing the victim unfavourably to a former partner, the narcissist maintains control over their emotions and keeps them in a state of anxiety.

This kind of triangulation is particularly effective because it creates doubt and mistrust within the relationship. The victim is left questioning their worth and feeling insecure about their place in the narcissist's life. This tactic reinforces the narcissist's power and keeps the victim emotionally dependent on them.

Long-Term Effects of Malignant Narcissism

The aftermath of a relationship with a malignant narcissist is a long and arduous journey. The effects of enduring this type of toxic relationship can be difficult to overcome, taking years to fully heal from.

The damage inflicted isn't just immediate; it can become deeply ingrained, sometimes leaving victims with scars that can take a lifetime to heal. These effects permeate every facet of the victim's life, from their mental and emotional well-being to their ability to trust, connect, and find happiness.

• Chronic Anxiety and Hypervigilance:

Living under the constant threat of the malignant narcissist's next move breeds unrelenting anxiety.

Victims become hyper-vigilant, always on edge, as they live under constant threat of harm, unable to relax or feel safe. This anxiety can persist long after the relationship ends because the trauma experienced becomes ingrained in their psyche.

Everyday interactions may feel like potential battlegrounds, with victims conditioned to expect conflict, manipulation, or betrayal at any moment.

• Severe Self-Doubt:

The relentless manipulation inherent in a malignant narcissistic relationship erodes the victim's confidence and self-worth. Emotional abuse creates a profound sense of self-doubt, making victims question their own judgment, abilities, and sanity. This self-doubt can cause them to lose trust in their own perceptions and instincts. Rebuilding this trust can be an uphill battle, requiring immense support and self-compassion.

• Trauma and Complex PTSD (CPTSD):

The psychological trauma inflicted by a malignant narcissist goes beyond the immediate effects of abuse, resulting in complex post-traumatic stress disorder (CPTSD). This condition is marked by persistent feelings of helplessness, hypervigilance, and emotional numbness related to the trauma they've endured.

Healing from this kind of profound trauma requires time, and often specialised therapy to truly rebuild your life.

Recognising Malignant Narcissism

Malignant narcissists leave a trail of destruction in their wake, particularly in the early stages of a relationship when their charm and charisma are on full display. However, there are consistent red flags that, when recognised, can serve as crucial warning signs.

Be wary of the following signs:

- ### Intense Charisma Followed by Control Tactics:

Malignant narcissists begin relationships with overwhelming affection, attention, and promises of loyalty.

This honeymoon phase is a calculated move to create dependency. Once the victim is sufficiently attached, the narcissist's true nature emerges, and the charm is replaced by manipulation, criticism, and control.

- ### Disregard for Rules or Social Norms:

A malignant narcissist shows little regard for personal boundaries or social conventions. Their behaviour is erratic, and they expect other people to cater to their every whim without question. They operate with an inflated sense of entitlement, believing that they're exempt from rules or personal boundaries. They demand compliance and submission from other people without offering any respect in return.

- ### Displays of Callousness and Cruelty:

Possibly the most telling sign of malignant narcissism is their blatant disregard for other people's emotions. These people show a lack of empathy in ways that are shocking and completely indifferent to other people's suffering.

They make cruel comments, cutting remarks, belittle other people without remorse, and even seem entertained by the pain they cause. Their actions reflect a deep-seated propensity for cruelty that's unnerving to witness. This is all part of their overall disregard for anyone other than themselves.

Coping Strategies for Dealing with Malignant Narcissists

Surviving a relationship with a malignant narcissist requires a combination of resilience, strategic action, and emotional fortification. While escaping their grip is never easy, it's possible with the right approach.

Here are some strategies to help you survive and heal:

- **Set Firm Boundaries and Stick to Them:**

Malignant narcissists thrive on breaking down boundaries, but boundaries are critical when dealing with a malignant narcissist. These people will test, push, and attempt to obliterate any limits set for them. Establishing and maintaining clear, non-negotiable boundaries is essential for protecting yourself from their manipulative behaviour.

- **Limit Contact When Possible:**

Minimising contact with a malignant narcissist can be one of the most effective ways to protect yourself and regain control of your life. Whether it's severing ties entirely or minimizing unavoidable contact, creating space from their toxic influence is vital to regain your sense of self. These people will continue to seek opportunities to manipulate and control you, so limiting interaction really is crucial.

- **Prioritise Self-Care and Mental Health Support:**

Healing from the trauma of a malignant narcissistic relationship requires consistent self-care and professional guidance. Therapy can be instrumental in addressing lingering emotional wounds, rebuilding self-esteem, and processing the complex emotions left in the wake of the malignant abuse you've endured.

- **Develop a Strong Support Network:**

Isolation is a hallmark of malignant narcissistic abuse. Malignant narcissists isolate their victims, which makes it critical to have a solid support system. Connections with trusted friends, family members, and support groups can provide invaluable validation and comfort as you recover.

- **Stay Grounded in Your Own Reality:**

One of the most damaging aspects of a malignant narcissist's manipulation is their ability to distort your perception of reality.

Regularly check in with yourself and trusted people to ensure that you're not being manipulated. Reaffirming your perception of reality will help you maintain your sense of self and sanity. Journaling, mindfulness practices, and open conversations can help anchor you in your own reality.

Moving Forward

Recognising and understanding malignant narcissism is the first step towards breaking free from its grip, reclaiming your life, and emotional health. The damage caused by these people can be deep and lasting, but with the right tools and support, recovery is possible.

Surround yourself with people who care about you, prioritise self-compassion, and work toward rebuilding your life. With time, patience, and healing, you can find freedom from the toxic hold of a malignant narcissist and move forward with confidence and resilience.

You've got the strength to rise above the devastation, reclaim your identity, and create a future life rooted in strength, authenticity, self-respect, and inner peace.

With each step forward, you move closer to freedom, proving that the hold of malignant narcissism isn't insurmountable.

Healing isn't only possible — it's within your reach, and it begins with recognising your worth and refusing to let anyone diminish it again.

Remember, you're not defined by the pain inflicted on you.

Chapter 13

The Dark Mask

Psychopathic Narcissism and Calculated Deception

Investigating the manipulative, remorseless traits of psychopathic narcissism and their real-world impact

Yes.......There are actually differences between psychopathic narcissism and malignant narcissism. Even though they're closely related, and despite common misconceptions, they're not exactly the same. While both terms describe severe forms of narcissism with overlapping traits, there are aspects that set them apart.

So, before I delve deep into psychopathic narcissism, I want to quickly compare some of these differences.

Malignant narcissism refers to an extreme form of narcissistic personality disorder, (NPD), characterised by a mix of narcissism, antisocial traits, aggression, and sadism. Malignant narcissists are manipulative, lack empathy, and have a grandiose sense of self-importance. They enjoy causing harm, exploiting other people, and maintaining power at all costs. Their behaviour is marked by cruelty and an intense need to dominate.

Psychopathic narcissism, on the other hand, merges traits of narcissism with psychopathy. While psychopathy itself is associated with superficial charm, lack of empathy, and impulsivity, when it's combined with narcissism, it amplifies grandiosity and entitlement.

A psychopathic narcissist will manipulate and exploit other people but in a more calculated and less overtly aggressive manner than a malignant narcissist.

They may not necessarily take sadistic pleasure in causing pain, but their actions still result in harm. In practice, the lines between these can blur, as both involve severe dysfunction and harm to other people. However, understanding the distinction between them helps when exploring their underlying motivations and behavioural patterns.

Psychopathic narcissism combines the need for power, admiration, and superiority found in narcissistic traits with the callous, remorseless, and ruthless tendencies typical of psychopathy.

Psychopathic narcissists excel at blending into their surroundings, wearing a mask of charm and normalcy that conceals their darker intentions. They are emotional predators, skilled at gaining trust, exploiting vulnerabilities, and leaving devastation in their wake.

They move through life like chameleons, manipulating with ease and leaving a path of emotional devastation, with long-lasting scars that can take years to heal. Victims who encounter this type of narcissist can be left reeling for a lifetime from the damage they cause.

In this chapter, I'll peel back the layers of psychopathic narcissism to expose the calculated and ruthless personality that thrives on control, dominance, and moral disregard.

I'll also provide a clear understanding of psychopathic narcissism, offering insights to help you recognise its traits and understand how to protect yourself from its devastating effects.

Personal Reflection:

The more time I spent with her, the more I felt a creeping sense of dread. There was a coldness underneath, an almost calculating cruelty hidden behind the friendly facade. It was like she enjoyed watching me unravel while keeping her own mask intact. She could charm a room, but behind closed doors, there was a stark absence of empathy — a void that was chilling to confront. By the time I realised what I was dealing with It was too late, the damage had already been done.

Psychopathic Narcissism: The Silent Predator

Psychopathic narcissism is a term used to describe a particularly dangerous personality type that blends traits of narcissistic personality disorder (NPD) and psychopathy.

While it's not an official diagnosis in diagnostic manuals, it provides a useful framework for understanding a certain kind of personality disorder that wreaks havoc in the lives of people who come into contact with it.

People who possess psychopathic narcissism exhibit a unique combination of traits that make them more harmful and manipulative than other types of narcissists. These people operate on a level of danger that can be difficult to spot until it's too late.

Unlike overt narcissists who openly display self-centeredness or arrogance, psychopathic narcissists are skilled at hiding their true nature behind a facade of charm, professionalism, and competence.

They pass themselves off as caring partners, supportive friends, or successful individuals, making their predatory behaviour even more dangerous. This disguise allows them to infiltrate the lives of their victims, gaining their trust before revealing their true, manipulative, and exploitative tendencies.

A psychopathic narcissist's combination of traits makes them master manipulators who operate without empathy or remorse. They view relationships as nothing more than transactional, where other people exist solely to serve their needs. Once someone is no longer useful to them, they're discarded without a second thought. For these people, emotions are tools to manipulate other people rather than genuine feelings to be experienced or shared.

How Psychopathic Narcissism Manifests

Psychopathic narcissists are often difficult to spot because their harmful behaviours are well concealed behind an outwardly charming and competent persona. However, their tactics are systematic, strategic, and designed to exploit other people for personal gain.

- **Charm as a Weapon:**

One of the most striking features of psychopathic narcissism is their ability to charm other people. Psychopathic narcissists tend to be charismatic, witty, and engaging; they can easily draw people into their influence. This charm, however, is not a reflection of any genuine warmth or feelings for other people. Instead, it's a calculated tool designed to manipulate and control. They know exactly what to say and do to make other people feel special, and their ultimate goal is to utilise them for personal benefit.

- **Cold Empathy:**

Despite their ability to mimic empathy, psychopathic narcissists don't genuinely truly understand or experience emotions in the same way other people do.

They might feign concern or compassion, but these expressions are hollow and are used only to further their own agenda. Their lack of empathy allows them to exploit other people without any sense of guilt or remorse. They might even appear to be caring, but this appearance is a calculated act designed to gain trust and manipulate people into doing their bidding.

- **Calculated Intent:**

Psychopathic narcissists aren't impulsive in their actions. Unlike other types of narcissists who might act on sudden desires or whims, psychopathic narcissists are meticulous planners. They study their victims carefully, identifying weaknesses and vulnerabilities that they can exploit.

Their ability to control and exploit other people isn't based on emotion, it's based on cold logic and self-interest. They actively coerce through a combination of charm, deceit, and calculated strategies.

- **Power Through Fear and Control:**

Another key aspect of psychopathic narcissism is the way in which these people maintain control over other people.

They create an atmosphere of fear, uncertainty, and insecurity, leaving their victims feeling trapped and powerless. This atmosphere of fear might not always be obvious, but it's a constant undercurrent that erodes the victim's sense of safety and autonomy. Once their victim's no longer useful to them, they're disposed of without hesitation or remorse, leaving them confused and devastated.

- **Masterful Manipulation:**

Psychopathic narcissists are experts in creating chaos and confusion to maintain control. They often spread misinformation, create conflicts, and subtly undermine other people to keep the focus on themselves.

Their mastery of psychological and emotional manipulation allows them to dominate and control the people around them, eroding their confidence and leaving them vulnerable to further exploitation.

Psychopathic Narcissism in Relationships

Being in a relationship with a psychopathic narcissist is an emotionally devastating experience. In the early stages, they may seem like the perfect partner, showering their victim with attention, affection, and care. This initial phase creates an illusion of an ideal relationship, which later turns into a manipulative power dynamic designed to control and exploit.

The Drip Mentality

Drip mentality is the gradual, subtle approach of manipulating or influencing someone over time. Instead of overwhelming them all at once, it involves a slow, consistent "drip" of actions or behaviours that slowly changes perception or behaviour. Narcissists undermine someone's sense of reality in these small doses, making it harder for them to notice or resist the shift until it's too late.

- **The Seduction:**

At first, psychopathic narcissists overwhelm their victim with affection, flattery, and material gifts. This intense attention is designed to make the victim feel unique and special.

It cultivates a sense of dependence and trust, laying the groundwork for future manipulation. The victim believes they've found someone wonderful, and the narcissist's charm and devotion make it hard to see the underlying control.

- **Emotional Deception:**

Once the trust is established, psychopathic narcissists begin to exploit it. They create a false sense of security by making their partner feel valued and significant, but it's just a tactic to gain emotional control. The narcissist crafts an illusion of care and support while preparing the ground for manipulation. Over time, the victim grows more emotionally dependent on the narcissist, making it harder to break free.

- **Isolation and Dependency:**

As the relationship deepens, psychopathic narcissists work to isolate their victim from family and friends. This isolation creates a sense of dependency, as the victim becomes even more emotionally reliant on the narcissist for validation and support.

It also makes it difficult for the victim to seek help or perspective from other people. Psychopathic narcissists use this isolation as a tool to control the victim, leaving them feeling alone and trapped.

- **Mind Games and Gaslighting:**

Psychopathic narcissists thrive on psychological manipulation, particularly through tactics like gaslighting. Gaslighting involves distorting the victim's perception of reality, making them question their own thoughts, memories, and experiences. This constant mental manipulation leaves the victim feeling confused, insecure, and emotionally drained. Over time, the victim's sense of self becomes eroded, and they start to doubt their own sanity.

- **The Devaluation Stage:**

Once the narcissist has successfully gained control over their victim, they begin the devaluation phase. This is where they start to gradually insult, criticise, and belittle their partner.

Insults are disguised as "helpful advice," and the victim's self-esteem is gradually chipped away.

Gaslighting and abuse becomes a vicious circle and the victim's emotional reliance on the narcissist increases. When the victim feels too emotionally dependent to leave, the psychopathic narcissist's behaviour becomes even more abusive.

- **The Final Discard:**

Eventually, the narcissist will discard their victim once they've extracted everything they need. This phase is abrupt and cold. The victim can be abandoned, betrayed, or emotionally withdrawn with little explanation or remorse. The narcissist has no genuine emotional attachment to the victim.

Recognising Psychopathic Narcissism and Protecting Yourself

Recognising a psychopathic narcissist can be challenging because they're very skilled at hiding their true nature. However, here are some signs that can help you protect yourself from their manipulation:

- **Surface Charms: Hidden Motives**

Psychopathic narcissists often come across as charming, friendly, and too good to be true. But beneath this mask is a hidden agenda. Their charming behaviour isn't a reflection of genuine kindness, it's a strategic ploy to gain your trust.

- **A History of Exploitative Relationships:**

Look for a pattern of short-lived, exploitative relationships. Narcissists tend to have a history of manipulating or deceiving other people, leaving a trail of broken relationships behind them.

They shift blame onto other people, portraying themselves as the victim while evading any responsibility for their actions.

- **Absence of Moral Restraints:**

Psychopathic narcissists lack a moral compass. They disregard rules, social norms, and boundaries when they believe they can get away with it. Their actions are driven purely by self-interest, and they'll exploit other people without hesitation, betraying trust and causing harm without remorse.

- **Frequent Blame-Shifting:**

A psychopathic narcissist never takes accountability for their actions. Instead, they consistently deflect blame onto other people ensuring they can continue manipulating and exploiting the people around them without facing any consequences.

Coping Strategies for Dealing with Psychopathic Narcissists

Recovering from a relationship with a psychopathic narcissist is challenging, but it is possible. Healing requires time, resilience, and a strong support system.

Strategies that can help you cope and protect yourself moving forward:

- **Build a Support Network:**

One of the most important steps in recovery is to reconnect with trusted friends and family members.

Their support and encouragement can help you regain emotional stability and begin the healing process. Surround yourself with people who value you and who can provide perspective on the relationship.

- **Educate Yourself:**

Understanding the tactics of psychopathic narcissists is an essential part of recovery. The more you know about their behaviour, the easier it will be to spot red flags in future relationships. Knowledge is empowering and can help you protect yourself from further harm.

- **Prioritise Boundaries:**

Establishing and maintaining firm boundaries is crucial when dealing with a psychopathic narcissist. These people will test your limits and attempt to manipulate you, so it's essential to be clear about what is acceptable and what's not. Stay resolute in your boundaries to avoid being taken advantage of.

- **Eliminate Contact:**

Eliminate, or at the very least minimise contact with the narcissist. This can help protect your mental health and allow you to begin healing. Do not engage in emotional conversations or share personal information, as the narcissist will likely use it against you.

- **Seek Professional Support:**

Therapy is an important part of healing from narcissistic abuse. A specialist who understands the dynamics of narcissistic abuse can help you navigate the recovery process, offering valuable strategies for coping with the emotional impact of the relationship.

- **Rebuild Your Identity:**

One of the most significant effects of narcissistic abuse is the erosion of your sense of self. Psychopathic narcissists work hard to undermine your confidence and self-worth.

Rebuilding your identity requires rediscovering your passions, values, and individuality. With time and support, you can regain confidence and trust in yourself.

Long-Term Psychological Impact of Psychopathic Narcissism

The effects of a relationship with a psychopathic narcissist can last long after the relationship has ended. Survivors can experience lasting emotional and psychological wounds that require time and healing to overcome.

- **Lingering Trauma:**

Survivors could experience symptoms of complex post-traumatic stress disorder (CPTSD), such as flashbacks, hypervigilance, and emotional numbness. These symptoms can make it difficult to feel safe in the world.

- **Insecurity and Self-Doubt:**

The constant manipulation and gaslighting that psychopathic narcissists engage in often lead to profound feelings of insecurity. Survivors might question their judgment, self-worth, and ability to trust their own instincts.

- **Erosion of Identity:**

Narcissistic abuse can leave survivors feeling as though they've lost their sense of being. The narcissist's constant criticism and manipulation can undermine their confidence, leaving them feeling disconnected from their true selves.

- **Erosion of Social Trust:**

Survivors might struggle to trust other people, even those with good intentions. The betrayal experienced at the hands of the narcissist can make it difficult to open up to other people, and rebuilding this trust can be a long and challenging process.

- **Relationship Challenges:**

After such profound betrayal, survivors might also find it difficult to trust in relationships again, or they can even become overly trusting, leaving them vulnerable to further exploitation. Learning to navigate relationships after narcissistic abuse requires time, patience, and self-compassion.

Moving Forward with Resilience

While psychopathic narcissists leave lasting emotional scars, recovery is possible. By understanding their tactics and protecting yourself from future harm, you can begin to heal and rebuild your life.

It's important to remember that the abuse you experienced was just a result — it was never your fault. With time, resilience, and the right support, you can emerge stronger.

You can reclaim your sense of self and move forward toward a healthier, more fulfilling future.

Healing is a process, but with effort and self-compassion, you can overcome the trauma and create a life that's free from manipulation and exploitation.

Chapter 14

Distorted Reflections

Narcissism and Co-occurring Disorders

Examining the relationship between narcissism and other mental health disorders

Narcissistic Personality Disorder rarely exists in isolation. Most people with NPD also experience other mental health disorders, known as comorbidities. These co-occurring disorders complicate both how narcissism manifests and its treatment, as the interaction between narcissistic traits and other psychological issues can create unique challenges.

Understanding Comorbidity in a Narcissist: A Layered Personality

Narcissism often coexists with other mental health disorders, like depression, anxiety, or substance abuse. Understanding these comorbidities is crucial for both treatment and recovery.

The relationship between narcissism and comorbid disorders often revolves around shared underlying psychological factors, like emotional dysregulation, trauma, and impaired self-concept. Narcissistic behaviours, like grandiosity, manipulation, and a lack of empathy, can become more pronounced or difficult to treat when combined with other conditions, making it crucial to understand how these disorders interact.

The Narcissist with Borderline Personality Disorder (BPD)

Emotional Instability Meets Narcissistic Entitlement:

BPD often overlaps with NPD due to shared traits like emotional instability and impulsivity.

The two do however differ in their core motivations. While NPD centres on a sense of grandiosity and entitlement, BPD focuses more on abandonment fears.

Narcissism and borderline personality disorder are an explosive combination. With BPD, there's a fear of abandonment, extreme emotional swings, and a pattern of unstable relationships. When combined with narcissism, this creates someone who isn't only deeply insecure but also expects everyone to cater to their needs without fail. The slightest hint of rejection can cause them to swing from idealisation to devaluation in an instant.

The Rollercoaster of Emotions:

On a Monday, the narcissist with BPD might praise their partner, showering them with attention and admiration because they feel adored. By Tuesday, a small perceived slight (like the partner being distracted or unavailable) triggers a borderline reaction, leading to rage or withdrawal. The narcissistic side then takes over, convincing them that they're too good to be treated this way, which results in punishing the partner, perhaps by giving them the silent treatment or demeaning them.

Imagine two people who both feel emotionally overwhelmed. One is the narcissist, who builds a fortress of arrogance to protect themselves from feeling vulnerable. They believe they're special and entitled, which keeps people at a distance. The other person, with BPD, has no such fortress.

Instead, they wear their heart on their sleeve, terrified of being abandoned and emotionally swinging between intense love and deep hatred.

When these two disorders mix, the narcissist's inflated ego clashes with the borderline's emotional chaos. One minute, the narcissist might feel on top of the world; the next, they can spiral into self-doubt, creating confusion in their relationships.

The Narcissist with Antisocial Personality Disorder (ASPD)

Manipulation and Callousness with a Narcissistic Veneer:

Narcissism can exist alongside ASPD with both disorders displaying manipulative and exploitative behaviour. However, while ASPD is marked by disregard for societal rules, NPD focuses on status and admiration.

Narcissists with antisocial traits don't just crave admiration; they'll do anything to get it, even if it means lying, cheating, or hurting other people. This person has the grandiosity of a narcissist, believing they're superior, but they're also willing to break rules and manipulate the people around them without remorse.

In this combination, the narcissist is cold, calculating, and willing to exploit other people to achieve their goals. They believe they deserve to be at the top, and if they have to walk all over people or break the law to get there, so be it. While a typical narcissist might crave admiration and recognition, a narcissist with ASPD has no problem using deception or even aggression to maintain control.

Picture someone who has no problem breaking the rules, bending people to their will, and doing whatever it takes to win. This is someone with ASPD, often labelled as sociopathic or psychopathic.

Now, add narcissism to the mix. Not only do they feel entitled to admiration and control, but they're also willing to lie, cheat, or manipulate without remorse to maintain their power. Think of a charming but ruthless politician or business mogul who will bulldoze anyone in their way to keep their status intact.

The Narcissist with Obsessive-Compulsive Personality Disorder (OCPD)

Perfectionism Taken to an Extreme:

When narcissism combines with OCPD, you get someone who's obsessed with perfection — not just in themselves, but in the people around them. They believe they deserve the best, and they'll hold themselves and other people to impossibly high standards. Any failure is met with harsh self-criticism or lashing out at other people.

Control and Rigidity:

The narcissist with OCPD will try to control every aspect of their life and expect other people to meet their exacting standards. If things aren't perfect, they experience anxiety or rage. For them, even minor imperfections feel like personal failures, but they'll project this disappointment onto other people, criticising them relentlessly for not being good enough.

Imagine this scenario: The narcissist with OCPD demands their partner organise the house in a way that reflects their ideals. When their partner moves a vase by an inch, the narcissist reacts by berating them for not being 'meticulous enough.' The narcissist's perfectionism dictates the terms of every relationship, leaving their partner feeling like they're walking on eggshells. Their obsession with perfection keeps them isolated, as no one can ever measure up to their standards.

The Narcissist with Substance Use Disorder (SUD)

Escaping Reality Through Self-Medication:

Narcissists with substance use issues often turn to alcohol or drugs to cope with the pressure of maintaining their grandiose self-image. This becomes a dangerous cycle when their reality doesn't match up with their inflated expectations; they turn to substances to numb their pain.

Over time, the addiction fuels their narcissism, and they start to blame other people for their problems and use manipulation to hide their addiction.

Self-medicating the ego:

Narcissists can sometimes drink excessively or use drugs to feel more powerful or to escape feelings of inadequacy. When challenged, they'll deny they have a problem, projecting the blame onto other people (e.g., "If my partner wasn't so critical, I wouldn't need to drink"). Their substance use reinforces their grandiosity while making it harder for them to face reality.

Imagine a scenario: After a particularly difficult week at work, where their talents were questioned, the narcissist turns to alcohol to numb their feelings of insecurity. By the weekend, they're drinking heavily at a party, bragging about their accomplishments and belittling other people.

When a friend mentions they're concerned about the amount the narcissist is drinking, they quickly turn the conversation around, blaming their friend for 'not understanding' their pressures. This denial helps them preserve their grandiose self-image but only deepens their sense of dissatisfaction and emptiness.

The Narcissist with Dysthymia

Navigating a Complex Battle Between Ego and Emptiness:

When narcissism and dysthymia combine, the narcissist experiences an ongoing internal struggle. They crave admiration and validation, but their chronic depression leaves them feeling perpetually unfulfilled, no matter how much attention they receive. This creates a cycle of seeking approval, only to feel empty and dissatisfied.

Their emotional instability swings between inflated confidence and deep self-doubt, making their behaviour unpredictable and draining for those around them.

Their need for validation is insatiable, yet no amount of recognition can fill the emotional void left by their depression.

This leads to frustration and conflict, with the narcissist blaming other people for not meeting their high expectations. They might also react defensively to criticism, magnifying their feelings of inadequacy.

In relationships, their constant need for reassurance can create tension, and when their partner's patience runs thin, they may respond with anger or withdrawal. Narcissists with dysthymia tend to be resistant to therapy, as their grandiose self-image conflicts with the reality of their depression. Their emotional struggles are intensified by their narcissistic traits, leading to a cycle of disappointment and frustration that's difficult to break.

Imagine this: Every morning, the narcissist with dysthymia wakes up hoping that today will be different — that they'll finally feel worthy of the praise they crave. They may start their day by boasting about their accomplishments to their partner, expecting admiration and validation.

But by mid-afternoon, a small comment — perhaps a remark about how tired their partner is — sends them spiralling into self-doubt. The praise they receive never feels enough, and they end up pushing their partner away, blaming them for not offering the reassurance they need. The emotional rollercoaster continues as they swing from arrogance to despair. In the evening, they might retreat into their loneliness, feeling like a failure despite the constant need for affirmation, and yet they continue to seek attention the next day, just to be met with the same emptiness.

The Narcissist with ADHD

A Dance of Intensity and Instant Withdrawal:

In relationships, the narcissist with ADHD creates an emotional dance that's as alluring as it is unpredictable. Their brilliant, magnetic personality is counterbalanced by sudden, disorienting shifts in focus and emotion — leaving you both exhilarated and exhausted as you try to navigate the constant push and pull of their affection and withdrawal.

Imagine falling for someone who, in one breath, sweeps you off your feet with grand declarations of love and a dazzling self-confidence that makes you feel special.

Then, without warning, a minor distraction — a stray thought or a fleeting moment of boredom — leads them to abruptly pull away, leaving you reeling from confusion. This is the turbulent interplay of narcissism and ADHD in a personal relationship.

A Rollercoaster of Emotional Highs and Lows:

At first, the narcissist with ADHD can be incredibly captivating. They shower you with compliments, elaborate promises, and passionate declarations that make you feel like the centre of their universe.

Their charm and flair for dramatics create an atmosphere of excitement and idealised romance. But as soon as a small setback or distraction arises—a comment you make, a change in the routine, or even just a momentary lapse in attention — they can suddenly swing into self-doubt and irritability. One moment, you're basking in their affection; the next, you're left wondering what you did wrong as they withdraw into themselves.

Unpredictable Demands for Connection:

Their need for constant validation means they oscillate between demanding your unwavering attention and disappearing into their own little world.

In a relationship, this leaves you constantly on edge, never quite sure if you'll be met with an eruption of warmth or an abrupt, inexplicable retreat. Imagine planning a quiet evening together, only for them to suddenly become restless, distracted by a new interest or a passing thought, leaving plans half-finished and emotions unsettled. Their inconsistency isn't about a lack of care — it's their struggle to stay focused that makes it so challenging to maintain the steady, reciprocal connection that relationships thrive on.

Picture This Scenario:

On a Saturday evening, they might start by planning an intimate dinner where they share heartfelt compliments and dreams of a future together. You feel appreciated and completely seen. But mid-conversation, a seemingly insignificant detail — a text message, a noise in the background — snaps their attention away.

Their tone shifts from warmth to indifference, and the conversation, once rich with emotion, abruptly fizzles out. You're left trying to piece together what happened, wondering if what you felt was genuine or just a spark that was quickly extinguished by distraction.

Challenges in Diagnosing and Treating Individuals with Multiple Disorders

Diagnosing comorbid NPD and other disorders can be tricky due to overlapping symptoms. It can be difficult to distinguish between narcissistic behaviours and symptoms of other disorders because of these shared characteristics and the complexity of someone's psychological presentation.

For example, depression in a narcissist might not appear as sadness but instead as anger or rage when their self-image is challenged. Emotional instability can be attributed to either NPD or BPD, which complicates accurate diagnosis.

In terms of treatment, when someone with NPD also has depression or anxiety, they won't always show it in expected ways. Instead of openly displaying sadness or worry, they might lash out or blame other people for their unhappiness. This makes it difficult to pinpoint the real issue, because narcissists rarely admit to feeling vulnerable or flawed.

When combined with other disorders that complicate emotional regulation or increase impulsivity, like BPD or substance abuse, the narcissist's motivation for change can become even more diminished.

Narcissists typically resist therapy, seeing themselves as above needing help or refusing to accept responsibility for their actions. This complicates treatment, as it's challenging to get them to engage in therapy when they won't acknowledge their problems.

Managing Comorbid Conditions

- **Addressing Comorbid Depression:**

Combining psychotherapy with medication is often necessary to tackle both NPD and depression.

Depression-specific strategies like cognitive restructuring and mood management can help alleviate symptoms by changing negative thought patterns and lightening the emotional load.

- **Managing Anxiety and Stress:**

Anxiety is another common issue. Relaxation exercises and stress management techniques can empower people to manage anxiety more effectively. Additionally, anxiety-specific therapies, like CBT and mindfulness-based approaches, can also help people handle anxiety.

- **Addressing Substance Abuse:**

For people struggling with both NPD and substance abuse, an integrated treatment plan is critical.

Addressing both issues simultaneously increases the chances of long-term recovery. Relapse prevention techniques are vital, offering people tools to manage cravings and maintain sobriety. A strong foundation of support and coping strategies is key to staying on the path to healing.

In cases of comorbid substance abuse, there's a high risk of relapse, which can derail any progress made in treating narcissistic traits.

Therapeutic Approaches for Treating Comorbidities:

- ### Cognitive Behavioural Therapy (CBT):

CBT can help address the thought distortions in both NPD and other disorders like depression or anxiety. Tailored interventions focus on reshaping the individual's belief systems around entitlement and self-worth.

Imagine helping a narcissist untangle the web of lies they tell themselves about their superiority and entitlement. CBT helps them recognise the negative thoughts driving their behaviour, like "I must always be admired" or "Failure is unacceptable." With time, they can learn healthier ways of thinking, which might help them manage their anxiety or depression.

- ### Dialectical Behaviour Therapy (DBT):

Originally designed for BPD, DBT can be effective in managing the emotional dysregulation found in narcissists, particularly those with comorbid BPD or mood disorders.

For a narcissist with emotional instability, DBT teaches them how to regulate their intense emotions and cope with distress in healthier ways. It can help them manage the swings between idealising and devaluing other people, especially in close relationships.

- ### Medication:

In some cases, SSRIs (Selective Serotonin Reuptake Inhibitors) or mood stabilisers are used to treat underlying anxiety or depression in narcissists.

In cases where anxiety or depression is severe, medication can help stabilise the narcissist's mood. However, it's crucial for therapists to be cautious, as the narcissist might misuse medication to avoid addressing deeper emotional issues.

- **Research on Genetic and Environmental Links:**

Studies suggest that certain genetic predispositions and early-life trauma might increase the likelihood of developing both narcissism and other disorders like BPD or mood disorders.

They also suggest that early childhood trauma or overindulgence can lead to both narcissism and other disorders. Imagine a child who was constantly praised and never disciplined — they grow up thinking the world owes them admiration.

On the other hand, a child who was neglected or abused might develop both narcissistic defences and depression or anxiety, using their inflated sense of self as a shield against a painful past.

Case Studies of Comorbid Presentations of Narcissism

Case Study 1: NPD with Borderline Personality Disorder (BPD)

Sarah is a 35-year-old woman diagnosed with both NPD and BPD. In relationships, she often starts out with intense idealisation of her partners, showering them with affection and admiration. However, when her partners fail to meet her high expectations, she quickly becomes hostile, devaluing them and expressing feelings of deep betrayal. Sarah oscillates between looking for constant reassurance and pushing people away due to her fear of abandonment, a common feature of BPD. Her relationships are marked by emotional chaos, as she alternates between grandiosity and intense vulnerability.

Case Study 2: NPD with Antisocial Personality Disorder (ASPD)

Tom is a 40-year-old man with NPD and ASPD. His combination of narcissistic entitlement and antisocial disregard for rules has led him to engage in manipulative, and even criminal behaviour. He frequently lies to gain financial advantages, exploiting other people without remorse.

While his narcissistic traits make him believe he's superior and deserving of success, his antisocial tendencies drive him to take shortcuts, like fraud and deception, to achieve his goals. Tom has little regard for the consequences of his actions on other people, making him dangerous and difficult to treat.

Case Study 3: NPD with Depression and Substance Abuse

John is a 50-year-old man with NPD, depression, and a history of alcohol abuse. On the surface, he presents as confident and self-assured, but privately, he battles feelings of deep inadequacy. His depression is triggered when he fails to live up to his own unrealistic expectations of success. To cope, John turns to alcohol, which exacerbates his mood swings and increases his irritability. His narcissistic need for admiration makes it hard for him to acknowledge his emotional struggles, leading him to avoid seeking help.

Final Thoughts:

When a narcissist has multiple comorbidities, these layers of dysfunction interact in complex ways. One minute, they might seem confident and in control, and the next, they're lashing out, spiralling into despair, or trying to manipulate other people. Their narcissism works as both a shield and a weapon, protecting them from facing their inner pain while hurting the people closest to them.

These comorbidities not only intensify their narcissistic traits but also make them harder to treat, as their personality disorder often obstructs their ability to see their own role in their problems.

By humanising the narcissist's experience with these comorbid conditions, it shows that they're not just a "villain" but someone grappling with a deep and complex set of psychological issues that make their behaviours difficult for them and devastating for the people around them.

Conclusion

This chapter's exploration of comorbid disorders with narcissism reveals the complexity and challenges of diagnosing and treating people with multiple mental health conditions. By understanding how disorders like BPD, ASPD, depression, and substance abuse interact with narcissistic behaviour, we can gain insight into the unique aspects that make these people difficult to engage in therapy and to sustain meaningful change.

Chapter 15

Lost in the Labyrinth

Denial and Ego After Narcissistic Abuse

An exploration of how survivors of narcissistic abuse navigate denial, self-deception, and the complex interplay of ego as they process their trauma

Narcissistic abuse can be an experience so disorienting that it feels like you're lost in an endless labyrinth, one where the walls seem to shift, trap you in confusion, and obscure the truth of reality. The labyrinth, formed by denial and ego, is a psychological web that protects you from the hard truth while simultaneously locking you into a cycle of distortion.

The forces of denial and ego are powerful allies in keeping you stuck, and their roles in the aftermath of narcissistic abuse can't be underestimated. They distort the painful reality, offering temporary relief but ultimately hindering recovery and true healing.

The journey out of this labyrinth is challenging, but it starts with the recognition and acceptance of these forces and understanding how they keep you tethered to the narcissist's world.

This chapter explores the aspects of denial and ego — how they initially protect you from the emotional impact of abuse and how, over time, they reinforce the damaging patterns that make it so difficult to break free.

Denial: The First Wall of the Labyrinth

Denial is often the first psychological defence mechanism that surfaces after experiencing narcissistic abuse.

When the pain of betrayal and manipulation is too much to bear, denial steps in to soften the blow.

It acts as a cushion that allows you to function, albeit with a skewed perception of reality. Instead of confronting the full gravity of what you've endured, denial creates an illusion that minimises the severity of the abuse, making it easier for you to process and continue on in the relationship, even though you know deep down something isn't right.

In the early stages, denial speaks in quiet whispers. It says things like, "It wasn't that bad," or "Maybe I overreacted," offering a false sense of peace. This inner voice serves to justify the narcissist's behaviour, making you believe their actions weren't as harmful as they appeared or that they didn't really mean to hurt you. These rationalisations allow you to stay in the relationship longer than you should, convincing yourself that their behaviour is something you can forgive or overlook — sometimes even labelling it as a "bad day" or an unfortunate misunderstanding.

Denial also plays a significant role in fuelling self-doubt. After every interaction with the narcissist, you might find yourself replaying events, trying to make sense of their words and actions. You look for logic in irrational behaviour, searching for signs of kindness or justification for their mistreatment. You might wonder what you could have done differently or how you could have "fixed" the situation.

This constant mental back-and-forth traps you in a cycle of confusion, where the truth of the abuse remains clouded by a desperate hope that things weren't as bad as they seemed.

However, denial isn't a true ally. It might protect you from the full emotional weight of the trauma, but it also keeps you tethered to the narcissist's world, obscuring your view of what's really transpired. Denial is the first wall in the labyrinth, and although it might provide short-term relief, it's ultimately a barrier to healing.

Ego: The Labyrinth's Deceptive Path

Once the initial barrier of denial begins to crack, ego steps in to provide further defence. Your ego, already bruised by the abuse, takes on the role of protecting you from vulnerability.

Admitting that you've been deceived feels like an assault on your self-image, so ego shields you from the harsh truth of being manipulated and gaslighted.

Ego plays out in a number of ways — through pride, resistance, and an unwillingness to accept the reality of the manipulation. It whispers that facing the truth would mean acknowledging failure, and for a lot of people, that's an unbearable thought.

The first signs of ego manifest as shame or self-blame. These thoughts make you feel inadequate, as if you somehow failed in your ability to protect yourself. It's hard to admit that you were manipulated, especially when you were so invested in the relationship. Acknowledging that you were deceived feels like admitting weakness, and your ego, in its need to maintain a sense of control, resists this vulnerability.

Ego also works to justify the narcissist's behaviour, even when deep down you know it was damaging. It might say, "They were stressed," or "They didn't mean it," attempting to rationalise away the abuse. This kind of thinking serves to protect your self-image, preventing you from confronting the truth that the narcissist's behaviour was intentional and abusive.

It allows you to excuse the narcissist's actions, creating a version where their faults are minimised and your responsibility for the situation is magnified.

For some people, ego manifests as a self-absorbed need to preserve pride. There's a fear of being perceived as weak or gullible, leading you to reject the idea that you were a victim. Instead, you might blame yourself for not being patient enough, understanding enough, or less "difficult."

You might start to internalise the narcissist's accusations, believing that their cruelty was a reaction to something you did. This self-blame, compounded by the narcissist's gaslighting, traps you within their version, preventing you from seeing the truth of the situation.

Like denial, ego distorts reality. While it might feel protective in the moment, it ultimately keeps you from accepting the full scope of the abuse you've endured.

It also reinforces the walls of the labyrinth, leading you to focus on preserving your pride or justifying your actions, rather than confronting the narcissist's calculated emotional manipulation.

The Cycle of Denial and Ego: A Self-Sustaining Trap

Denial and ego don't work in isolation. They feed off one another, creating a self-sustaining trap that makes it nearly impossible to escape the labyrinth. Denial provides a cushion by distorting the truth, while ego works to protect your sense of self, keeping you stuck in a cycle of justification and confusion.

For example, denial convinces you that the narcissist's behaviour wasn't intentional. Meanwhile, ego reinforces the idea that you could have changed the outcome, if you had only tried harder or been more patient.

This interplay of denial and ego forms a kind of mental loop, where the truth remains elusive. Denial keeps you from seeing the full reality of the abuse, while ego tries to preserve your dignity by deflecting blame and responsibility.

The narcissist is complicit in maintaining this cycle. They understand how your mind works and use your ego against you. They can manipulate you into believing that you're the problem or that they're the victim. They might even tell you that you're lucky to have them, or that no one else would ever treat you as well as they do.

This kind of manipulation further entrenches you in denial and ego, reinforcing the belief that you're in the wrong and keeping you tethered to them.

The Walls of Justification

A particularly insidious aspect of the labyrinth is the wall of justification. Denial and ego work together to create a story that explains away the narcissist's behaviour, this is what allows you to continue to invest emotionally in the relationship, even when the signs of abuse are all around you.

You tell yourself that the narcissist was simply under stress, that they didn't mean it, or that their childhood trauma is to blame for their actions. These justifications create a false sense of control, convincing you that the solution lies in your ability to change yourself, rather than recognising that the narcissist's behaviour is rooted in their own dysfunction.

The trap of justification is dangerous because it places the responsibility for the relationship's failure on your shoulders.

You begin to think that if only you could be better, more understanding, or kinder, the abuse would stop. This line of thinking keeps you focused on changing yourself, rather than recognising the abuse for what it really is: a deliberate, calculated, predatory effort to control and manipulate you.

But justification only deepens the labyrinth. It inflates the ego by making you believe you have the power to fix the situation, while further entangling you in a cycle of guilt and self-doubt.

Breaking Free: Confronting the Denial and Ego

Escaping the labyrinth of denial and ego isn't easy, but it is possible. The first step is acknowledging that the abuse was real and that it wasn't your fault. It means accepting the uncomfortable truth that you were manipulated, and that the narcissist's behaviour was intentional and cruel. This requires courage, vulnerability, and a willingness to face the pain head-on.

Next, addressing the role of ego is crucial. You have to recognise the ways in which your pride and self-blame have distorted your perception of reality.

Letting go of the need to protect your self-image allows you to see the situation for what it really was. It's important to understand that being manipulated doesn't mean you're weak or foolish — it means you were deceived by someone who knew exactly how to exploit your vulnerabilities.

Finally, dismantling the walls of justification is key:

You have to reject the false versions that the narcissist has crafted. You're not responsible for their actions, and no amount of understanding or patience on your part could have changed their behaviour. You have the right to hold them accountable for the abuse they inflicted on you, and you deserve to heal without carrying the weight of guilt and self-doubt.

The Uncertainty of Narcissistic Love: Decoding Their Intentions

Breakups are never simple. They leave behind a tangled mess of emotions, doubts, and questions that claw away at your sense of reality. And when you're dealing with a narcissist, the mess becomes even harder to unravel. You don't just question the relationship; you start questioning them — the person they were, and the intentions behind everything they did.

You're left wondering: were they a conscious narcissist, fully aware of how they manipulated you? Or were they an unconscious narcissist, so wrapped up in their own world that they couldn't even see the damage they caused?

Or was it something worse — were they a predator, intentionally targeting you for what they wanted, knowing full well the wreckage they'd leave behind?

This confusion doesn't just sit at the surface. It eats away at you. You replay every moment, every conversation, trying to uncover their motives.

Were they building you up just to tear you down?

Did they actually love you, even in their own flawed, distorted way?

Or were you simply a means to an end — a source of validation, security, or something else they needed?

The uncertainty is unbearable because every possibility brings its own unique kind of pain.

Here's the real struggle:

If they were a conscious narcissist, a master manipulator, it feels like every moment you thought was real wasn't. You can't stop thinking about how carefully they seemed to know what to say, what to do, and how to make you feel special — only to rip it all away when it suited them. That thought alone can break you. It makes you question every shared experience, every memory, and every ounce of trust you gave.

Then there's the idea that they were an unconscious narcissist. Maybe they didn't mean to hurt you. Maybe they were so consumed by their own needs that they couldn't see past them. But does that make the pain any less real? Does it mean they cared, even if they couldn't show it in a way that made sense? Or were you just collateral damage — caught in the storm of their inability to fill their own emptiness?

And then, there's the darkest possibility: that they were a predator. This thought stops you cold. What if they knew exactly what they were doing and only cared about what they could take from you? What if you were just a target — chosen for your vulnerability, your kindness, or your willingness to give everything for a dream? This is the possibility that shatters you the most. It leaves you feeling used, discarded, and questioning your own worth.

The worst part is that these possibilities don't stay separate. They bleed into each other, swirling in your mind, and feeding your confusion.

One day, you're sure they knew exactly what they were doing, and your anger surges like a wave, giving you a brief sense of power. But the next day, you find yourself wondering if they were just broken — incapable of genuine feelings but not intentionally malicious — and you feel pity, tangled with a flicker of regret. Then, there are the moments when the predator theory takes hold, and your sadness collapses into despair.

This internal tug-of-war traps you, keeping you from moving forward. You want so desperately to believe they loved you, even in their own flawed way, because that would mean your love wasn't wasted. But the thought that they didn't — that it might have all been a game, whether conscious or unconscious — eats you away.

And here's the truth: it's not just about them. It's about you. It's about trying to reconcile the person you were, and the person you've become. How could you not see it? How did you fall so deeply for someone who might have never genuinely cared?

The hardest part of all this isn't even about understanding their intentions. It's about making peace with your own truth. It's about finding a way to make sense of the love you gave, the pain you're carrying, and the person you are now.

Because no matter who they were — conscious, unconscious, or predatory — the fact remains: you loved them. That love was real, even if they weren't.

The challenge is untangling their intentions from your truth. It's figuring out how to acknowledge what you felt and give it its due, without letting the unanswered questions consume you.

The Truth Beyond the Labyrinth

While the labyrinth of denial and ego seems endless, there's a way out. The truth is the key that unlocks the labyrinth, and every step you take toward confronting the reality of the abuse brings you closer to freedom. It requires immense strength, but each layer that you peel away — whether it's denial, ego, or justification brings you closer to the way forward.

Chapter 16

The Labyrinth of the Lost Souls

Narcissistic Personality Disorder: Perception of Victimhood and Despair

Exploring narcissists' self-perception as victims, their emotional turmoil, and the impact on relationships

In the complex landscape of human psychology, people grappling with narcissistic personality disorder often find themselves ensnared in a web of confusion and emotional turmoil. This condition manifests in behaviours that can be self-centred and harmful to other people, but it's essential to recognise that these people aren't necessarily inherently bad people. Instead, they can be lost souls, trapped in a labyrinth of their own making, struggling with a profound sense of despair and victimhood that they might not even realise is affecting them, but this still doesn't mean that they shouldn't be held accountable for the way they treat you.

Personal Reflection:

Witnessing her constant need for validation was heartbreaking. She seemed like an actress performing in a tragic play, always looking for applause but never satisfied. It felt like I was watching someone drown while they insisted, they could swim, trapped in a cycle of need and despair.

Recovering from a toxic narcissistic relationship, takes you into the darkest corners of your soul — places you never thought you'd visit — maybe places you didn't even know existed. It's a toxic journey through an emotional labyrinth of perception, confusion, resentment, rejection, anger, frustration, acceptance, abandonment, and even perceived guilt — all waiting to be unravelled, processed and understood.

Personal Reflection:

For me it was a surreal experience, it consumed me pulling me in, leaving me hoping that this adoration would last forever. You give in completely, desperate to keep it going, pouring everything you have into the illusion. But when the love bombing fades and reality starts to creep in, confusion hits hard. You've given it your all, but somehow, it was never enough. The demands pile up, and self-victimisation becomes their constant agenda, consuming every part of you, bit by bit — like piranhas stripping you down to the bone. After a while, there's simply nothing left to give.

Self-preservation finally kicks in:

They'll keep telling you they're not happy but won't be able to explain why. Their unhappiness comes from deep internal struggles and feelings of inadequacy, but they're not self-aware enough to recognise or express it. Acknowledging the reasons would mean admitting that their behaviour and expectations are unreasonable, something they avoid at all costs. Instead, they deflect by simply saying they're unhappy and shifting the blame onto you.

This is where resentment festers — you've sacrificed so much, and it's still not enough. You get frustrated, trying to find some way to make it work without losing yourself entirely.

But as time goes on, the narcissist's demands only get fiercer, twisting reality to fit their needs, ignoring your logic, and completely disregarding any empathy you try to offer.

Their focus sharpens on one thing: exactly what they want, and they'll stop at absolutely nothing to get it.

Confrontations are inevitable. Frustration boils over, and you're met with accusations, anger, and manipulation. Suddenly, "you're the villain," and "they're the victim."

They weaponize your love, twisting your dedication to extract even more, pushing you to sacrifice everything for their benefit.

They'll even say things like, "If you loved me, you'd make it work," attempting to guilt-trip you into giving up everything just to get their own way and keep them satisfied. They'll even suggest reckless solutions to financial issues — anything to fulfil their desires without considering the lasting consequences.

The Call of the Void

The mental exhaustion can feel suffocating, pulling you into deep reflection about where you are. In psychology, "The Call of the Void" is also known as "High Place Phenomenon", or HPP).

It's the sudden, unsettling urge to engage in a risky action — thoughts that come and go without the intention of following through.

You might notice your mind drifting to thoughts that feel disconnected from your reality. These moments don't reflect a real desire to act, but rather how the mind explores potential danger.

Research suggests that the "High Place Phenomenon" could be the brain's way of reinforcing self-preservation, pushing us to stay safe by imagining threats.

This experience is common and doesn't always point to mental health issues. It's just the mind briefly exploring danger to remind you why you need to stay safe. When you're drained, it's easy for your thoughts to spiral out of control.

Acceptance and Self-Preservation

But then comes acceptance. You recognise that you can't save the narcissist. Their needs and demands are far beyond anything grounded in reality. You wrestle with your conscience, wondering if you're strong enough, and good enough, to pull them out of this dark place.

You try talking to them, reasoning like you would with a child, hoping they'll understand. But you could talk until you're blue in the face, and your voice gives out; it won't change anything.

Then denial sets in because you know you're a good person, and you've given everything you can. You plead, pointing out all you've sacrificed, hoping they'll see the truth for just a moment.

Personal Reflection:

I remember watching as she would ruthlessly cut people out of her life without a second glance or thought, blaming everyone for abandoning her. It stirred something up inside me and convinced me that maybe I could finally be the one to help her.

But eventually, reality hits. Once you're completely drained, they become even more desperate, pulling harder until you have nothing left.

The cycle continues — anxiety, depression, sleepless nights, and guilt — all because you refuse to abandon them "like everyone else has."

But whatever you give, it's never enough. When they accuse you of deserting them at their lowest, despite everything you've done, the weight becomes unbearable.

In the end, they suggest they "you" go to therapy — convincing themselves, of course, that: "it's you"; who needs fixing.

They can't see the pain they've inflicted, nor do they care. They offer you the idea of at least clinging on to "friendship," but even this is only as long as it serves their needs.

Trying to comprehend the mind of a narcissist — especially a covert one — is like trying to understand the vastness of the universe.

They're locked in a prison of their own mind, oblivious to the reality of other people. They paint themselves as victims, twisting literally every situation to fit their version of events.

If they sense that you find yourself breaking down, questioning everything, doubting your sanity, they'll immediately pounce, and gaslight you into wondering if maybe you're the narcissist. Real introspection isn't something that they can grasp.

The Saviour Complex

Those of us who've lived through this nightmare know how deeply it can wound. This toxic bond is tangled with something we call in psychology "The Saviour Complex" — a part of you that wants to be the one to finally help them. Also known as "White Knight Syndrome," it comes from a place of compassion, but the narcissist thrives on it. They'll bleed you dry, like a pack of wolves, consuming everything until there's nothing left. They drain you of every last drop of energy, empathy, and compassion, before moving on to their next target

The Illusion of Superiority

At the heart of NPD lies a fragile self-image. A lot of people with this disorder present an outward appearance of confidence and superiority, masking deep-seated insecurities. They crave admiration and validation, believing they're entitled to it.

But beneath this facade lurks a sense of emptiness that they can't fully comprehend. They can be oblivious to the fact that their behaviours are rooted in a desperate need for external validation, a need that regularly goes unfulfilled.

This relentless pursuit of admiration creates a distorted reality. They see themselves as victims, convinced that the world is out to get them. When faced with criticism or rejection, their instinct is to lash out defensively.

This behaviour isn't necessarily an intentional effort to harm other people; instead, it's a desperate attempt to protect their fragile self-esteem from what they perceive as threats. They fail to see how this defensive posture alienates other people, reinforcing their feelings of isolation.

The Cognitive Dissonance

Navigating the emotional landscape of someone with NPD is complex. Cognitive dissonance plays a significant role in their experiences. They long for connection and acceptance, but their fear of vulnerability keeps them at arm's length from other people. This internal conflict breeds confusion and despair, leaving them trapped in a cycle of emotional turmoil.

Consider the scenario where someone with NPD desperately wants a close relationship but they're terrified of being hurt. Their protective mechanisms can lead them to sabotage potential connections, leaving them feeling more isolated. When they witness other people thriving in relationships, envy and resentment bubble to the surface.

They interpret the successes of their peers as personal failures, which deepens their despair and sense of victimhood. The irony is that their fear and self-preservation often push away the very people they want to connect with. This creates a vicious cycle of emotional suffering, reinforcing their belief that they're misunderstood and victimised by a world that fails to recognise their worth.

The Abyss of Despair

Despair is a constant companion for a lot of people with NPD. They can chase success, relationships, or validation, but feel a nagging emptiness that nothing can fill. This emotional void can become overwhelming, leading to self-destructive behaviours or unhealthy coping mechanisms that only exacerbate their suffering.

When they encounter jealousy or resentment toward other people, it often stems from an underlying sense of inadequacy. Their perception of other people's achievements as threats only amplifies their emotional pain. Each failure to meet their own unrealistic expectations reinforces their belief that they're victims of an unfair world, perpetuating this feeling of despair.

This cycle of despair manifests in various emotional responses; anger, frustration, sadness, and regret. But acknowledging these feelings can be insurmountable.

They're so wrapped up in their self-perception that they're not willing to confront the reality of their emotional state.

The fear of vulnerability can be paralysing, trapping them in a labyrinth of negative thoughts and emotions.

The Mask of a Narcissists Denial

Denial is a prevalent aspect of the lives of most narcissists. They cling to the belief that they're victims, even when confronted with evidence to the contrary. This refusal to acknowledge their behaviour not only perpetuates their pain, but also adversely affects the people around them.

Confronting uncomfortable truths about themselves can be excruciating. Now, imagine facing that discomfort while simultaneously believing that you're blameless. The resulting cognitive dissonance can feel unbearable. However, there are fleeting moments when people with NPD can actually catch a glimpse of their reflection and feel a flicker of doubt. These moments can lead to profound insights, but are often accompanied by fear, because they threaten to shatter their carefully constructed self-image.

During these rare flashes of self-awareness, they feel a vulnerability that they're not prepared to handle. The thought of confronting their true selves can send them retreating back into denial, reinforcing the cycle of despair.

They might even, also momentarily recognise the pain they inflict on other people but quickly dismiss it to protect their fragile self-image.

The Emotional Isolation

One of the most poignant aspects of living with NPD is the deep emotional isolation it creates.

Narcissists feel disconnected from other people, unable to form meaningful relationships because of their self-centred behaviours.

Their constant need for validation leaves them feeling alone, craving connection, but unable to figure out how to achieve it, even when they're surrounded by people. Ironically, the very behaviours that push other people away — manipulation, defensiveness, and grandiosity — only deepen their loneliness.

This isolation fuels a longing for connection that always feels just out of reach. They watch other people build meaningful relationships and feel a sharp pang of envy, convinced they're the only ones who can't. This perceived failure reinforces their belief that they're victims, forever trapped in the labyrinth.

The Void of Connection

The void of connection experienced by people with NPD is painfully evident when it comes to vulnerability.

They see emotional intimacy as a threat, not an opportunity for growth, fearing that showing their true selves will only lead to rejection. This fear strengthens their defensive behaviours, creating a wall they can't seem to get past.

For someone with NPD, exposing their vulnerabilities feels like standing on the edge of a precipice. The fear of falling into the abyss is stronger than their desire for connection. They settle for superficial interactions, convincing themselves that solitude is better than risking the pain of emotional intimacy.

This avoidance of vulnerability traps them in a cycle of loneliness and despair. Superficial relationships provide fleeting relief but lack the depth they crave. The resulting void leaves them grappling with emptiness and isolation, caught in a struggle they can't fully express.

The Impact on Relationships

The struggles faced by people with NPD have far-reaching implications for their relationships. Their inability to recognise and empathise with the emotions of other people often leads to misunderstandings and conflict.

While they might genuinely desire connection, their behaviours frequently alienate the people closest to them.

Friends and family often find themselves walking on eggshells, unsure of how to navigate the emotional minefield created by a loved one with NPD.

The constant need for validation can be exhausting, leading to resentment and frustration. The narcissist's perception of themselves as a victim complicates matters further, as they fail to recognise the toll their behaviour takes on other people.

This leads to a cycle of blame and defensiveness, as the narcissist deflects criticism and shifts the burden of their emotional struggles onto the people around them.

Relationships become transactional, built on a foundation of unmet emotional needs, rather than genuine connection. The resulting disconnect leaves both parties feeling isolated and unheard.

The Relentless Search for Validation

For people with NPD, the relentless search for validation is all-consuming. They pursue achievements, status, or recognition with obsession, convinced that these external markers of success will fill the void within. However, the satisfaction derived from such accomplishments is fleeting.

Each success is very quickly overshadowed by a new set of expectations, leaving them in a perpetual state of dissatisfaction.

This cycle creates a pressure cooker of emotions, as they wrestle with feelings of inadequacy, even after achieving success. The need for validation becomes a double-edged sword — providing temporary relief while reinforcing their sense of emptiness.

The Trappings of Comparison

Comparison is another dominant theme in the lives of people with NPD. They constantly measure their worth against other people, viewing the successes of peers as personal affronts. This constant comparison only deepens their feelings of inadequacy, leading to jealousy and resentment.

When they see someone else succeeding — whether in looks, status, or achievements — it can trigger an emotional crisis. Rather than using these comparisons as motivation, they spiral into despair, convinced they're unworthy of love and admiration. This cycle of comparison reinforces their victimhood, as they feel victimised by a world that seems to favour other people over them.

This comparison extends beyond individual interactions, influencing their relationships, career choices, and self-worth. They can feel compelled to one-up other people, trying to outshine their peers as a means of validating their self-worth. This competitive drive can trap them in a cycle of frustration, as they become trapped in a constant race for validation that never really satisfies.

The Weight of Expectations

People who suffer with NPD grapple with constant unrealistic expectations, both from themselves and other people.

They set impossibly high standards for achievement, convinced that meeting these benchmarks will finally lead to the validation they crave.

However, the pressure to succeed is suffocating, leaving them feeling on the verge of failure. The weight of these expectations breeds anxiety and self-doubt, amplifying their feelings of inadequacy.

The fear of not living up to their own standards can paralyse them, leading to a cycle of avoidance that entrenches them in emotional turmoil.

This avoidance can manifest in procrastination or a reluctance to engage in situations where they might not excel.

They can convince themselves that they're unworthy of the opportunities presented to them, leading to missed chances and reinforcing their victim mentality. The dissonance between their aspirations and perceived shortcomings creates a profound sense of despair that can be difficult to navigate.

The Influence of Early Experiences

The roots of NPD can trace back to early life experiences, where these people received inconsistent messages about their worth and value. Some people with NPD have grown up in environments where they were either excessively praised or severely criticised. This inconsistent feedback can lead to a distorted sense of self, where their self-worth becomes tied to external validation.

As children, they learn to associate love and approval with performance, laying the groundwork for a lifelong struggle with self-acceptance. This conditioning leads to coping mechanisms that prioritise image over authenticity, driving them to chase superficial achievements rather than build meaningful connections.

In adulthood, these internalised beliefs create a deep sense of emptiness. They seek relationships based on status or appearances, often ignoring the emotional depth needed for genuine connection. This fixation on the surface leaves a void, as the deeper, more meaningful connections they crave always feel just out of reach.

The Cycle of Anger and Regret

For people grappling with narcissistic personality disorder (NPD), anger frequently emerges as a companion, stemming from feelings of inadequacy and a sense of being victimised.

When they perceive slights or injustices, their emotional reactions can quickly intensify, resulting in outbursts or defensive behaviour.

These responses don't only damage their relationships but also contribute to their isolation, as other people hesitate to interact with someone who displays frequent anger.

This pattern of anger often turns into regret. After heated arguments, they can sometimes experience fleeting moments of clarity, recognising the damage caused by their words or actions. However, the fear of vulnerability and the unwillingness to admit mistakes forces them back into defensiveness, keeping them trapped in emotional turmoil.

During these rare moments of reflection, the weight of regret can be crushing, but it's always overshadowed by their desperate need to preserve their self-image. This internal struggle can amplify their emotional distress as they confront the difference between who they actually are, and who they want to be.

The Existential Crisis

As people with NPD grow older, they can encounter an existential crisis that forces them to confront their life choices and the path they've taken. This often stems from a growing awareness of their emotional struggles and the impact their actions have had on the people around them. They might begin to question their sense of self-worth, realising that the constant pursuit of external validation hasn't provided genuine fulfilment.

In rare moments of introspection, they're faced with the consequences of their behaviour — broken relationships, missed opportunities, and the emotional damage they've caused to themselves and other people. This awareness can be deeply unsettling, stirring feelings of hopelessness and despair.

As they grapple with this internal conflict, the fear of change can become overwhelming. Acknowledging their vulnerabilities and taking steps toward self-improvement can feel impossible.

The thought of facing their shortcomings leaves them paralysed, caught between the instinct to protect themselves and the desire to grow.

The Longing for Connection

A deep yearning for connection lies at the heart of their struggles. Despite their self-centred nature, most people with NPD crave genuine relationships.

They long for acceptance and validation but often don't know how to foster it. This creates a paradox, as their desire for connection clashes with an intense fear of vulnerability.

In trying to form bonds, they might resort to grandiosity or manipulation, mistakenly believing these tactics will draw other people in.

Unfortunately, these methods often backfire, leading to even greater isolation and despair. Their inability to establish meaningful connections exacerbates feelings of loneliness, reinforcing their sense of victimhood.

In the search for connection, they might unintentionally alienate the people who genuinely care about them. This pattern can lead to feelings of rejection and misunderstanding, further entrenching their victim mentality. They can again convince themselves that the world is against them, which only deepens their isolation from the support they so desperately need.

The Burden of Shame

Shame plays a significant role in the emotional landscape of people with NPD. They often grapple with profound feelings of shame related to perceived failures, inadequacies, or their struggles to connect with other people. This shame can be paralysing, creating barriers that hinder their ability to seek help or support. The fear of judgement can lead to a reluctance to engage in self-reflection or seek constructive feedback.

Instead of confronting their shame, they turn defensive, projecting their insecurities onto other people. This behaviour serves as a coping mechanism, deflecting attention away from their vulnerabilities, but the weight of shame can be unbearable, leading to an inner dialogue that's frequently harsh and critical.

This negative self-talk only intensifies feelings of inadequacy, trapping them in a cycle of despair. The struggle to reconcile their self-image with their behaviours can culminate in a fundamental crisis, prompting them to question their very worth.

Conclusion

The complex struggles faced by people with narcissistic personality disorder are deeply intertwined with emotional turmoil, distorted self-perception, and the patterns of their relationships.

Their experiences highlight a profound sense of despair and victimhood, exacerbated by their inability to recognise how their behaviours impact other people.

While their pursuit of validation might seem self-serving, it's vital to recognise that beneath the surface lies a genuine need for connection and acceptance. As they navigate the intricate labyrinth of their own minds, they remain trapped in a cycle of anger, regret, and existential questioning, often feeling like lost souls in an unforgiving world.

The journey through this emotional abyss is fraught with challenges, underscoring the complexities of the human experience. By understanding these struggles, we can cultivate empathy and compassion, shedding light on the darker aspects of a condition that remains largely misunderstood.

Chapter 17

Tangled Intersections

Narcissism in Romantic, Familial, and Friendly Relationships

How narcissism distorts romantic, familial, and friendship dynamics, leaving emotional scars and shattered connections

Narcissistic relationships tend to follow the same painful cycle: idealisation, manipulation, and discard. Each type of relationship also has its own unique traits, but the experience of being involved with a narcissist leaves you feeling used, emotionally drained, and shattered.

Personal Reflection:

After the end of the relationship, I found myself questioning everything I'd believed about love, trust, and partnership. I'd been idealised and showered with affection, only to be torn down and discarded once I no longer served a purpose in her world.

In hindsight, I now see how my relationship wasn't unique — most victims of narcissism describe eerily similar experiences. The highs of being adored, the constant walking on eggshells during the devaluation phase, and the gut-wrenching discard can leave you feeling like you were the one to blame. But this is a cycle that narcissists orchestrate to maintain control.

This chapter looks at how narcissism shows up in romantic, family, and friendship dynamics. I'll dive into the unique challenges each of these relationships faces and share practical strategies for managing and improving them.

I'll also explore the specific tactics narcissists use to manipulate the people closest to them. You'll find straightforward advice on recognising and breaking free from these toxic patterns.

Narcissism and Its Impact on Relationships

Relationships are a fundamental part of our lives, shaping our emotional experiences and social interactions. When narcissism enters the equation, it dramatically alters everything around them, leaving the people involved feeling frustrated, drained, and often lost.

Narcissism isn't just a personal trait; it ripples through every interaction, affecting how these people relate to partners, family members, and friends alike.

The issue goes beyond romantic relationships. Narcissists struggle to form meaningful friendships too. Their self-centred focus can push people away when they begin to feel that they're only valued for what they can contribute, rather than for who they are.

The impact on relationships is profound. A narcissist's constant need for validation, control, and admiration creates toxic patterns. These relationships are often manipulated, mistreated, and ultimately discarded when they no longer serve a purpose. This leads to ongoing conflict and emotional damage for everyone involved.

Whether in a romantic partnership, a family setting, or among friends, narcissistic behaviours like idealisation, devaluation, and discarding create an emotional rollercoaster. These cycles of extreme highs and crushing lows leave people feeling confused, hurt, and emotionally drained. Over time, trust is worn away, leaving significant emotional, psychological, and even physical scars for those caught in the chaos.

When these traits take hold, they make genuine connection almost impossible. Narcissists focus on their own needs for validation and attention, often leaving other people feeling neglected, undervalued, or even invisible.

In romantic relationships, this dynamic becomes particularly destructive. The constant need for attention from one partner can create a deep sense of rejection in the other, who may feel like they're never enough or that their needs are irrelevant.

Without empathy, understanding, or compromise, conflict becomes inevitable. Resentment builds, trust breaks down, and the relationship begins to crumble under the weight of unmet needs and unresolved tensions. This pattern of behaviour doesn't just destroy relationships; it leaves lasting wounds on those involved, creating a legacy of pain and mistrust.

Therefore, understanding the impact of narcissism on relationships is vital. Recognising these behaviours not only fosters healthier connections but also empowers people to protect themselves from the damage narcissism can cause.

Narcissism in Romantic Relationships

Romantic Relationships: The Intense Highs and Destructive Lows

When it comes to personal relationships, narcissism can create substantial challenges. Narcissistic partners can struggle with empathy and reciprocity, leading to imbalanced patterns. Grandiose narcissists seek constant admiration and validation, while vulnerable narcissists crave endless reassurance and support. This combination can result in a tumultuous relationship.

Romantic relationships with narcissists are characterised by intense initial attraction followed by deep emotional pain.

Narcissists often begin relationships by idealising their partners, creating an illusion of the perfect connection. Their charm, attentiveness, and grand gestures can make their partners feel special and unique, often referred to as love bombing.

In personal life, narcissistic behaviours create an imbalance. The constant need for admiration and validation overshadows the needs of other people. This leaves partners feeling neglected or even exploited. Recognising these patterns is essential for finding ways to restore balance and ensuring that both partners' emotional needs are met.

Being in a relationship with a narcissist can feel like being on a rollercoaster. Their relationships often swing between extreme idealisation and sharp devaluation, mirroring the chaos inside them. At first, when they see someone as a source of validation, they can seem incredibly generous, even adoring. But the moment that person stops feeding their ego or doesn't live up to their unrealistic expectations, they can quickly discard them or become hostile.

This cycle of lifting someone up, only to later tear them down, is driven by the narcissist's need to protect themselves from the overwhelming pain of their own wounds. It's not so much about the other person as it is about their desperate need to avoid feeling vulnerable or exposed.

However, this initial phase is fleeting. Once the narcissist's partner begins to assert their needs or challenge the narcissist's grandiosity, the narcissist quickly shifts into devaluation, where they criticise, belittle, and emotionally abuse their partner.

The relationship becomes a constant battle for control, with the narcissist using tactics like gaslighting, emotional blackmail, and manipulation to maintain dominance.

The final phase is often discarding, where the narcissist might abruptly end the relationship or begin emotionally detaching, leaving their partner confused and devastated.

Narcissists might return to the relationship later, engaging in what's called hoovering, to draw their partner back into the toxic cycle. This pattern of idealisation, devaluation, and discarding creates profound emotional turmoil for their partners, who often struggle with feelings of self-worth and identity after being in such a relationship.

Characteristics of Narcissistic Partners

Grandiosity and Self-Centeredness:

Being in a relationship with a narcissist can feel like a one-way street. These people are deeply engrossed in their own needs and desires, constantly looking for admiration and validation from other people while offering little in return. The relationship becomes fundamentally unbalanced, with the narcissist's requirements always taking precedence. For example, a narcissistic partner might dominate conversations with stories of their achievements while dismissing their partner's experiences as unimportant. This lack of reciprocity can lead the non-narcissistic partner to feel like an afterthought, spiralling into feelings of inadequacy and frustration.

Manipulation and Control:

Narcissistic partners frequently resort to manipulation to maintain control in the relationship. They employ tactics like gaslighting — making their partners question their own reality — or emotional manipulation, which leaves the other person feeling disoriented and isolated. For instance, if a partner confronts a narcissist about their behaviour, the narcissist might twist the story, making their partner feel guilty for expressing their feelings. This constant tug-of-war for control can create an environment where the non-narcissistic partner feels powerless.

Impact on Relationship Dynamics

Emotional and Psychological Effects:

The emotional toll of being involved with a narcissist can be severe. Partners can find themselves feeling anxious, depressed, or even worthless due to the lack of emotional support they receive. It's like pouring into a cup that never fills; this imbalance can be utterly exhausting, eroding your self-esteem over time. Most partners in these relationships feel like they're walking on eggshells, constantly trying to appease their narcissistic partner's needs while neglecting their own.

Challenges in Communication:

Communication with a narcissist often resembles a one-sided conversation. They tend to dismiss their partner's feelings and opinions, which hinders meaningful conversation. For example, during conflicts, a narcissistic partner might deflect blame or refuse to acknowledge their partner's concerns, leading to unresolved conflicts. This lack of reciprocity further fuels resentment and frustration on both sides, creating a cycle that feels inescapable.

Strategies for Managing Narcissism in Romantic Relationships

• Setting Boundaries:

One of the most effective ways to cope with a narcissistic partner is by establishing clear boundaries. It's crucial to protect your emotional well-being. Define what is acceptable and what isn't; if you don't take a stand, the narcissist will continue to disregard your needs. For example, if your partner frequently belittles your achievements, it's important to communicate that this behaviour is unacceptable and discuss the consequences of continued disrespect.

• Seeking Professional Help:

Therapy can be transformative for people in narcissistic relationships. A professional can provide tools to enhance communication, help you set and maintain boundaries, and guide you through the emotional challenges associated with these relationships. Engaging in couples therapy can also be beneficial, as it provides a neutral ground for discussing issues within the relationship, although it's important to approach this with caution, because narcissists try to manipulate the therapeutic process to their advantage.

• Building a Support Network:

It's vital to maintain relationships outside of your romantic partnership, especially when dealing with a narcissistic partner.

Friends and family can provide a necessary support system, helping you regain perspective and reminding you of your worth. Engaging in social activities can also help bolster your self-esteem and reduce the isolating effects of a narcissistic relationship.

Narcissism in Family Relationships

Familial Dynamics with Narcissistic Parents, Siblings, and Children:

In each of these family roles, narcissism can lead to emotional abuse, neglect, and chronic feelings of inadequacy, as the family unit revolves around the narcissist's needs and desires.

Narcissism within families creates deeply entrenched power imbalances and toxic patterns that can last for generations. In a family system, narcissists dominate by controlling the emotional and psychological space of their relatives.

Family Dynamics:

In family settings, narcissistic traits can create tension and conflict. Narcissistic parents can be controlling or manipulative, making it hard for their children to thrive. Additionally, narcissistic siblings can engage in rivalry, turning what should be a supportive environment into a battleground.

Narcissistic Parents:

Children of narcissistic parents often grow up feeling inadequate and unloved. Narcissistic parents readily use their children to enhance their own status or project an image of perfection, all while being emotionally unavailable or abusive. The constant need for the child to meet the parent's expectations, combined with the parent's emotional neglect, leads to lifelong challenges with self-esteem and identity.

Narcissistic Children:

When a child displays narcissistic traits, they can manipulate and control their parents to fulfil their desires, lacking respect for authority and boundaries.

Narcissistic children can grow up to become more domineering and entitled, creating difficult family relationships where their needs are prioritised above all else.

Narcissistic Siblings

Narcissistic siblings create sibling rivalry by constantly looking for attention and validation from their parents at the expense of their brothers or sisters. They manipulate family relationships using their charm to become the favoured child, pitting other siblings against each other, leaving their siblings feeling overlooked, alienated, unloved and resentful.

Extended Family:

Extended family relationships can suffer from manipulation and control, creating a tense environment during family gatherings and events. Narcissistic family members can attempt to pit relatives against each other, fostering distrust and division within the family unit.

Impact on Family Dynamics

Emotional and Psychological Effects:

Family members dealing with narcissistic behaviour often feel inadequate, frustrated, and emotionally drained. The perpetual need for validation from the narcissist can leave other people feeling overlooked and unappreciated. This emotional toll can result in family members developing anxiety, depression, and strained relationships with one another.

Challenges in Family Communication:

Conversations in narcissistic family settings are frequently dominated by the narcissist, leading to ongoing tensions and unresolved conflicts. This lack of healthy communication can create an atmosphere of resentment and misunderstanding among family members. Often, non-narcissistic family members feel that they can't express their true feelings or concerns without facing backlash or manipulation.

Strategies for Managing Narcissism in Familial Relationships

- **Establishing Boundaries:**

Setting firm boundaries with narcissistic family members is essential for maintaining emotional health. This can involve limiting contact or specifying what behaviours you won't tolerate. For example, if a parent frequently belittles your achievements, you could choose to limit conversations about your personal life. Being clear about your boundaries can help protect your well-being.

- **Seeking Support and Therapy:**

Counselling and support groups can provide people with coping strategies and a safe space to express their feelings. Engaging with other people who've experienced similar situations can help you gain perspective and feel less isolated. Family therapy could also be an option for addressing issues within the family unit, although as previously said, it should be approached carefully if a narcissist is involved, because they regularly believe that they can manipulate the process.

- **Developing Emotional Independence:**

Cultivating emotional independence is crucial when dealing with narcissistic family relationships. This involves recognising that your self-worth isn't contingent upon the approval of narcissistic family members.

Engage in activities that promote self-esteem and self-acceptance, whether through hobbies, friendships, or personal achievements.

Building a strong sense of self can help mitigate the negative impact of narcissistic behaviour on your emotional well-being.

Narcissism in Friendships

Characteristics of Narcissistic Friends

Friendships:

Friendships can become tricky when you're dealing with someone who exhibits narcissistic tendencies.

These people often approach relationships with a self-centred mindset, focusing primarily on their own needs and desires. This can turn what should be mutual support into a one-sided, transactional relationship.

True friendship is about balance, care, and respect — qualities that are often overshadowed in relationships involving a narcissistic friend.

How Narcissists Use and Discard Friends:

Friendships with narcissists are often short-lived and one-sided. Narcissists typically don't view friendships as reciprocal relationships, but as opportunities to gain admiration, validation, or advantage.

In the early stages of a friendship, the narcissist might seem charming, engaging, and even generous, making their new friends feel valued., however, this attention comes with strings attached.

Narcissists often use friendships as a way to boost their self-image, either by associating with people they see as successful or influential, or by having someone who admires and praises them.

Over time, these friendships can become draining for the other person, as the narcissist demands constant attention and emotional effort, but offers little in return. When the narcissist no longer finds the friendship beneficial, they can discard their friend abruptly, leaving them feeling confused and betrayed.

In some cases, narcissists will maintain a friendship for the sole purpose of maintaining control over their friend's emotions or social circle. They engage in triangulation, pitting friends against each other to maintain power or feel superior.

The unpredictability of a narcissist's friendship can cause emotional turmoil and leave lasting scars for the people who considered them close friends.

Self-Centeredness and Validation Seeking:

Narcissistic friends often prioritise their own needs, which lead to one-sided friendships. They only reach out when they want something, neglecting the reciprocal nature of friendship.

For example, a narcissistic friend might dominate conversations with their problems or achievements while failing to show interest in their friend's life. This one-sided interaction can leave genuine friends feeling undervalued and taken for granted.

Manipulation and Exploitation:

Friends exhibiting narcissistic traits can use charm or emotional manipulation to control and exploit the people around them. This can leave genuine friends feeling drained and unappreciated, as the narcissist uses their emotional energy for self-serving purposes. For instance, a narcissistic friend could leverage guilt to extract favours or support from other people, leading to a cycle of manipulation that's difficult to break.

Impact on Friendship Dynamics

Emotional and Psychological Effects:

Friendships with narcissists are often emotionally taxing. Friends can find themselves feeling frustrated and undervalued, leading to diminished self-esteem and overall dissatisfaction with the relationship.

Over time, these feelings can contribute to anxiety and loneliness, as the non-narcissistic friend struggles to find fulfilment in a one-sided friendship.

Challenges in Maintaining Authentic Friendships:

Authentic connections can be challenging to maintain when the narcissistic friend prioritises self-promotion and control over mutual support and understanding.

The imbalance can leave the non-narcissistic friend feeling isolated and neglected. This can also lead to resentment, as the non-narcissistic friend grapples with feelings of being used or taken for granted.

Strategies for Managing Narcissism in Friendships

- ### Setting Boundaries and Managing Expectations:

Clearly defining acceptable behaviours within the friendship is crucial. This can help protect your emotional well-being and set the tone for how the friendship operates. If your friend continually crosses those boundaries, it might be time to reevaluate the friendship. For instance, if a friend frequently interrupts you or dismisses your concerns, you could choose to address these behaviours directly by telling them how it affects you and expressing your need for more balanced communication. If they continue to disregard your feelings, it's an indication that the friendship might be one-sided, and you might need to reassess its value.

- ### Evaluating the Relationship:

Regularly assessing the value of friendship is vital. Ask yourself whether the relationship brings you joy or leaves you feeling drained. It's okay to prioritise your emotional health. If you find that the friendship consistently falls short of your expectations and needs, it could be time to distance yourself. Sometimes, taking a step back can provide clarity about the friendship's true nature and whether it's worth continuing.

- **Looking for New Connections:**

Don't hesitate to seek out friendships that are more reciprocal and fulfilling. Surrounding yourself with supportive, genuine people can significantly boost your emotional well-being.

Engage in activities that interest you, join clubs or groups, and cultivate relationships that encourage mutual support and understanding. Authentic friendships can act as a buffer against the negative impact of narcissistic people in your life.

Conclusion

The emotional toll of dealing with narcissism leaves people feeling frustrated, drained, and even lost. Narcissists have a unique way of turning every situation to their advantage, leaving the people around them to struggle with feelings of inadequacy and self-doubt.

Navigating relationships with narcissists—whether they're romantic partners, family members, or friends—can be a challenging experience. However, understanding the patterns and employing effective strategies can make a significant difference.

Throughout this chapter, I've explored the various ways narcissism manifests in relationships and the specific challenges it presents. More importantly, we've discussed practical strategies for managing these interactions.

Whether you're dealing with a narcissistic partner, family member, or friend, remember that you have the power to shape your emotional reality.

Chapter 18

Reflections of The Puppet and the Master

Who's Who in the Narcissist's Labyrinth

Unravelling the complex roles in the labyrinth of narcissistic relationships

Being in a relationship with a narcissist can feel like being trapped in a maze with no clear way out. The roles you and your partner play can become so tangled that it's hard to tell where their narcissistic behaviour ends, and your reactions begin. Narcissistic traits aren't always obvious — they can be learned over time, subtly appear, or exist outside the relationship altogether, showing up in both quiet and more obvious ways.

This reflection tool is here to help you step back and look at your relationship more clearly. It's designed to help you spot patterns of behaviour — whether in yourself or your partner — that might point to narcissistic traits. The goal isn't to label anyone but to encourage self-awareness, understanding, and a more balanced view of your relationship.

Disclaimer:

This questionnaire is purely for self-reflection and isn't a diagnostic tool. It's based on common behaviours seen in narcissistic relationships but isn't a substitute for professional psychological advice.

Your answers are meant to offer insight, not provide a final solution. If you're worried about narcissistic behaviour or your emotional well-being, it's important to speak with a qualified mental health professional.

This tool is meant to guide your reflection and build awareness. Any steps you decide to take should be made with the support of appropriate professionals.

Assigning Criteria to the Questions

Each question asks for a "Yes" or "No" answer. Your responses can help you reflect on whether certain behaviours in your relationship might reflect narcissistic traits or reactions to them.

Here's how the answers can be interpreted:

Yes" to Narcissistic Traits:

Answering "Yes" may suggest that someone is showing behaviours or attitudes linked to narcissism. These behaviours can appear in either person, whether as isolated actions or as part of a deeper pattern within the relationship.

"Yes" to Victim Response:

A "Yes" here could mean the person is feeling emotional distress caused by narcissistic behaviours, rather than showing narcissistic traits themselves. It's crucial to recognise the difference between a victim's reaction and narcissistic behaviour. A victim's response is often a reaction to unhealthy relationship patterns, not an inherent personality trait.

I have left space below each section for any notes you may wish to take.

Self-Reflection:

1. Sense of Entitlement and Special Treatment

Do I expect special treatment in situations where most people wouldn't?

Do I get frustrated or upset when things don't go my way or when I don't get the attention, I feel I deserve?

Do I expect other people to prioritise my needs without doing the same for them?

Do I believe certain rules or expectations shouldn't apply to me?

Do I feel I deserve more than other people, even if their achievements match or surpass mine?

Do I resent people who get recognition or rewards I think should be mine?

Do I often feel like I'm not given the respect or recognition I deserve?

Do I believe my time is more valuable than other people's?

Summary: Answering "Yes" may suggest narcissistic traits linked to entitlement and a tendency to expect special treatment.

2. Need for Validation and Attention

Do I often look for admiration or validation from other people to feel good about myself?

Do I feel disappointed or upset when my achievements aren't praised or recognised?

Do I regularly compare myself to other people to measure my own success or importance?

Do I feel uneasy when I'm not the centre of attention?

Do I often seek compliments or recognition for how I look or what I've accomplished?

Do I get anxious or upset if I don't receive quick feedback or acknowledgment?

Do I feel like I constantly need to prove my worth to other people?

Do I actively look for situations where I can be the focus of attention?

Summary: Answering "Yes" may point to a strong need for external validation and attention.

3. Empathy and Sensitivity to Other People's Emotions

Do I struggle to empathise with other people's feelings when their emotions don't directly impact me?

Do I sometimes ignore or dismiss someone's pain, sadness, or vulnerability?

Am I more concerned with how other people can meet my needs than how I can support them?

Do I find it hard to understand why someone's upset when it doesn't involve me?

Do I have trouble seeing things from someone else's perspective in emotional situations?

Do I often feel detached or indifferent towards other people's problems?

Do I find it difficult to offer comfort or support to friends or family during tough times?

Do I often think other people are just being too sensitive or emotional?

Summary: Answering "Yes" might suggest a lack of empathy and sensitivity towards other people's emotions.

4. Emotional Reactions and Defensiveness

Do I get angry, defensive, or irritated when someone criticises or challenges me, even over minor things?

Do I feel like I have to "win" arguments, no matter how it affects the other person?

When someone points out my flaws, do I blame them or deflect instead of reflecting on my own behaviour?

Do I struggle to take constructive feedback without feeling personally attacked?

Do I often justify my actions, even if they've hurt someone else?

Do I feel the need to prove people wrong, even when they're right?

Do I often feel misunderstood or like I'm being treated unfairly?

Do I find it hard to admit when I'm wrong?

Summary: Answering "Yes" may suggest defensiveness and a struggle to accept criticism.

5. Impulse Control and Decision-Making

Do I make decisions on impulse, without thinking about the long-term effects or how they might affect other people?

Do I act without thinking, especially when it's about getting attention or approval?

Do I struggle to reflect on my actions or understand why I made certain choices?

Do I often regret acting too quickly or without enough thought?

Do I find it hard to delay gratification for future rewards?

Do I often act on sudden desires without considering what might happen next?

Do I struggle to stick with plans or commitments when they no longer hold my interest?

Do I make promises I can't follow through on?

Summary: Answering "Yes" may suggest impulsivity and difficulties with self-reflection.

6. Relationship Dynamics and Emotional Intimacy

Do I find it hard to form deep, lasting emotional connections other's despite having many surface-level interactions?

Do I push people away when they don't meet my emotional needs, even when they've shown care and loyalty?

Am I hesitant to be vulnerable with other people, or do I avoid emotional closeness in relationships?

Do I often feel misunderstood, creating emotional distance between me and other people?

Do I put my own needs ahead of the emotional needs of those close to me?

Do I often feel like relationships are more about what I can get than what I can give?

Do I struggle to maintain long-term friendships or romantic relationships?

Do I often feel like other people aren't as invested in the relationship as I am?

Summary: "Yes" responses may indicate difficulties with emotional intimacy and connection.

Partner Reflection:

1. Need for Admiration and Attention

Do they get upset or angry when they feel ignored or unappreciated?

Do they frequently dominate conversations, leaving little room for your input?

Do they often boast about their achievements or talents, always seeking validation?

Do they expect other people to recognise their superiority without having to explain it?

Do they often interrupt you, steering the conversation back to themselves?

Do they feel envious or resentful when other people get attention or praise?

Do they exaggerate their accomplishments to impress other people?

Do they expect special treatment in social or professional settings expect to be treated like the most important person in the room, no matter the situation?

Summary: "Yes" responses suggest your partner may be seeking constant validation and attention, potentially overshadowing your needs and creating an imbalanced dynamic in the relationship.

2.   Lack of Empathy and Understanding of Your Feelings

Does your partner disregard your feelings, especially when you're upset, hurt, or in need of emotional support?

When you're open or vulnerable about your emotions, do they dismiss or belittle your personal experiences?

Do they often lack compassion for other people, even when empathy is clearly needed?

Do they struggle to understand or acknowledge your perspective during disagreements?

Do they seem indifferent to your emotional needs or well-being?

Do they often minimise your feelings or tell you to "get over it"?

Do they often make you feel guilty for expressing your emotions?

Do they rarely apologise or take responsibility for actions that hurt you?

Summary: "Yes" responses suggest a lack of empathy and understanding, which can lead to emotional neglect or invalidation of your feelings, making it difficult to form emotional connection.

3. Emotional Manipulation and Control

Does your partner emotionally manipulate you to get what they want, using guilt, threats, or gaslighting?

When you express dissatisfaction or stand your ground, do they make you feel guilty or responsible for their emotions?

Do they try to control aspects of your life, from your relationships to your choices, in subtle or overt ways?

Do they exploit your vulnerabilities to maintain control?

Do they often play the victim to gain sympathy and manipulate your actions?

Do they make you question your own perceptions or memories?

Do they withhold affection or communication as a form of punishment?

Do they often make you feel like you're walking on eggshells around them?

Do they use your insecurities to influence your behaviour?

Do they make promises they don't keep to keep you hopeful?

Summary: "Yes" responses may point to emotional manipulation, where your partner uses tactics like guilt, gaslighting, or controlling behaviour to maintain power in the relationship, affecting your sense of autonomy.

4. Sensitivity to Criticism and Conflict

Does your partner react to criticism or feedback with anger, defensiveness, or an over-the-top response?

Do they shut down emotionally or become distant when you express concern or dissatisfaction?

Do they often deflect blame onto you, even when they're in the wrong?

Do they use the silent treatment or withdraw as a way to punish you when upset?

Do they often become hostile or aggressive when confronted?

Do they dismiss your concerns as unimportant or invalid?

Do they accuse you of being overly sensitive or unreasonable?

Do they refuse to have constructive discussions about relationship issues?

Do they often make you feel like you're the problem in the relationship?

Summary: "Yes" responses may reveal your partner's difficulty handling criticism or conflict, leading to emotional withdrawal, defensiveness, or blaming behaviour, which hinders productive communication.

5. Superiority and Entitlement

Does your partner expect other people to meet their needs, even when those needs are unreasonable or excessive?

Do they disregard boundaries, rules, or conventions, acting as though they're above them?

Do they often belittle or demean other people to feel superior?

Do they expect special treatment or privileges without earning them?

Do they boast about their status or achievements to assert dominance?

Do they disregard the feelings or needs of other people in favour of their own?

Do they often make decisions without consulting you, assuming their choice is best?

Do they expect you to prioritise their needs over your own?

Do they often make you feel inferior or unimportant?

Summary: "Yes" responses suggest your partner may feel entitled and superior, expecting special treatment while showing a disregard for boundaries. This can impact the balance and equality in your relationship.

6. Emotional Intimacy and Connection

Does your partner struggle to connect with you emotionally, or avoid meaningful conversations about feelings and personal growth?

Do they only show affection or care when it serves their purpose or when they want something from you?

When you try to deepen your emotional connection, do they distance themselves or deflect the conversation?

Do they often put their own needs first, showing little regard for your emotional well-being?

Do they often leave you feeling emotionally drained or neglected?

Do they rarely initiate intimate or heartfelt conversations?

Do they often seem uninterested in your day-to-day experiences or feelings?

Do they avoid talking about important issues that affect the relationship?

Do they often make you feel like you're the only one invested in the relationship?

Summary: "Yes" responses suggest your partner struggles with emotional intimacy, avoiding deep connections and prioritising their own needs, leaving you feeling distant or neglected.

7.   Shifting Behaviour (Idealisation and Devaluation)

Does your partner often switch between being overly affectionate and then emotionally distant or cold?

Do you feel like you're walking on eggshells, always trying to "earn" their approval or love?

When their mood changes, do you feel uncertain about where you stand with them?

Do they often devalue you after idealising you, leaving you feeling inadequate?

Do they withhold affection or attention to punish or control you?

Do they often make you feel like you're never good enough for them?

Do they frequently change their opinions or attitudes towards you without explanation?

Do they often make you feel like you're the cause of their mood swings or emotional reactions?

Summary: "Yes" responses may point to a pattern of idealisation followed by devaluation, which causes confusion and emotional instability, creating a cycle of seeking approval and emotional distance.

Interpreting and Understanding Your Results

Now that you've completed the questionnaire, it's time to step back and look at the bigger picture. Your answers can reveal patterns in your behaviour or your relationship that are worth exploring. Use this guide to help you understand what your responses might be telling you.

Self-Reflection:

- **Mostly "Yes" Answers:**

If you've answered "yes" to most questions, you might recognise some narcissistic traits in yourself. These patterns could be affecting your relationships but recognising them is a powerful first step. It's worth exploring these behaviours more deeply — whether that's through therapy, self-help resources, or simply taking time to reflect. With greater self-awareness, you can start building healthier, more fulfilling connections.

- **Mostly "No" Answers:**

If you answered "no" more often, narcissistic traits probably aren't a major factor in your behaviour. That said, even subtle patterns can impact relationships, so it's still helpful to reflect on any areas that stood out. Personal growth is a lifelong process, and small insights can lead to meaningful change.

Partner Reflection:

- **Mostly "Yes" Answers:**

If most of your answers were "yes," your partner may be showing behaviours linked to narcissism. This could be affecting your emotional well-being and the balance in your relationship.

It's important to reflect on how this dynamic is impacting you. You might want to talk to your partner about what you've noticed or seek professional support to help you decide on the next steps.

- **Mostly "No" Answers:**

If you mostly answered "no," your partner likely doesn't display strong narcissistic traits. Still, no relationship is perfect, and there may be other challenges worth addressing. Honest conversations about your relationship can help strengthen your emotional connection.

- **A Mix of "Yes" and "No" Answers:**

If you noticed that both you and your partner show some narcissistic traits, it suggests that the relationship may need more mutual understanding and effort. Open communication is key here, and it might be helpful to work through these issues with a counsellor. Together, you can create a more balanced and supportive dynamic.

What to Do Next

1. Reach Out for Professional Support

If you've identified narcissistic behaviours in yourself or your partner, speaking to a therapist or counsellor can offer clarity and guidance. They can help you understand how these traits are affecting your relationship and how to navigate them in a healthy way.

2. Have Honest Conversations

If you feel safe doing so, talk to your partner about what you've discovered. Honest, open communication can be challenging but is vital for making positive changes in your relationship.

3. Focus on Your Own Growth

If you've recognised narcissistic tendencies in yourself, that doesn't define who you are. It's an opportunity for growth. Therapy or self-development work can help you develop empathy, accountability, and healthier ways of relating to other people.

Final Thoughts

Be kind to yourself as you reflect on these results. Self-awareness is a powerful tool, and recognising unhealthy patterns — whether in yourself or your relationship — is the first step towards change. If things feel overwhelming, remember that professional support is always there to help guide you forward. Taking this time to reflect shows a commitment to healthier relationships and personal growth.

You're already on the right path !

Chapter 19

The Veiled Strategies

Manipulative Tactics of the Narcissist

A look at various manipulative tactics used by narcissists

Navigating the world of narcissism can feel like walking through a minefield, the dangers are hidden beneath the surface. Narcissists are experts at using disguised tactics that mask their true intentions, making it hard for other people to recognise their manipulation until it's too late.

Personal Reflection:

When I think back to my engagement, I remember the initial thrill of love, filled with promises and plans for our future. But over time, her compliments turned into something more sinister, they became a double-edged sword.

At first, I was drawn in by her charisma, but the subtle criticisms hidden beneath her praise began to chip away at my self-esteem. It became clear that her affection was conditional, always tied to how well I met her expectations. I found myself constantly striving for her approval, only to feel more lost as I navigated her ever shifting emotional needs. It was only after our breakup that I recognised how her veiled strategies had kept me trapped, making me doubt my worth, while she maintained the illusion of support.

In this chapter, I'll explore the veiled strategies narcissists use in personal relationships, showing how these tactics subtly manipulate those around them. Dissecting these behaviours will help dismantle the complex web narcissists create, bringing clarity and understanding to your interactions. By recognising these methods, you'll be better equipped to protect yourself from their damaging effects.

100 Tactics Narcissists Use to Maintain Control in Relationships: Different Slants on Similar Traits

Narcissists are skilled at using a range of tactics to maintain control in their relationships, these manipulative strategies allow them to dominate the emotional landscape leaving those around them confused, hurt, and emotionally scarred. Recognising these tactics will help toward breaking free from the web of narcissistic control.

1. Tactical Incompetence

Narcissists often pretend they can't handle basic tasks, leaving you to pick up the slack. They'll act clueless when it comes to household chores, decision-making, or managing responsibilities. This forces you into the "caretaker role", making you believe it's easier to handle everything yourself. Over time, you feel overwhelmed, while they sit back comfortably. This calculated helplessness keeps you trapped, emotionally exhausted, and dependent on them, because they know you won't let things fall apart.

2. Intermittent Reinforcement

They create a toxic cycle of love and punishment. One moment, they're full of affection, making you feel special, and the next, they withdraw or lash out. This inconsistency hooks you emotionally, as you constantly chase the fleeting moments of kindness. You start believing that if you just behave the 'right' way, you'll earn their love again. This unpredictable behaviour keeps you anxious and desperate for their approval.

3. Manipulated Victimhood

Narcissists expertly twist situations to make themselves the victim, even when they're at fault. If you confront them about their behaviour, they'll bring up their own struggles or accuse you of being cruel. Suddenly, you find yourself apologising and comforting them. This manipulation not only deflects blame but also keeps you emotionally entangled. It's a clever way to dodge accountability and maintain control over the relationship.

4. Sabotaging Your Success

Your achievements threaten a narcissist's fragile ego. They'll subtly undermine your confidence by criticising your goals, distracting you, or belittling your accomplishments. They might 'forget' to support important events or plant seeds of doubt in your mind. This sabotage ensures you don't surpass them, keeping you small and dependent. They can't stand the idea of you thriving without them, so they quietly work to hold you back.

5. Backhanded Compliments

Narcissists deliver compliments that double as insults. They might say, "You're smarter than I thought you'd be", or "I can't believe that outfit actually looks good on you." These comments leave you confused and second-guessing yourself. If you confront them, they'll claim you're being too sensitive or that it was just a joke. This constant underhanded criticism chips away at your self-esteem while allowing them to deny any wrongdoing.

6. Emotional Invalidation

Your feelings are dismissed as overreactions. If you express hurt or frustration, they'll tell you to "calm down," or accuse you of being dramatic. Over time, you begin doubting your own emotions, questioning whether you're the problem. This emotional invalidation forces you to suppress your feelings to avoid conflict, leaving you feeling isolated and misunderstood. It's a subtle but powerful way to silence you.

7. Manufactured Crisis

They create chaos to keep your attention on them. Whether it's a sudden health scare, financial 'emergency,' or drama with friends, they always seem to be at the centre of some kind of crisis. These constant disruptions drain your emotional energy, leaving little room for your own needs. You're always in damage control, too exhausted to question their behaviour or focus on your own well-being.

8. Gaslighting the Past

Narcissists will outright deny past actions or twist facts to make you question your memory. They'll tell you "That's not how it happened" or "You weren't paying attention," making you doubt your own perception. Over time, this distortion of reality makes you unsure of what's true. You begin to rely on their version of events, which gives them total control over how you view the relationship and yourself.

9. Provoking Emotional Reactions

They deliberately push your buttons to make you react emotionally. Once you explode or break down, they accuse you of being irrational or 'crazy.' Meanwhile, they stay calm, making it seem even more like you're the problem. This calculated behaviour leaves you feeling guilty and embarrassed, making you suppress your emotions in the future. It's a cruel tactic that shifts the blame onto you.

10. Public Charm, Private Cruelty

In public, narcissists are charming and charismatic, making it hard for anyone to believe they could be abusive. Behind closed doors, they're cold, critical, and manipulative. This dual personality isolates you because when you try to speak out, no one believes you. Their public mask allows them to quietly discredit you while maintaining their flawless image, leaving you feeling completely alone.

11. Non-Apology Apologies

Their apologies are meaningless. They'll say things like, "I'm sorry you feel that way," which shifts blame back onto you. These hollow apologies give the appearance of remorse without any real accountability. You're left feeling unresolved and invalidated because nothing ever changes. It's a clever way for them to silence conflict without admitting any fault or making amends.

12. Pretending to Be "Just Like You"

Narcissists will copy your interests, routines, and opinions to make you believe you're perfectly matched. They'll agree with your views, take up your hobbies, and act like they share your values. It feels natural, like you've found someone who just gets you. But it's all for show. Once they've gained your trust, the mask slips, and you're left wondering who they really are.

13. Chronic Lying

Narcissists lie effortlessly about everything — big or small. They fabricate stories, hide truths, and distort facts to suit their agenda. You'll catch them in lies, but they'll deny or justify them, making you second-guess yourself. This constant dishonesty keeps you disoriented and vulnerable, giving them total control over the situation while you're left scrambling for the truth.

14. Controlling the Flow of Information

They selectively share information to keep you off-balance. Whether it's hiding financial details or omitting important plans, they control what you know. This leaves you feeling powerless and dependent on them for answers. By keeping you in the dark, they ensure you can't make independent decisions, tightening their grip on your life and your choices.

15. Constant Comparisons

Narcissists frequently compare you to other people to make you feel inadequate. They might say, "My ex never did that" or praise someone else's looks or success. This makes you feel like you're constantly competing for their approval. Over time, these comparisons erode your self-esteem and keep you chasing validation, making it easier for them to control you.

16. Weaponizing Vulnerabilities

Anything you share in confidence becomes a weapon. They'll bring up your deepest insecurities in arguments or mock your past mistakes to humiliate you. This betrayal of trust makes you hesitant to open up again. You become guarded, knowing anything you reveal could be used against you. It's a calculated way to weaken you emotionally while maintaining power.

17. Twisting Your Morals

They manipulate your values to control you. If you value kindness, they'll guilt-trip you for setting boundaries. If family loyalty is important, they'll accuse you of abandoning them. They exploit your principles to make you feel guilty for standing up for yourself, leaving you torn between staying true to yourself and keeping them happy.

18. Strategic Disappearance

During conflicts, they vanish. They ignore your messages, disappear for hours or days, and leave you panicking. This is a form of punishment, forcing you to chase them for answers. You're left feeling desperate and powerless, willing to do anything to restore peace. This disappearance makes you fear abandonment, keeping you in their control.

19. Love Bombing

At first, they overwhelm you with constant attention, grand gestures, and promises of a perfect future. It feels like you've finally met someone who truly gets you. But once they know you're hooked, the affection fades. What you're left with is criticism and control, and you're left chasing the illusion they created.

20. Conditional Favour

They may help you, but they'll expect something in return, usually more than you can give. If you don't meet their expectations or fail to repay them the way they want, they'll make sure you feel guilty, it's never about kindness or generosity; it's always about creating a debt they can call in whenever it suits them.

21. Moving the Goalposts

No matter how hard you try to meet their expectations, narcissists constantly shift the standards. One day, they praise you for something, and the next, it's not good enough. This endless game leaves you feeling like you're always falling short. You're left exhausted, trying to meet demands that were never meant to be achievable. They do this to keep you chasing for their approval, keeping you in a cycle of self-doubt and frustration.

22. Triangulation

Narcissists love dragging other people into your relationship to stir jealousy and insecurity. They might mention how a friend or ex admires them or suggest someone else treats them better than you do. This tactic makes you feel like you're in competition, forcing you to work harder for their attention. It divides relationships and isolates you, making them the centre of your world while causing conflict between you and other people.

23. Guilt-Tripping

They make you feel guilty for having your own needs, desires, or boundaries. If you say no or stand up for yourself, they'll remind you of everything they've done for you or suggest you're selfish. They exploit your empathy, turning your kindness against you. Over time, you give in just to avoid feeling guilty, slowly losing your ability to say no.

24. Smear Campaigns

When they sense they're losing control over you, narcissists start spreading lies and half-truths about you to friends, family, or even on social media. They paint you as unstable or abusive, gaining sympathy and support from other people. This isolates you further and makes it harder to seek help because people already have a distorted view of you. It's a cruel but effective way to punish you and protect their image.

25. Future Faking

They make grand promises about your future together — marriage, kids, business ventures — but never follow through. These empty promises are designed to keep you hooked and hopeful. You invest more time and energy into the relationship, waiting for these dreams to come true. But they never intended to make them happen; it was just another way to control you and stop you from leaving.

26. Divide and Conquer

Narcissists will openly turn you against the people closest to you. They'll say things like, "Your friend's jealous of you" or "Your family's trying to control you." They might even twist the truth or spread lies to spark arguments. The goal is simple — to cut you off from your support system so you have no one else to rely on but them.

27. Passive-Aggressive Behaviour

Instead of addressing issues directly, narcissists express their anger through subtle digs, backhanded compliments, or deliberate procrastination. They might "forget" important dates or do things poorly, so you'll stop asking. This passive-aggressive behaviour creates tension and confusion, making it hard to confront them because they always have an excuse. It's their way of expressing hostility without appearing outright cruel.

28. Financial Control

Money becomes a tool for control. They might restrict your access to funds, criticise your spending, or make you financially dependent on them. Even if you have your own income, they'll find ways to make you feel guilty for spending, or pressure you to share finances. This keeps you trapped because leaving feels impossible without financial freedom.

29. Projection

They accuse you of the very things they're guilty of. If they're cheating, they'll accuse you of being unfaithful. If they're lying, they'll call you dishonest. This constant projection confuses you and forces you to defend yourself against false accusations. It's a distraction tactic that shifts attention away from their own behaviour and puts you on the defensive.

30. Shutdown

When upset, they'll completely shut down communication — ignoring your calls, texts, or even your presence. This isn't just about needing space; it's a deliberate punishment. You're left anxious, wondering what you did wrong and desperate to fix things. This emotional abandonment makes you feel invisible and keeps you walking on eggshells to avoid it happening again.

31. Overstepping Boundaries

Narcissists have no respect for your personal boundaries. If you set limits, they'll push back, ignore them, or make you feel guilty for having them. Whether it's invading your privacy, making decisions for you, or dismissing your feelings, they constantly test how far they can go. Over time, your boundaries erode because it feels easier to give in than fight back.

32. Playing Dumb

They pretend they don't understand what you're saying or act clueless when confronted about their behaviour. It's a subtle way to frustrate you and avoid responsibility. They might say, "I don't know what you're talking about"; or "You're overthinking." This makes you question whether you're explaining things poorly or being unreasonable, causing you to back down.

33. Excessive Flattery — (Love Bombing Continued)

Beyond just love bombing, they'll shower you with compliments, calling you perfect or saying no one has ever understood them like you do. It feels incredible — like you've found your soulmate. But this flattery isn't genuine. It's a tactic to lower your defences and make you emotionally attached before their true colours start to show, keeping you stuck in the toxic cycle.

34. Using Jealousy as a Weapon

They intentionally flirt with other people or talk about how attractive someone else is to spark jealousy. This makes you feel insecure and more eager to win back their full attention. It's a way of keeping you off-balance, making you feel like you have to compete for their affection, and reinforcing their control over how you feel about yourself.

35. Creating Dependency

They subtly make you dependent on them for emotional support, decision-making, or even daily routines. They'll discourage your independence, making you feel like you can't succeed without them. Over time, you start relying on them for things you used to handle easily. This dependency makes it much harder to leave, even when the relationship becomes toxic.

36. Rewriting History

Narcissists will rewrite past events to suit their narrative. If you recall something they did, they'll insist it happened differently or deny it entirely. They'll say things like, "You're remembering it wrong"; or "That's not what I meant." This constant rewriting of history makes you question your memory and gives them control over the truth.

37. Playing the Martyr

They act like they're constantly sacrificing everything for the relationship. If you dare to complain about something, they'll paint themselves as the long-suffering partner. This is designed to guilt-trip you into silence and make you feel like you owe them. It's a clever way to avoid addressing their own toxic behaviour.

38. Weaponizing Intimacy

They use affection and sex as tools for control. When you're in their favour, they might shower you with intimacy. But when you upset them, they withdraw affection completely. This hot-and-cold pattern keeps you craving their approval and confuses emotional closeness with control.

39. Selective Amnesia

They suddenly "forget" promises or agreements that don't benefit them. If they agree to help or support you, they'll act like it never happened. But anything that benefits them is remembered in vivid detail. This selective memory allows them to dodge accountability while keeping you confused and frustrated.

40. Overreacting to Boundaries

If you try to set a boundary, they explode. They accuse you of being selfish, cold, or controlling. Their exaggerated reaction makes you feel like you've done something wrong, pushing you to drop the boundary to restore peace. This teaches you that it's safer not to stand up for yourself.

41. Gaslighting through Flattery

Narcissists use flattery not only to charm but to gaslight you. They'll shower you with compliments and praise, only to later make you feel unworthy or insecure. This confusing back-and-forth makes you doubt your perception of reality. You begin questioning your worth because the praise is often followed by subtle criticisms that make you feel like you don't deserve it.

42. Blaming You for Their Problems

When things go wrong, they'll turn the tables and make you feel like it's your fault. If they fail at something, they'll accuse you of not supporting them enough or not doing your part. This tactic shifts the focus off their own behaviour and places the burden on you, leaving you feeling guilty and responsible for their failures.

43. Lying to Make You Look Crazy

Narcissists are notorious for twisting the truth and creating elaborate stories. They'll tell lies about situations to make you appear paranoid, crazy, or delusional. If you confront them about something, they'll deny it or claim you've misunderstood. This manipulative tactic forces you to question your own reality, making you second-guess everything.

44. Using Your Vulnerabilities Against You

They'll remember everything you've confided in them, especially your weaknesses, and later use those details to manipulate you. If you're having a tough time, they might bring up personal struggles you've shared to belittle or control you. This premeditated tactic exploits your trust to get what they want, turning your vulnerability into a weapon against you.

45. Setting Unrealistic Expectations

Narcissists will often set standards so high that you're set up to fail. They make demands that are unreasonable, and when you don't meet them, they criticise you. This tactic keeps you constantly striving for something you'll never reach. They use it as a way to undermine your self-esteem and keep you chasing after their approval.

46. Triangulating with Your Own Emotions

They manipulate your emotions by bringing up past situations or people, trying to make you feel inferior. They might tell you how someone else handled a similar situation better than you or how you used to be more competent. This makes you question your own emotional responses and leads to an unhealthy comparison, leaving you doubting your value.

47. Empty Promises

They'll assure you that they're going to change, make an effort, or treat you better, but nothing ever changes. These empty promises are just a way to keep you hopeful and invested, waiting for a better future. Eventually, you realise it's just another tactic to keep you hooked, with no intention of making any real changes.

48. Weaponizing Your Success

If you achieve something, they'll either diminish it or use it against you. They might say you're lucky or that you didn't work hard enough for it. If you get attention for your success, they'll shift the focus onto themselves. This strategy keeps you from ever feeling truly proud of your achievements and makes sure it's always overshadowed by their need to dominate.

49. Playing the Victim to Gain Sympathy

When confronted with their bad behaviour, narcissists often turn the situation around and portray themselves as the victim. They'll claim you're attacking them for no reason or accuse you of being insensitive. This emotional manipulation distracts from their wrongdoing and forces you to feel guilty for standing up for yourself. It keeps them in control by drawing sympathy from other people.

50. Minimising Your Needs

When you express your feelings or needs, narcissists will downplay them, telling you that you're overreacting or that your concerns are not a big deal. This tactic makes you feel like you don't deserve to have your needs met. Over time, it erodes your sense of self-worth, leaving you to constantly suppress your feelings in order to maintain peace.

51. Testing Your Loyalty

They will often test your loyalty by pushing boundaries or asking you to choose between them and someone else. These tests can come in the form of questions like, "Who would you choose if you had to pick between me, and your friends?" The goal is to manipulate your responses and make you feel guilty for supporting anyone but them.

52. Offering Help to Gain Control

Narcissists offer help in a way that puts you in debt to them. They make grand gestures of assistance, but it always comes with strings attached. Whether it's fixing something for you or offering emotional support, their help is never unconditional. They expect something in return, using your gratitude to manipulate and control you further.

53. Gaslighting Through Silence

When you challenge their actions, they refuse to acknowledge you. This silence forces you into submission as you become anxious, trying to figure out what went wrong. The lack of communication leaves you feeling isolated, doubting yourself, and questioning whether your concerns were ever valid in the first place.

54. Exploiting Your Empathy

Narcissists have a way of making you feel responsible for their emotions. If they're upset, they'll make you feel like you need to fix it. They use your natural empathy to control your behaviour, making you prioritise their feelings over your own. This emotional burden leaves you feeling drained and constantly second-guessing your decisions to ensure they don't feel neglected.

55. Disguising Criticism as 'Constructive Feedback'

When they criticise you, they often disguise it as constructive feedback, making it seem like they're helping you grow. In reality, it's an underhanded way to make you feel inferior or inadequate. They claim they're doing you a favour by pointing out your flaws, but it's really just a way to maintain power and keep you feeling small.

56. Playing on Your Insecurities

Narcissists will use your insecurities to manipulate you. If they know you're self-conscious about something, they'll bring it up subtly, making you feel worse. Whether it's about your appearance, intelligence, or abilities, they'll exploit these feelings to keep you on edge. This constant targeting of your vulnerabilities weakens your confidence and strengthens their hold over you.

57. Undermining Your Confidence

If you express pride in your accomplishments, they'll minimise or dismiss them. They'll tell you that you're being arrogant or that your achievements aren't significant. This tactic is designed to make you second-guess yourself and undermine your confidence. Over time, you start doubting your abilities and questioning whether you deserve to feel proud of yourself.

58. Blaming Your Past

When they're caught in the act, narcissists will deflect blame by pointing to your past. They'll claim, "Well, you've always been like this," or "You're just bringing up old stuff again." This tactic shifts the focus away from their bad behaviour and makes you feel like your past is the real problem, rather than their actions.

59. Offering Unsolicited Advice

Narcissists love to give unsolicited advice, often in a way that makes you feel inadequate. They position themselves as the expert, offering their "wisdom" on everything from your career choices to your personal life. This constant advice undermines your confidence and makes you feel like you can't make decisions without their input, further solidifying their control.

60. Using Your Love Against You

Narcissists know how much you care for them, and they'll exploit that by threatening to leave or withholding affection. They'll tell you, "If you really loved me, you'd do this," or use love as a bargaining chip to get what they want. This emotional manipulation keeps you hooked, constantly working to prove your love to them in unhealthy ways.

61. Pretending to Be Vulnerable for Sympathy

Narcissists often feign vulnerability when it suits them. They may exaggerate personal struggles or act helpless to get sympathy or manipulate other people into taking care of them. This tactic allows them to gain attention and control, as people feel compelled to step in and "help" them, thinking they're in a genuine emotional crisis.

62. Subtly Competing with You

Instead of openly competing, narcissists will covertly undermine your success by comparing you to other people or belittling your achievements. They'll make small, snide remarks that question your abilities or dismiss your hard work. This tactic creates an ongoing sense of rivalry, where you're constantly left wondering if you measure up in their eyes.

63. Making You Feel Like a Burden

They'll use guilt to make you feel like your needs or requests are unreasonable. If you ask for help or attention, they'll respond with frustration or annoyance, implying that you're being a burden. Over time, you'll hesitate to ask for anything because you'll feel guilty for demanding too much from them.

64. Creating a False Sense of Intimacy

A narcissist may act overly affectionate or tell you personal details to make you feel like you share an intimate bond. They'll do this to lure you in, making you believe that you are the most important person in their life. However, this false sense of closeness is designed to manipulate you into trusting them completely, so they can later betray that trust when it benefits them.

65. Using the "We" Language

Narcissists will frequently use "we" when talking about their successes or problems, trying to make everything about the two of you. They might say, "We're so successful together," or "We're facing challenges, but we'll get through them." This tactic blurs the line between their own needs and yours, subtly forcing you to take on their struggles as your own.

66. Narcissistic Perception Manipulation

Narcissists will twist your view of events to make themselves look better. They'll deny or distort facts to fit their agenda. If you challenge them, they'll accuse you of being too sensitive or not seeing things clearly. This leaves you confused, making you doubt your own experiences and weakening your trust in your understanding of them.

67. Demanding Loyalty Without Reciprocity

They will expect unwavering loyalty from you, demanding that you always have their back, regardless of how they treat you. At the same time, they won't return this loyalty. They may betray your trust, ignore your needs, or act as if you're disposable. This one-sided expectation is a method to maintain control while denying you the same respect and loyalty.

68. Distracting You from Their Behaviour

When confronted about their actions, narcissists often divert the conversation away from their behaviour. They might bring up an irrelevant issue or attack your character to make you feel guilty for even raising concerns. These distraction tactics keep the focus off their wrongdoings and make you feel like you're the one at fault for bringing it up.

69. Manipulating Other People to Isolate You

Narcissists will subtly turn your friends, family, or co-workers against you. They'll spread rumours or twist the truth about your actions, making other people doubt your intentions. Over time, this manipulation leaves you feeling isolated and alone. This ensures you have no one to turn to, while they maintain control and continue to distort the truth, deepening your sense of abandonment and vulnerability.

70. Overloading You with Complaints

They will barrage you with complaints or issues that seem trivial but are meant to exhaust and overwhelm you. These constant grievances can range from small annoyances to exaggerated problems, making you feel like you're always in the wrong. This overload tactic wears you down mentally and emotionally, leaving you drained and questioning your worth.

71. Portraying You as the Cause of Their Misfortune

If something goes wrong for them, narcissists will turn the blame onto you. They may claim that your actions or decisions led to their problems, even if you had nothing to do with it. This tactic keeps you in a state of guilt and confusion, always trying to make things right while they avoid taking any accountability.

72. Demanding Unwarranted Apologies

They'll demand an apology from you, even when they've done something wrong. Narcissists often use this tactic to shift the blame, forcing you to admit fault for things you didn't do. They'll use phrases like, "I can't believe you would act like that," or "You owe me an apology for how you treated me." This manipulation tactic ensures they remain in control of the situation.

73. Evoking Fear of Abandonment

To keep you emotionally attached, narcissists will frequently evoke a fear of abandonment. They might say things like, "If you really loved me, you wouldn't leave me," or "You'll regret this if you walk away." This tactic plays on your insecurities and fear of losing them, making it harder for you to break free from the toxic cycle.

74. Pretending to Have Your Best Interests at Heart

Narcissists will often act like they're looking out for your well-being, giving you advice that seems caring on the surface. However, their true intent is to control you. They'll tell you what to do, how to think, and who to trust, all while maintaining the appearance of a concerned friend or partner. This guise of caring makes it difficult for you to see their true manipulative intentions.

75. Using Confusion to Avoid Responsibility

When caught in a lie or bad behaviour, narcissists will often try to confuse you with conflicting statements or contradictory actions. They might deny things they've said or done, making it difficult for you to get a clear answer. This constant state of confusion prevents you from holding them accountable, leaving you second-guessing yourself and unable to address their harmful behaviour.

76. Playing the Victim of Your Reaction

When confronted about their harmful actions, narcissists will often twist the situation by claiming that your response is the real problem. They may accuse you of overreacting or being overly emotional, effectively shifting the focus from their behaviour to your feelings. This tactic is meant to invalidate your perspective and make you feel guilty for expressing yourself.

77. The Silent Treatment as a Punishment

Narcissists will use the silent treatment as a way to punish you and regain control. By refusing to engage with you or acknowledge your presence, they make you feel isolated and desperate for their attention. This method is intended to create emotional distress, forcing you to grovel or apologise, even when you're not at fault.

78. Discrediting You in Public

When a narcissist wants to undermine your reputation, they may discredit you in front of other people. They might make subtle or overt criticisms, spreading rumours or exaggerating your flaws. This tactic not only diminishes your credibility but also isolates you socially, as people begin to view you through the narcissist's distorted lens.

79. Giving You the "Cold Shoulder"

The narcissist might withdraw emotionally, giving you the "cold shoulder" when they don't get their way. This passive-aggressive behaviour is designed to make you feel like you're being ignored or rejected, forcing you to seek their approval and re-establish a connection, all while they maintain the power dynamic.

80. Making You Question Your Own Worth

Narcissists frequently attack your self-esteem by subtly questioning your abilities, looks, or character. They might make backhanded compliments, telling you that you're "pretty for someone your age" or suggesting that your achievements aren't as impressive as you think. This constant undermining erodes your confidence, leaving you doubting your worth.

81. Using Your Emotions Against You

Narcissists often exploit your emotional responses to manipulate you. If you're upset, they might accuse you of being irrational or oversensitive. They might even turn your tears into a tool for further control, using your vulnerability to guilt-trip you into doing what they want. This manipulation makes you feel like your emotions are invalid or inconvenient.

82. Gaslighting Through Denial

When you catch a narcissist in a lie or dishonest behaviour, they may deny it completely, even in the face of undeniable evidence. They'll insist that you're imagining things, gaslighting you into doubting your own reality. This denial tactic keeps you in a constant state of confusion and forces you to question your perception of events.

83. Shifting Blame to Avoid Accountability

Rather than taking responsibility for their actions, narcissists will quickly shift the blame onto you or someone else. They might accuse you of being the one to cause the problem or make you feel guilty for bringing it up in the first place. This constant deflection ensures that they avoid accountability and continue to control the narrative.

84. Using "Jokes" to Criticise You

Narcissists often hide their insults behind humour, making hurtful comments seem like jokes. They'll say something like, "Just kidding, but you really should lose a few pounds," or "I didn't mean to offend you, but you've always been a bit touchy." This tactic allows them to get away with criticism while leaving you unsure whether it's meant to be taken seriously.

85. Encouraging You to Doubt Your Relationships

A narcissist works more quietly here. They'll drop subtle comments like, "Do you really think they have your back?" or "Funny how they only call when they need something." It's not full-blown conflict — it's slow, creeping doubt. Over time, you start pulling away from the people who care about you, leaving the narcissist in full control.

86. Mirroring Your Identity

They don't just copy your interests — they study you. They mirror your deepest values, your dreams, and even your insecurities. It feels like you've met your soulmate, someone who understands you in ways no one else has. But it's manipulation. Once they've pulled you in, they drop the act, leaving you confused and questioning what was ever real.

87. Omitting Critical Facts

In relationships, narcissists may withhold key details to keep you in the dark, making it harder for you to make informed decisions. They may omit important facts, manipulate timelines, or deliberately forget things that are relevant to you. This control of information puts you at a disadvantage, leaving you at their mercy.

88. Making You Fear Their Temper

Narcissists often use intimidation to manipulate and control other people. They may threaten to lose their temper or act outrageously angry, causing you to walk on eggshells in fear of their outbursts. This tactic is used to maintain control over the situation, making you reluctant to challenge their behaviour or voice concerns.

89. Dismissive Apologies

When they are caught or forced to acknowledge their wrongdoings, narcissists will often offer apologies that lack sincerity. These apologies are just a way to end the conversation or avoid consequences, without actually acknowledging the harm they caused rather than taking responsibility for their actions.

90. Playing Both Sides

In conflict situations, narcissists may engage in a tactic called "playing both sides," where they subtly manipulate each party against the other. They will tell one person one thing and another person something completely different, ensuring that everyone is at odds. This tactic causes confusion and division, allowing the narcissist to remain in control of the situation.

91. Overemphasising Their Sacrifices

Narcissists often boast about their self-sacrifice to guilt-trip other people. They will tell you how much they've given up for you or how hard they've worked to make things right, exaggerating their efforts to make you feel indebted. This tactic is designed to make you feel like you owe them, regardless of whether their sacrifices were genuine or not.

92. Creating an "Us Versus Them" Mentality

To maintain control, narcissists often create an "us vs. them" mentality, where they position you as part of a team and everyone else as an enemy. They will vilify other people and make you believe that you need to protect them from the outside world. This tactic fosters dependency and blinds you to their manipulative behaviour.

93. Blurring Boundaries for Control

Narcissists often blur personal boundaries to gain control over your life. They may invade your privacy, push you into uncomfortable situations, or pressure you to reveal more than you're comfortable with. By violating your boundaries, they ensure you feel like you owe them access to your personal space, time, or emotions.

94. Dismissing Your Achievements

When you share your accomplishments, a narcissist will often dismiss them or downplay them as insignificant. They might say things like, "Anyone could have done that," or "It's not a big deal." This tactic makes you feel like your achievements are unimportant, reinforcing their position as the only one who deserves recognition. It's calculated to make you question the value of your own success while maintaining their sense of superiority.

95. Making You Justify Their Actions

Narcissists often manipulate you into justifying their hurtful or selfish behaviour. They might say, "I wouldn't have done that if you hadn't..." or "I only acted that way because you made me." This tactic shifts the responsibility onto you, making you feel like you're the one who needs to explain why they acted in a certain way.

96. Using Your Past Against You

A narcissist will sometimes use your past mistakes or vulnerabilities as ammunition to discredit you. They may bring up old issues, private matters, or past wrongs you've made to undermine your self-worth or make you feel inferior. This strategy serves to keep you stuck in a cycle of guilt, preventing you from moving forward.

97. Making You Fear Their Reaction

They'll often use threats, intimidation, or passive-aggressive behaviour to make you fear their reaction to your decisions. Whether it's how you spend your time, who you talk to, or what you choose to do, they'll make it clear that their approval is essential for your peace of mind. This fear creates an unhealthy power dynamic.

98. Creating False Expectations

A narcissist will set up unrealistic expectations for you to meet, only to change the goalposts when you get close. They'll build up an idea of what you should do, how you should behave, or what you should provide, only to later criticise you for not meeting the constantly shifting standards.

99. Keeping You in a State of Uncertainty

Narcissists love to keep people in a state of confusion or doubt, never quite knowing where they stand. They will make contradictory statements or promises that they never follow through on, creating a sense of uncertainty. This tactic keeps you on edge and makes it harder for you to make decisions or assert yourself.

100. False Sense of Change

After a blow-up or period of bad behaviour, narcissists will often claim they've "changed" to draw you back in. They'll promise to be better or admit their past mistakes, only to repeat the same harmful patterns once you're emotionally invested again. This strategy lures you into a false sense of hope, keeping you stuck in a cycle of disappointment.

Conclusion

What you're looking at here are textbook examples of narcissistic behaviour. It's a pattern that's all about manipulation, and believe me, there's no room for understanding or compromise.

Narcissists always view everything through a black-and-white lens, where it's always about their own self-interest. They either try to control you or completely dismiss what you're saying. That's how they operate; there's no space for real emotional connection.

Understand this: for narcissists, it's all about power and feeling superior. They dictate the terms of every interaction, turning the relationship into a one-sided game. When you confront them, their response shows they simply don't care about you, your feelings, or needs. To them, there's no grey area — it's all about maintaining control and dominance.

In a nutshell, when you're dealing with a narcissist, you're stuck in a situation that lacks healthy communication. Your feelings take a back seat, and their needs are always front and centre. Recognising this pattern is crucial. It's about taking back your power and learning to build healthier, more balanced relationships.

Chapter 20

The Narcissistic Cycle

Twists and Turns of Idealisation, Devaluation, and Discard

An overview of the cycle of abuse in narcissistic relationships and it's psychological impact

Understanding the "Narcissistic Cycle" is essential for anyone who's experienced the emotional ups and downs that come with loving a narcissist and the confusing pattern that leaves victims reeling.

Personal Reflection:

One day, I was her world. Everything I did was perfect, and I was showered with love and affection. But as quickly as it came, it vanished. She began criticising literally everything — my work, my friends, the way I dressed, even the way I cut the grass. I just couldn't understand what I did wrong. And then, she was gone. I was left wondering what happened to the person who once idolised me.

Narcissists follow a distinct pattern in relationships, especially romantic ones. This cycle involves three phases: Idealisation, Devaluation, and Discard. Each phase serves to manipulate and control the victim before ultimately casting them aside.

The process begins with seduction, where narcissists overwhelm their target with charm, attention, and flattery, making them feel special and unique. They may seem like the perfect match, showering you with affection and praise, but this intense attention isn't genuine — it's part of a strategy to manipulate you emotionally. At first, it may feel like a dream come true, but it's important to remember that their flattery is a tactic to gain control.

Phase 1: Idealisation – The Honeymoon Phase

- **Let's begin with the Idealisation Phase:**

This phase is marked by what's commonly known as love bombing. Narcissists make you feel like you're the centre of their world. They shower you with affection, compliments, and attention, creating an illusion of harmony.

During idealisation, the narcissist presents themselves as the perfect partner, someone who understands you better than anyone else. The goal is to make you emotionally dependent on them, setting the stage for future manipulation.

While this attention can be intoxicating, it's essential to recognise it as a tactic, not genuine affection. The narcissist is building dependency, so you'll feel special, needed, and ultimately controlled.

Characteristics of Idealisation

- **Excessive Praise:**

During this phase, the narcissist showers you with compliments that can feel a bit overwhelming. You might hear things like, "You're the smartest person I've ever met," or "You're so beautiful; I can't believe someone like you is with me."

While these words might feel amazing at first, they're designed to create a sense of dependency on their approval. You start to crave that validation, making you feel like your worth is tied to how they see you.

- **Love Bombing:**

Love bombing describes the overwhelming and rapid affection a narcissist showers on you. They might want to spend every moment by your side, making you feel special. This kind of attention can be intoxicating, almost like a drug or dream come true. At first, it feels amazing to be the centre of someone's world, but it's important to remember that this intensity can be a way to draw you in and create a deep emotional bond quickly.

- **Creating a Fantasy:**

The narcissist creates a fantasy about the relationship, putting you on a pedestal and projecting their desires onto you. In their eyes, you become the perfect partner, embodying everything they've ever wanted. You're not just you; you're the person who fulfils all of their dreams and desires, which can feel unbelievably flattering at first. However, this idealised version of you doesn't necessarily align with who you really are, and that can put you under pressure to maintain that fantasy as the relationship progresses.

- **Isolation:**

During this phase, the narcissist begins to isolate you from your friends and family, in an attempt to make you feel like they're the only one who genuinely understands you. They subtly start to suggest that your loved ones and friends don't have your best interests at heart or that they just don't get you the way your partner does.

This tactic not only deepens your reliance on them but also helps them maintain control over the relationship.

While it seems like they care, this isolation can leave you feeling lonely and disconnected from the support system you once had.

The Impact of Idealisation

While this phase can feel exhilarating, it's important to understand that it's not built on genuine love. The narcissist is mainly focused on their own need for admiration and validation. Their affection often comes with conditions, depending on how well you meet their needs and expectations.

This phase can create a strong bond that makes it hard to notice any red flags. When you're being showered with love and attention, it's easy to overlook the subtle signs of manipulation. Even though you might feel like you've found "the one," it's crucial to remember that the love you are experiencing is more about fantasy than reality. Recognising this can help you stay grounded and aware of the true nature of the relationship.

Phase 2: Devaluation – The Shift in Dynamics

Once the narcissist has gained emotional control, the relationship shifts. The same qualities that once attracted them to you become points of criticism. They begin belittling you, gaslighting you, and using emotional manipulation. The contrast between the initial affection and the harsh criticisms is jarring, leaving you confused and questioning your worth.

The narcissist can criticize you, use passive-aggressive tactics, or emotionally withdraw to reinforce their control. This behaviour can chip away at your self-esteem and make you question your reality.

Manipulation and guilt are often employed to make you feel responsible for their happiness. The emotional rollercoaster can leave you feeling trapped and unsure of how to escape.

Characteristics of Devaluation

- **Criticism and Blame:**

The partner that you once adored begins to turn into your biggest critic. Instead of the compliments that filled your early days together, you start hearing hurtful things like not being as smart as they thought you were, or being accused of letting yourself go.

These criticisms are jarring, especially after the intense idealisation. It's hard to go from being perfect in their eyes to being blamed for everything. You feel lost and unsure of yourself. This sudden shift massively affects your self-esteem and makes you question the whole foundation of the relationship.

- **Manipulation and Control:**

As the relationship progresses, the narcissist tightens their grip on your actions and emotions. They resort to guilt and intimidation to get you to comply with their demands. You hear phrases like, "If you really loved me, you would do this."

This kind of manipulation is literally suffocating, because it places your worth in their hands, and it's calculated to make you feel responsible for their happiness. It's unsettling to realise that your feelings for them are being weaponised against you, this creates a sense of confusion and anxiety, making it harder to trust your own instincts, feelings, and judgement.

- **Gaslighting:**

The narcissist starts to twist reality in a way that makes you question your own perceptions. They deny conversations you've had and manipulate events to make you feel like you're losing your grip on reality. This leaves you doubting your memories and instincts.

It leads you to wondering if you're overreacting or losing your mind. This kind of psychological manipulation erodes your confidence and makes it challenging to trust yourself, leaving you feeling isolated and confused.

- **Withdrawal of Affection:**

During this phase, the narcissist pulls back their affection as a way to punish you. This sudden shift leaves you feeling bewildered and craving their approval, creating a desperate need to win back the love that they used to give you.

You find yourself in a constant cycle of trying to please them, feeling as though you're chasing something that feels like it's just out of reach all the time. The emotional withdrawal is painful and confusing, making you question what you did wrong and intensifying your desire to restore the connection you once shared.

The Impact of Devaluation

When the mask of perfection starts to slip it reveals the narcissist's true nature. You find that the person who once showered you with love and affection is now critical, demanding, and emotionally distant.

When the narcissist starts to twist things and pick apart your appearance, your choices, or your personality — criticising things you once felt good about or belittling your achievements with subtle put-downs or sarcasm — and this becomes the norm, it becomes even more damaging, making you question your own self-worth or sanity.

The gaslighting makes you doubt your perception of events and even your own reality.

The devaluation phase is also when the narcissist employs tactics like silent treatment or triangulation.

The silent treatment involves refusing to communicate with you, leaving you feeling isolated and helpless.

Triangulation occurs when the narcissist brings another person into the relationship — whether real or imaginary — to create jealousy, insecurity, and competition.

You can experience a mix of confusion and emotional pain because the person you saw as loving and kind is now acting in ways that feel cruel and dismissive.

The emotional rollercoaster is intentional; it keeps you in a state of uncertainty, making it hard to leave or even to see the truth. One moment, you feel like royalty, and the next, you're left feeling worthless.

The constant stream of criticism and manipulation chips away at your self-esteem and your ego, making it difficult to see your own worth.

You find yourself walking on eggshells, constantly worried that anything you say or do will trigger another onslaught.

The sense of dependency keeps you clinging to the memories of the idealisation phase, hoping to get back to the love you had in the beginning.

The stark contrast between these two experiences leaves you feeling lost and trapped in a toxic cycle, unsure of how to break free and reclaim the happiness that once seemed so attainable.

Phase 3: Discard – The Final Break

The discard phase is the most painful. After the narcissist has worn you down emotionally, they abruptly end the relationship, often without warning or explanation. This is a tactic designed to regain control and reaffirm their dominance.

The victim is left heartbroken and confused, searching for answers that will never come. The narcissist will rewrite the relationship's narrative, casting themselves as the victim, and use "flying monkeys" to reinforce their false version of events. This phase can leave you feeling empty, questioning everything, and struggling to heal.

Characteristics of Discard

- **Boredom and Devaluation:**

Firstly, they often get bored. The initial excitement fades, and suddenly you're not the shiny object they once adored. They start focusing on your flaws, magnifying everything that annoys them. In their eyes, you've gone from a treasure to someone they feel they can easily replace. They can also turn to flying monkeys to help paint a negative version that reinforces their own view of playing the victim.

- **Sudden Withdrawal:**

The narcissist suddenly cuts off communication and withdraws emotionally, leaving you in a state of shock.

You can find yourself questioning what went wrong or trying to understand why they've changed so drastically.

The unexpected silence is disorienting, making you feel as though you've been blindsided, and you struggle to find answers and make sense of the sudden shift in their behaviour.

This confusion is overwhelming, leaving you grappling with a mix of emotions and the uncertainty about the relationship's end.

- **Blame and Projection:**

During this phase, the narcissist now shifts the blame onto you for the relationship's failure. You hear hurtful comments like, "You were never good enough for me," or "You pushed me away."

These phrases can be massively damaging because they're not only denying any accountability on their part, but they also leave you questioning your own worth.

This blame game is emotionally draining, making you feel like you're the one at fault for everything that went wrong, which only adds to the pain of the breakup.

- **Emotional Shutdown:**

While you're left reeling from the discard, they switch off emotionally. You notice how cold and indifferent they become; it's like they've built a wall around themselves to avoid feeling any guilt or remorse. For them, it's easier to shut down than to confront their emotions. However, they might still use flying monkeys to reach out during emotional shutdown, either to echo their version or to discourage you from moving on completely, just in case they need you again in the future.

- **Rewriting the Story:**

Here's the kicker: narcissists will rewrite the story of how the relationship went down. They'll paint themselves as the victim and you as the villain, convincing themselves and other people that they did nothing wrong. They'll also use flying monkeys to help them craft and spread a false version that vilifies you, making it harder for you to recover. It's a way to maintain their inflated self-image while deflecting any blame.

- **No Closure:**

During the discard phase, you often feel like there's no sense of closure. You might be left with lingering questions and unresolved emotions, which can make it challenging to heal and move on with your life.

- **The Hoovering Game:**

Even after the relationship discards, they might try to suck you back in; this is known as hoovering. They'll reach out, act like they miss you, or throw out breadcrumbs of fake empathy and care. Once again, they'll use flying monkeys to further confuse or manipulate you, making it seem as though the narcissist had genuine concern or missed you. But beware, in fact, this is just another strategy to regain control. It's just another ploy to get their supply back before they toss you aside again.

- **Emotional Self-Protection:**

At the end of the day, their main goal is to protect their fragile ego. When they feel threatened or bored, they end the relationship to regain control. It's all about avoiding vulnerability and feeling weak. For them, discarding the relationship is a way to shield themselves from any emotional fallout, nothing more.

- **Seeking New Supply:**

Once they're done with you, they're usually already scouting for someone else to fill that void. Narcissists thrive on attention and admiration, so they quickly move on to a new source of validation. They need that fresh hit of admiration to feel good about themselves, and the cycle starts all over again.

By introducing someone new into the situation, whether as a partner or confidant, the narcissist ensures you feel even more diminished. This not only serves to validate their superiority but also leaves you questioning your worth and desirability.

- **Moving on Quickly:**

Narcissists often have a new source of supply, admiration, and validation lined up, leading them to move on quickly. This can leave you feeling discarded and devalued, as if you were just a stepping stone in their search for validation.

The Sudden Rejection and Discarding of Victims

The rejection can come in a lot of forms. Sometimes the narcissist will simply stop communicating or disappear without any warning. Other times, they'll devalue the victim in a way that the victim is left feeling unworthy. In extreme cases, the narcissist might even provoke a dramatic breakup, trying to make the victim feel as if they were the one at fault.

Regardless of the method, the discard is orchestrated as a seemingly final psychological blow. This is to ensure that the victim is left questioning what went wrong, struggling to make sense of the sudden rejection.

It can feel as if everything they shared with the narcissist — the love, the good moments, the connection — was a lie. In truth, the discard is a way for the narcissist to regain control and reinforce their power.

The validation is that the victim then becomes another trophy of the narcissist's discards once it's no longer useful.

The emotional toll can be overwhelming. Victims feel confused, betrayed, and deeply hurt, longing for closure that the narcissist refuses to give. This leaves the victim in a state of limbo, trying to make sense of what happened while also grappling with feelings of inadequacy.

Being discarded so suddenly can be traumatic. This experience can make it hard to trust other people in future relationships, leaving a lasting mark on your emotional health.

Breaking the Cycle

Now that I've broken down the narcissistic cycle into its three phases, let's talk about how to break free from it. If you've found yourself in this cycle, know that you're not alone, and healing is possible.

- **Recognise the Cycle:**

Awareness is paramount in breaking the cycle. Understand that what you're experiencing isn't normal and that you deserve healthier relationships.

- **Setting Boundaries:**

It's important to establish clear boundaries with the narcissist, whether that means limiting communication or severing ties entirely. Boundaries are vital for safeguarding your emotional well-being.

- **Seek Support:**

Don't hesitate to ask for help. Whether it's from friends, family, or a therapist, surrounding yourself with supportive people can provide perspective and strength.

- **Prioritise Self-Care:**

Make nurturing your mental and emotional health a priority. Engage in activities that make you happy, practice mindfulness, and focus on your well-being.

- **Process Your Emotions:**

Give yourself permission to grieve the loss of the idealised relationship. It's completely normal to feel a wide array of emotions, and taking the time to process these feelings is crucial for your healing journey.

- **Educate Yourself:**

Knowledge is power. Understanding the pattern of narcissism is empowering. Gaining knowledge about it helps you spot red flags in future relationships, helping you to make healthier choices for yourself.

- **Consider Professional Help:**

If you're struggling to navigate the aftermath of a narcissistic relationship, therapy can provide you with the tools and support you need to heal and move forward.

Moving Forward with Strength

Breaking free from the narcissistic cycle isn't easy, but it is absolutely achievable. By understanding the phases of idealisation, devaluation, and discard, you can reclaim your story and work toward building healthier relationships in the future. Remember, you deserve love, respect, and genuine connections.

As you progress, cherish the lessons you've learned and the strength you've developed. Don't allow the cycle to define who you are. You've got the ability to create a future filled with authentic relationships that uplift and support you.

Embrace your worth, prioritise your happiness, and keep in mind that healing is a journey; one that you're fully capable of navigating.

Acknowledge your experiences, break the cycle, and embrace the life you deserve. You 're not alone, and a brighter future is on the horizon. It's time to rise above and thrive.

Conclusion

In summary, narcissists discard relationships not because of any deep emotional reflection but to preserve their inflated sense of self, find new supply, and avoid facing their own flaws. The process is cold, calculated, and entirely self-serving.

The discard phase can hit you hard, leaving you reeling. You might feel a whirlwind of emotions, including confusion, anger, betrayal, and profound sadness. It often takes time to process what's occurred and to accept the reality of the relationship's end.

But remember, when a narcissist discards, it's not about you; it's all about them, and their need to maintain their inflated sense of self.

You deserve so much better than being a pawn in their strategy of life.

Chapter 21

The Unseen Traps

Co-dependency and Empathy in Narcissistic Relationships

Understanding co-dependency dynamics and strategies for building emotional independence

Co-dependency and excessive empathy are common traps for people entangled with narcissists, often leading to years of emotional and psychological harm.

Personal Reflection:

At the time I was convinced that loving someone meant always being there for them, no matter what. So, when she demanded more and more from me, I gave it. I didn't realise that my empathy and my desire to help were feeding her narcissism. The more I gave, the more she took, and it took me years to see that our relationship wasn't based on love — its aim was purely transactional and based on control.

In this chapter, I'll explore the relationship between narcissism and co-dependency, providing insights into how empathy can be both a strength and a vulnerability in these relationships.

In the intricate labyrinth of human relationships, narcissism can lead to complicated and painful interactions, particularly with people who are codependent or highly empathetic.

The combination of these traits can create a tangled web that traps both narcissists and their partners, perpetuating a cycle of dysfunction that's challenging to escape. To heal and build healthier connections, it's essential to understand these hidden traps of co-dependency and empathy in relationships shaped by narcissism.

Understanding Co-dependency and Empathy

To fully understand the dynamics at play, we need to define both.

Co-dependency describes a pattern where someone relies excessively on other people for emotional support, self-worth, and identity. Codependent people often prioritise the needs of other people above their own, leading to self-neglect.

This behaviour frequently stems from early life experiences, particularly in dysfunctional or addictive family environments, where the codependent person assumes a caretaker role to maintain peace.

In adulthood, codependents may be drawn to narcissists, seeking validation through self-sacrifice and the pursuit of making their partner happy.

Empathy, on the other hand, is the ability to understand and share the feelings of other people. While empathy fosters connection and compassion, it can also create challenges. Empathetic people regularly absorb the emotional struggles of the people around them, especially when involved with a narcissist who manipulates and controls.

The Dance Between Narcissism and Co-dependency

The relationship between narcissists and codependents can feel like a complex dance, where each partner plays a role that caters to the other person's needs. Narcissists possess an inflated sense of self-worth, and seek constant admiration, relying on other people for validation to bolster their fragile egos. Their need for control drives them to manipulate people, especially people with codependent tendencies.

Codependents can become drawn to the charisma and confidence narcissists display.

The initial phases of the relationship can feel exhilarating, as narcissists shower their partners with attention and praise. However, this phase is fleeting. As the narcissist grows comfortable, their behaviour tends to shift to devaluation and emotional neglect.

At this stage, codependents can find themselves trapped in a cycle of giving without receiving. They tend to internalise the narcissist's criticism, believing they can regain affection if they become even more accommodating. In doing so, they gradually lose their sense of identity, sacrificing their own needs and boundaries, in favour of the narcissist to keep the relationship intact.

The Impact of Empathy in the Relationship

Empathy can further complicate this already challenging situation. Empathetic people are often drawn to narcissists, because they see beyond their confident exterior, recognising the vulnerabilities and insecurities driving their behaviour.

This ability to empathise can initially create a strong bond, making the narcissist feel uniquely understood. However, empathy can quickly become a double-edged sword. Narcissists often exploit their partner's empathy, manipulating them by leveraging their vulnerabilities.

Empathetic partners may then try to rationalise the narcissist's harmful behaviour, believing they can "fix" or "heal" their partner through compassion. This belief sustains the cycle of emotional abuse, as the narcissist continues to exploit the empathetic partner's willingness to overlook their harmful actions.

Additionally, empathetic people often struggle with guilt or a sense of responsibility for the narcissist's well-being. They can feel compelled to stay in the relationship, fearing that leaving would cause the narcissist further emotional pain.

This internal conflict can lead to further self-neglect, with the empathetic partner consistently prioritising the narcissist's needs over their own well-being.

The Unseen Traps of the Relationship

The interplay between co-dependency and empathy in relationships with narcissists creates multiple unseen traps that can harm both partners, leading to long-lasting emotional damage.

Some common traps include:

- **Loss of Identity:**

The most profound consequence of co-dependency is the erosion of your sense of self. In their quest to please the narcissist, codependents can sacrifice personal interests, values, and friendships. Over time, they can struggle to identify who they are outside of the relationship, resulting in feelings of emptiness and confusion.

- **Emotional Exhaustion:**

Empathetic people can feel drained from continuously trying to navigate and manage the narcissist's emotional landscape. This emotional exhaustion can lead to burnout, leaving the empathetic partner feeling overwhelmed and anxious.

- **Cycle of Blame:**

In most narcissistic relationships, blame regularly shifts. Narcissists are skilled at deflecting responsibility for their actions, causing codependents to internalise the blame for any issues in the relationship. This cycle simply serves to perpetuate the feelings of inadequacy and guilt.

- **Fear of Abandonment:**

The fear of being abandoned can be particularly powerful in codependent relationships. Narcissists leverage this fear to maintain control, threatening to leave or withdraw affection. This fear keeps the codependent trapped, clinging to the hope of regaining the narcissist's love and approval.

- **Disruption of Boundaries:**

Codependents face a significant struggle to establish and sustain healthy boundaries. The narcissist's need for control can erode the codependent's ability to assert their needs, resulting in further emotional turmoil and resentment.

- **Cycle of Idealisation and Devaluation:**

Most narcissistic relationships experience this cycle. Codependents feel extreme emotional highs during the idealisation phase and then encounter devastating lows during the devaluation phase. This instability can leave the codependent in a state of perpetual anxiety and longing.

- **Isolation:**

Narcissists frequently seek to isolate their partners from friends and family, deepening the codependent's reliance on them. This isolation can make it even more challenging for the codependent to recognise the unhealthy patterns at play.

Awareness is the first step toward breaking free from the traps of co-dependency and empathy in narcissistic relationships. If you're feeling drained or overwhelmed by your partner's needs on a consistent basis and struggling to maintain personal interests or friendships outside of the relationship, they could be signs that you're in this type of relationship.

Recognising the Traps

Here are the things to look out for:

- **Feeling responsible for your partner's emotions:**

Believing that you need to manage your partner's feelings can lead to neglecting your own emotional needs and sacrificing your well-being.

- **Regularly putting their needs before your own:**

Consistently prioritising your partner's needs over your own can leave you feeling drained and disconnected from your personal desires and goals.

- **Experiencing extreme emotional highs and lows tied to your partner's behaviour:**

When your emotional state depends on your partner's mood, it becomes difficult to maintain a sense of stability or inner peace.

- **Rationalising or excusing their hurtful behaviour:**

Making excuses for your partner's harmful actions can prevent you from recognising the damage being done to you and the relationship.

- **Believing you can change or 'fix' them:**

The belief that you have the power to change or heal your partner can keep you trapped in a cycle of disappointment and emotional drain.

Recognising these patterns can be the catalyst for change. Once you identify the issues at play, you can start to reclaim your sense of self and work toward healthier relationships.

Strategies for Breaking Free

Breaking free from the cycle of co-dependency and empathy in narcissistic relationships takes intention and effort.

Things to consider:

- **Establish Boundaries:**

Learning to set healthy boundaries and to maintain them is crucial. Start small by asserting your needs and desires, gradually building up to more significant boundary-setting. Remember, boundaries are protective measures rather than barriers.

- **Prioritise Self-Care:**

Make self-care an essential part of your routine. Participate in things that feed your mind, body, and soul. Whether it's spending time with friends, pursuing hobbies, or practising mindfulness, prioritise your well-being.

- **Seek Professional Help:**

Therapy can be invaluable for unpacking the complexities of co-dependency and empathy in relationships. A mental health professional can provide support, tools, and strategies to help you navigate the healing process.

- **Cultivate a Support System:**

Surround yourself with people who uplift and support you. Maintaining a healthy reliable support system can offer perspective and encouragement as you face the challenges of breaking free from a narcissistic relationship.

- **Educate Yourself:**

Understanding the aspects of narcissism, co-dependency, and empathy can empower you to make informed decisions.

Read books, attend workshops, or join support groups to learn more about these issues and how to address them.

- **Practice Mindfulness:**

Mindfulness techniques, like meditation or journaling, can help you stay positive and reconnect with your feelings and desires. Taking the time to reflect on your experiences can foster self-awareness and clarity.

- **Focus on Personal Growth:**

Invest in your personal development by setting goals for yourself, exploring new interests, and nurturing your passions. Rebuilding your sense of self outside the relationship can help in reclaiming your identity.

Moving Toward Healthier Connections

As you begin to recognise and address the traps of co-dependency and empathy in narcissistic relationships, shifting your focus toward healthier connections becomes paramount. This shift requires patience and self-compassion, as healing from emotional trauma takes time.

Finding a balance between empathy and self-care is crucial. While empathy can be a strength, it's vital to recognise when it becomes detrimental. Strong relationships are grounded in mutual respect, support, and understanding, where both people feel appreciated and genuinely listened to.

Psychological and Emotional Toll on Victims

The narcissistic abuse cycle leaves a lasting emotional and psychological toll on its victims. After experiencing idealisation, devaluation, and discard, victims often feel shattered. Their self-esteem is eroded, their sense of self-worth undermined, and they might even question their own sanity.

The idealisation phase creates a false sense of security and love, leading the victim to believe that they've found someone who genuinely cares.

When this illusion is broken in the devaluation stage, the victim feels deeply betrayed, as they're confronted with a person who seems completely different from the one, they initially met.

Gaslighting and other manipulative behaviours can cause the victim to doubt their perceptions of reality. This often leads to cognitive dissonance, where the victim struggles to reconcile the idealised version of the narcissist with the abusive behaviour they're experiencing.

The victim can feel torn between wanting to believe in the good times and the growing realisation that the narcissist isn't who they once seemed to be.

After the discard, victims regularly suffer from a range of psychological symptoms, including anxiety, depression, and PTSD. They might find themselves unable to trust other people, feeling unworthy of love, or constantly questioning their judgement.

The cycle of abuse, combined with the sudden and unexpected rejection, can create a deep emotional scar that takes time to heal.

Recovery from Each Stage of the Cycle

Recovering from the narcissistic abuse cycle is a gradual and challenging process. The first step in recovery is recognising the cycle and accepting that the abuse wasn't your fault. This can be difficult, especially after enduring the emotional highs of idealisation, the lows of devaluation, and the crushing final discard.

- **Idealisation:**

Begin by acknowledging that the narcissist's attention and flattery were manipulative. The key to recovery here is to stop looking for validation from other people, and instead, focus on rebuilding your sense of self-worth. Therapy can help, as can self-care practices that promote healing.

- **Devaluation:**

In this stage, victims often struggle with self-blame and emotional confusion. Recovery involves understanding that the abuse was a tactic to control you, not a reflection of your shortcomings. Establishing boundaries and cutting ties with the narcissist is essential for healing.

- **Discard:**

After the discard, the emotional pain can be intense. To recover, it's vital to process the grief, surround yourself with supportive friends and family, and resist the temptation to go back.

Understanding that the narcissist will likely try to re-enter your life to repeat the cycle can help you prepare to stay strong and resist.

Conclusion

Navigating the complex world of the unseen traps can be insidious, leading to emotional pain and confusion. By recognising these aspects and implementing strategies to break free, you can reclaim your identity, foster healthier connections, and ultimately find a path to emotional well-being. Through understanding and self-reflection, you can step out of the labyrinth and toward a more fulfilling and balanced life.

Chapter 22

Inheriting the Labyrinth

Children of Narcissists and the Generational Cycle

Exploring the generational impact of narcissism and pathways to healing

Narcissism often trickles down through generations. Children of narcissists either become victims themselves or, in some cases, develop narcissistic traits as a means of survival. The emotional toll of being raised by a narcissistic parent leaves deep scars that can take a lifetime to heal. This generational cycle can feel like an inescapable maze, but understanding its impact is the first step toward healing and breaking free.

Personal Reflection:

Growing up, she didn't realise the signs of narcissism that permeated her family. Her parents' need for control and validation overshadowed her own emotional needs, leaving her feeling invisible. Love was conditional, given only when she excelled or fulfilled their expectations. As she navigated her childhood, she internalised the belief that her worth was tied to pleasing other people.

It wasn't until much later in life that these patterns influenced her relationships. She often mirrored her parents' behaviour: emotionally unavailable or overly controlling. These patterns stemmed from the unresolved wounds of her childhood.

Let's break down and clarify what I mean when I talk about narcissism in a parenting context.

Understanding Narcissism and Parenting

Narcissistic parents often engage in behaviours that seriously hinder their children's emotional development, making it more likely for the children to adopt narcissistic traits and potentially develop narcissistic personality disorder (NPD) themselves.

Narcissistic parents are often characterised by a few key traits: not only an inflated sense of self-importance, a craving for admiration, a lack of empathy, but also a tendency to manipulate their own children for their own needs.

They prioritise their desires over their child's emotional well-being, making the child feel more like an extension of the parent than a person with their own rights and feelings.

This self-centred behaviour manifests in several ways. A narcissistic parent might only praise their child when they're performing well or meeting expectations but quickly withdraw love and support when the child falters. They can be overly critical, leaving lasting scars on the child's self-esteem. They also use both physical and verbal abuse, guilt, or emotional blackmail to keep their children compliant and focused on the parent's needs.

This behaviour often leads to profound emotional neglect, leaving the child feeling abandoned and unworthy. Over time, the child learns that love is conditional; something to be earned through achievement and compliance.

The long-term effects of having narcissistic parents can be profound, potentially leading to a cycle of narcissism in future generations. Recognising this generational cycle is the first step toward breaking free from it.

This chapter will explore how narcissistic traits are passed down and how children of narcissists can begin to heal.

Growing Up with a Narcissistic Parent

When we talk about narcissism, we tend to focus on the narcissist themselves. However, their behaviour doesn't just impact their own lives — it leaves deep emotional scars on their children.

Growing up in a household with a narcissistic parent profoundly impacts a child's emotional and psychological development. It shapes their self-esteem, identity, and future relationships.

Children of narcissists can experience neglect, emotional invalidation, and manipulation, leading them to feel unworthy, confused, and anxious. From a young age, they become conditioned to seek their parent's approval constantly. Their worth is measured by how well they can meet the narcissistic parent's needs or make them look good in public. This reinforces the belief that love, and acceptance are conditional and have to be earned.

The emotional neglect in these families often leads to feelings of emotional emptiness or self-doubt. Children can feel like they're not good enough or that their needs are unimportant.

This manifests in adulthood as difficulty in forming healthy balanced relationships, as they either overcompensate to please other people or struggle with a lack of self-worth.

In severe cases, the emotional abuse from a narcissistic parent can lead to attachment disorders, resulting in insecure relationships, fear of abandonment, or excessive dependency on other people. The damage is long-lasting, often affecting the child's ability to trust and feel safe in future relationships.

How Children of Narcissists Develop Trauma, Identity Struggles and Narcissistic Traits

Trauma is one of the most significant outcomes of growing up with a narcissistic parent, as it can leave deep emotional scars that can affect a child's development into adulthood. Constant emotional manipulation, gaslighting, and neglect from the parent can distort the child's perception of reality. The child begins to question their own perceptions and develop a distorted sense of self.

Children of narcissists often struggle with identity formation. Since they're taught that their value is dependent on the narcissistic parent's approval, they grow up unsure of who they are outside of their parent's needs and desires. This lack of a solid identity can lead to low self-esteem, depression, anxiety, and a deep sense of not belonging.

Sometimes, children of narcissists develop narcissistic traits as a coping mechanism. They mirror their narcissistic parent's behaviour, adopting a superiority complex to shield themselves from feelings of inadequacy. Alternatively, they might become excessively people-pleasing, seeking validation in an attempt to avoid the emotional pain they experienced as children.

How Parenting Can Lead to This Outcome

- **Parental Narcissism:**

Narcissistic parents regularly neglect their children's emotional needs, focusing instead on their own desires and aspirations. This neglect can have a lasting effect on a child's development, self-esteem, and ability to form healthy relationships in adulthood. A child raised by a narcissistic parent can constantly crave validation from other people, trying to fill the emotional void left by their parent's self-centredness.

- **Lack of Empathy:**

Narcissistic parents generally struggle to understand, care about, or share their children's feelings. This emotional neglect deprives children of the ability to recognise and express emotions in a healthy way. As a result, they can struggle to empathise with other people, an important trait in the development of narcissism.

- **Conditional Love:**

Narcissistic parents show love and approval only when their children meet certain expectations or achievements. This conditional love teaches children that their worth is tied to their accomplishments rather than being inherent. Over time, this leads to fragile self-esteem reliant on external validation, a hallmark of narcissism.

- **Overvaluation or Undervaluation of Different Children:**

Narcissistic parents can fluctuate between either overvaluing, or undervaluing their children, pushing them to achieve unfulfilled dreams or making them feel inadequate. This inconsistency can leave children confused about their identity and self-worth, often leading them to adopt narcissistic traits as a way to cope with these conflicting messages.

- **Manipulation and Control:**

Narcissistic parents often use manipulation to maintain control over their children. This behaviour can distort a child's self-perception and make it difficult for them to form healthy relationships. Children can become self-centred or overly concerned with how other people view them.

- **Role Reversal:**

In some cases, children of narcissistic parents take on the caregiving roles, focusing on meeting their parent's emotional needs rather than their own. This role reversal can lead to co-dependency, where the child is made to feel responsible for the parent's happiness. This prevents them from establishing healthy boundaries and developing a true sense of self.

Case Study: Narcissistic Parent

Sam grew up with a narcissistic mother who was obsessed with projecting the image of the perfect family. She constantly sought praise from other people, often at the expense of Sam's emotional well-being. Any achievement of Sam's was presented as her own success, while any mistake was criticised. Sam's mother showed little genuine affection or interest in Sam's emotional needs, focusing instead on how Sam's actions reflected on her. As an adult, Sam struggled with feelings of inadequacy and worked through therapy to untangle the emotional damage caused by her mother's narcissism.

Even though not every child of narcissistic parents will become narcissistic, the combination of these unhealthy parenting behaviours creates an environment that significantly increases the risk. The child's temperament, the presence of supportive relationships, and personal experiences can all influence how they develop. However, the impact of their upbringing tends to play a critical role in shaping their personalities and relationships later in life.

The Effects on Children and Long-Term Impact

As these children transition into adulthood, the effects of their upbringing don't simply disappear.

They carry these patterns and struggles into their adult lives, affecting their personal relationships, professional environments, and overall mental health. The psychological scars of having a narcissistic parent can lead to various issues:

- **Anxiety and Depression:**

Alot of adults raised by narcissistic parents experience chronic anxiety and depression. The weight of unmet emotional needs and the inability to develop a healthy self-image manifest in mental health struggles that need significant attention and care.

- **Low Self-Esteem and Self-Worth:**

One of the most significant impacts of being raised by a narcissistic parent is the development of low self-esteem. Children of narcissists often feel unworthy or undeserving of love and validation. They internalise their parent's criticisms, leading them to believe their value is determined by their achievements or the attention they can attract. This mindset follows them into adulthood, making them overly critical of themselves and constantly seeking external validation.

- **Fear of Rejection and Abandonment:**

The emotional rollercoaster of living with a narcissistic parent creates this constant fear of rejection and abandonment. Children learn early on that their parent's love is conditional, and this fear manifests in various ways in their adult relationships; through clinginess, avoiding intimacy, or self-sabotaging behaviours to prevent being hurt. Trust issues plague their relationships, leading to cycles of conflict and dissatisfaction.

- **Emotional Dysregulation:**

Children of narcissistic parents often struggle with emotional dysregulation. They might experience intense emotions like anger, sadness, or anxiety but struggle to process or express them healthily. This leads to various coping mechanisms, such as substance abuse, self-harm, or engaging in toxic relationships. The inability to manage emotions can create a cascade of issues affecting their mental health and overall well-being.

- **Struggles in Relationships:**

Adult children of narcissists often find it difficult to maintain healthy relationships. They might attract narcissistic partners or struggle with commitment and intimacy due to childhood fears. Trust issues can lead to cycles of conflict and dissatisfaction.

- **Difficulty with Boundaries:**

Narcissistic parents blur the lines of appropriate boundaries, leading children to struggle with asserting their own limits. They may grow up feeling responsible for their parent's emotions or needs, which leads to co-dependency. This struggle makes it difficult for them to set boundaries, prioritise their own needs, or say no, creating a cycle of unhealthy relationships.

- **Imposter Syndrome:**

Many children of narcissists carry a sense of being a fraud, despite their achievements. This is known as "Imposter Syndrome," which leads to chronic feelings of inadequacy, anxiety, and fear of being "found out."

This mental paralysis makes it difficult to pursue opportunities, leading to significant professional and personal setbacks.

- **Repetition of Patterns:**

One of the more troubling outcomes for children of narcissists is the unconscious repetition of unhealthy patterns in their relationships.

They can become involved in toxic friendships or mirror their parent's behaviour in their own parenting styles. Without conscious intervention, these patterns can perpetuate the cycle of narcissism and emotional harm across generations.

- **Difficulty in Professional Life:**

In the workplace, adult children of narcissists often struggle with assertiveness and self-promotion. They can downplay their accomplishments due to Imposter Syndrome or become overly competitive, seeking validation through behaviours that mirror their childhood experiences. These patterns can hinder career advancement and satisfaction.

The Origins of the Wound

At the heart of every child of a narcissist is a profound and regularly unacknowledged wound. This wound, whether it originates in early childhood or from past trauma, drives their distorted sense of self as an adult. Understanding this wound is crucial not only to unravelling narcissistic behaviour but also to seeing past the facade that conceals the deep-seated and concealed pain.

Narcissists typically carry a history of emotional neglect, criticism, or even outright abuse. Contrary to the common misconception, narcissists are not born arrogant or self-important. Instead, their inflated sense of self-worth is a protective shield developed to defend against feelings of inadequacy.

This mask conceals the hurt they endured during their formative years when their emotional needs were either ignored or invalidated. In many cases, the narcissist's wound stems from a failure of emotional connection in early relationships, whether with a parent, caregiver, or someone they were close to.

Children who feel unloved or unworthy of attention can develop a false sense of superiority as a way of compensating for these unmet needs. They attempt to prove to themselves and other people that they matter, that they're important, and that they are special. But this compensatory behaviour doesn't heal the wound; it only deepens it.

The Role of Shame in a Narcissist's Damage

Shame plays a significant role in a narcissist's inner world, even though it often hides beneath the surface.

It's the silent driver behind much of their behaviour. Deep down, narcissists live with a constant nagging fear of being exposed as flawed or inadequate. This fear manifests as arrogance, entitlement, or even contempt for other people, but at its core, it's about evading the intense shame they feel. To them, vulnerability equals weakness, and they'll stop at nothing to keep their vulnerabilities hidden.

This shame often originates from those early childhood experiences of rejection or neglect, leaving the narcissist with the belief that something is fundamentally wrong with them. To avoid confronting this painful reality, they overcompensate by building up their egos.

They try to appear larger than life, but the more they do this, the more fragile their self-esteem becomes. Ultimately, they rely heavily on external validation, needing other people to reinforce their sense of worth.

Breaking the Cycle and Healing from Parental Narcissism

Breaking the cycle of narcissistic abuse and dysfunction that spans generations is difficult, but it is possible. Healing from the wounds inflicted by a narcissistic parent requires self-awareness, boundaries, and the courage to confront painful truths about the past.

The first step toward healing is acknowledging the narcissistic abuse. A lot of children of narcissists grow up believing the abuse they suffered was normal or feel guilty for even recognising it.

Accepting that their parent's behaviour was harmful is crucial in beginning the healing process.

Therapy plays a vital role in this journey. A trained therapist can help children of narcissists navigate the complex emotions tied to growing up with a narcissistic parent.

Therapy can also address issues like low self-esteem, anxiety, and identity struggles, while providing tools for setting healthy boundaries, understanding emotional needs, and rebuilding a sense of self-worth outside of the narcissist's influence.

Self-care becomes an essential practice in healing. Reclaiming time for yourself, pursuing passions, and nurturing healthy relationships all play significant roles in moving past the damage caused by a narcissistic parent. Children of narcissists have to learn to validate their feelings, trust their instincts, and prioritise their own emotional needs.

Finally, breaking the cycle means confronting the possibility of continuing narcissistic patterns in future generations. This relies on actively choosing to parent differently by modelling empathy, respect, and self-awareness.

Breaking the generational chain of narcissistic behaviour takes courage, but it can create lasting change for future generations.

Strategies for Healing

Healing from the effects of a narcissistic upbringing is challenging, but it can be alleviated with the right tools, starting with developing self-awareness.

Here are some key strategies to facilitate this journey:

1.   Therapy and Counselling:

Engaging with a mental health professional provides a safe space to process feelings and experiences. Cognitive Behavioural Therapy (CBT) and Schema Therapy, in particular, can help address the thought patterns and beliefs formed in childhood.

2.   Developing Self-Compassion:

Learning to be kind to yourself is essential. Practise self-compassion by acknowledging your feelings without judgment, treating yourself with the same compassion and kindness you'd give to a friend. This can help combat feelings of unworthiness and foster a healthier self-image.

3.   Setting Boundaries:

Identifying your boundaries and asserting them is critical. This might involve distancing yourself from toxic family members or learning to say no to protect your emotional well-being and autonomy.

4.   Building a Support System:

Surround yourself with people who understand your struggles and provide healthy emotional support. This might include friends, support groups, or online communities, where you can connect with other people who've faced similar challenges.

5.   Journaling and Reflection:

Journaling is a powerful tool for self-exploration. Writing about your feelings, experiences, and insights helps you process emotions, recognise patterns, and celebrate progress.

6.   Practising Mindfulness and Emotional Regulation:

Engaging in mindfulness practices like meditation or yoga helps you process your thoughts and feelings without becoming overwhelmed. This can promote emotional regulation, helping you to respond to challenges in healthier ways.

7.   Educating Yourself:

Knowledge is power. Reading books, articles, or listening to podcasts about narcissism and healing from emotional trauma can validate your experiences and help you recognise patterns.

8.   Cultivating Independence:

Focus on developing your own identity outside of your family. Explore your interests, set personal goals, and take part in activities that you enjoy. Building a sense of self, independent of your upbringing can be empowering.

9.   Engaging in Healthy Relationships:

Surround yourself with people who value you for who you are and encourage your growth. Healthy relationships provide a stark contrast to the toxicity you might have experienced growing up.

10.   Celebrating Progress:

Healing is a journey, not a destination. Every step that you take toward self-discovery and healing is worth recognising and cherishing.

The Cycle of Narcissistic Generations: Exploring How Narcissistic Traits Are Passed Down

Narcissism can be passed down through generations — not only through genetics but also via learned behaviour.

Narcissistic parents serve as primary models for how relationships, emotions, and self-worth are understood, absorbed, and expressed.

Children of narcissists are often taught to prioritise the narcissist's needs above their own, internalising self-worth based on external validation.

They can also learn to suppress their own emotions, as their feelings are often invalidated in favour of the narcissist's desires.

Narcissistic traits can be perpetuated when the boundaries between parents and children are blurred, making it difficult for children to develop a separate identity. In this way, narcissism can become a generational cycle; one that continues until it's actively addressed.

Case Studies of Intergenerational Narcissistic Families

Case studies reveal how narcissism can perpetuate over time and its impact across generations. These examples demonstrate the emotional dysfunction that can repeat across family lines.

- **The Johnson Family:**

The father, a narcissist, demanded constant attention and belittled his wife and children for failing to meet his high expectations. His eldest daughter grew up feeling inadequate and developed anxiety.

She later married a man with narcissistic traits, continuing the cycle of emotional neglect and abuse. Her adult children now struggle with self-worth issues and tend to form relationships with narcissists.

- **The Williams Family:**

In this case, the grandmother was the narcissist, and the mother, though emotionally neglected, was more resilient. However, she unconsciously carried the same patterns into her parenting. As a result, her son grew up with emotional insecurity and developed co-dependency tendencies. Eventually, he recognised these patterns and worked to break the cycle through therapy, learning to build healthy relationships and set boundaries with his narcissistic mother.

These case studies highlight the importance of recognising narcissistic patterns and the need for self-reflection and therapy in breaking the cycle. While the effects of a narcissistic upbringing are profound, they don't have to dictate the future. With intentional healing, it's possible to break the generational cycle of narcissism.

Moving Forward

Healing from a narcissistic upbringing isn't straightforward. However, each day offers an opportunity to reclaim your story, reshape how you view yourself, and foster healthier relationships.

You deserve a life free from the emotional burdens of your childhood.

Conclusion

Growing up with a narcissistic parent creates long-lasting struggles with emotional regulation, self-worth, and relationships. But the cycle can be broken with awareness, therapy, and a commitment to healthier patterns.

Remember, healing isn't only possible; it's also within reach.

Chapter 23

The Psychological Pitfalls

Narcissism's Impact on Mental Health

Mental health effects for both narcissists and their victims

Narcissism harms not only the people around the narcissist, but also profoundly affects the narcissist's own mental health. Their struggle to form real connections, their constant need for admiration, validation, and their fragile self-esteem often lead to inner turmoil and distress. For the people trapped in their web, the emotional toll can be severe, leading to anxiety, depression, and even Complex PTSD.

In this chapter, I'll explore the impact of narcissism on both the narcissist, and the people they harm. I'll delve into the psychological fallout that accompanies these toxic behaviours, shedding light on both sides of the experience. I'll also examine the therapeutic approaches that can make a real difference, offering insights into building healthier relationships; and improving emotional well-being.

Personal Reflection:

Although she admitted feeling empty and unfulfilled during counselling, she tried to manipulate the therapist into agreeing with her point of view. When she failed, she became frustrated and angry, refusing to return and abandoned therapy after just one session.

Narcissism doesn't just affect the person displaying the traits; it ripples through everyone around them. Let's dive in and uncover how narcissism impacts both those with narcissistic tendencies and the people caught in their orbit. Understanding these patterns is the first step towards healing and creating more meaningful connections.

The Psychological Impact of Narcissism

Narcissism is often linked to self-centeredness, a lack of empathy, and an inflated sense of superiority. However, the effects go beyond just the narcissist. Both they, and their victims suffer from the dysfunction that narcissistic behaviour creates.

What Does This Mean for Relationships

Understanding the neuroscientific underpinnings of narcissism doesn't excuse the behaviour, but it does help explain it. For people who've been in relationships with narcissists, these insights can provide a sense of closure and understanding. The narcissist didn't choose to be incapable of empathy, or prone to outbursts; it's the way their brain is wired, making these behaviours more likely.

That said, recognising a biological basis doesn't mean tolerating their abusive behaviour. Boundaries are still essential regardless of when dealing with narcissists, just as is the understanding that change if it happens, is a long and difficult process. Therapy can be effective, but only if the narcissist is genuinely committed to confronting and altering their patterns of thought and behaviour.

For people recovering from narcissistic relationships, understanding the neuroscience behind these behaviours can be a powerful first step toward healing.

It provides a framework to understand that the emotional pain caused by narcissists isn't solely about their choices; it's also rooted in how their brain functions.

This knowledge can help people release the burden of believing they could have changed the narcissist and instead refocus their energy on their own recovery and growth.

Why This Matters to Victims of Narcissism

The neurological underpinnings of narcissism offer more than just a clinical perspective; they provide a pathway to compassion for people who've been affected by narcissists. While this doesn't excuse the hurtful actions of a narcissist, it helps make sense of why they behave the way they do. For victims, recognising that narcissism is tied to brain structure and function can ease feelings of confusion, frustration, or self-blame. It helps you realise that their inability to connect with your emotions wasn't a failing on your part; it was a byproduct of how their brain processes emotions and self-perception.

However, understanding the neuroscience behind narcissism, has to be balanced with self-protection. Just because narcissism has a neurological basis it doesn't mean you're obligated to endure abuse or emotional harm. Setting boundaries, seeking support, and stepping away from toxic relationships are vital for your own mental well-being.

By understanding these behaviours, you're better equipped to make informed decisions about navigating relationships with narcissists, whether that means stepping away, offering support for genuine efforts toward change, or protecting your peace in other ways.

Chronic Envy and Resentment

Narcissists tend to grapple with intense feelings of envy; not just towards other people, but anyone they perceive as a threat to their self-image. This envy can reveal itself in various ways, such as belittling your achievements, downplaying your successes, or even attempting to sabotage you out of jealousy.

Sometimes, their envy is concealed beneath a facade of false admiration or subtle condescension, making it difficult to recognise at first.

Over time though, you may notice a pattern — they rarely celebrate your successes and may even go out of their way to undermine them.

If someone consistently diminishes your accomplishments, it could be a reflection of their deep-seated insecurity and narcissistic tendencies.

For Narcissists

- ### Self-Esteem Issues:

Narcissists often appear extremely confident, but this facade masks deep-seated insecurities. Their sense of self-worth is heavily dependent on external validation, which traps them in a constant cycle of internal conflict.

They crave compliments, admiration, and recognition to feel valued. However, this need creates a fragile sense of identity that can easily crumble when they don't receive the attention they seek. When the admiration doesn't come, a narcissist can feel as though the rug has been pulled out from under them.

Personal Reflection:

"Each time she received a compliment, her mood would brighten, but as soon as the praise faded, so did her sense of self-worth. She needed constant reminders of her own greatness, and when those reminders weren't there, she fell into a pit of self-doubt, victimhood, and anger."

This reliance on external sources of validation regularly leads to anxiety and depression.

Imagine constantly feeling like you're standing on unstable ground, only as secure as the last compliment you received. When they feel unsupported, narcissists can become irritable, resentful, and even hostile.

- **Emotional Regulation:**

Most narcissists struggle with managing their emotions effectively. They tend to find it difficult to accept criticism or handle situations where they're not in control. This challenge leads to frequent mood swings, irritability, and emotional outbursts. These behaviours can strain their relationships, making it hard for people to connect with them on a deeper level.

Their inability to self-regulate strains these relationships even more, regularly alienating those around them. Despite their desire for social acceptance, these emotional eruptions push people away, ultimately isolating them even more.

- **Interpersonal Struggles and Isolation:**

Social isolation is common among narcissists, although it's often self-inflicted. Their manipulative and self-centred behaviour tends to push people away, even those initially drawn to their charisma or confidence, leaving them feeling lonely and disconnected.

Although they may believe they enjoy being the centre of attention, narcissists often end up alone, on the pedestal they built for themselves, refusing to admit their role in the isolation that they experience.

For Those Affected by Narcissism

- **Emotional Stress:**

Living with someone who exhibits narcissistic traits can be emotionally exhausting and deeply draining.

Their constant manipulation and criticism create an environment that fosters anxiety, depression, and burnout, leaving other people always preparing for the next wave of negativity. The ongoing manipulation, gaslighting, and criticism create an emotionally charged atmosphere where people feel as though they're constantly walking on eggshells.

For victims, this relentless emotional strain can manifest in physical symptoms of stress, such as insomnia, fatigue, and headaches. It's common for people in relationships with narcissists to develop a hypervigilant state, constantly anticipating the next criticism or manipulation. This perpetual state of alertness is draining and can gradually erode mental well-being.

- **Identity Struggles and Self-Worth Erosion:**

Victims of narcissists often suffer significant blows to their self-esteem. Narcissists tend to devalue other people in order to feel superior, which leads to persistent belittling and criticism. The constant devaluation by the narcissist takes a heavy toll on self-worth, leading to self-doubt, and feelings of inadequacy. You could start to question your value, wondering if you'll ever be enough in their eyes; or in your own.

Every time a narcissist dismisses your opinions or invalidates your feelings, part of you can start to feel insignificant. Over time, you can find yourself unsure whether you're genuinely wrong all the time, or if they simply want you to feel that way.

This behaviour creates a state of perpetual inadequacy, eroding self-confidence in ways that can take years to rebuild, even after the relationship ends.

- **Response to Criticism:**

Everyone can feel hurt or defensive when criticised, but people with NPD often react with intense anger, rage, or contempt. Their fragile self-esteem is so dependent on external admiration that even the slightest criticism can trigger disproportionate reactions.

In contrast, someone with normal narcissistic traits might feel hurt but can still maintain emotional control and reflect on the situation.

- **Impact on Daily Life:**

The most significant difference between normal narcissism and NPD is the extent to which the behaviours impact daily life. While normal narcissism can lead to occasional challenges in relationships or self-perception, it typically doesn't interfere with a person's ability to maintain a functioning life. In contrast, for someone with NPD, the symptoms cause consistent problems, such as difficulty maintaining friendships, challenges at work, and strained personal relationships. This level of dysfunction is a key indicator that narcissistic traits have become pathological.

- **Relational Challenges and Emotional Drain:**

Dealing with a narcissist isn't just exhausting; it requires immense emotional labour. Balancing boundaries while trying to maintain some semblance of a relationship can leave you feeling emotionally drained and depleted, making it a steep uphill battle.

Victims of narcissistic abuse often try to salvage the relationship by constantly adapting to the narcissist's needs. This usually leads to burnout and a deep sense of emotional destruction. Over time, the toll of this makes it difficult to summon the energy or focus needed for other relationships.

The Brain's Reward System: Validation and Attention-Seeking

Narcissism thrives on a constant need for admiration, and this goes beyond a superficial desire; it's rooted in how the brain responds to validation. Dopamine, the brain's "feel-good" chemical, plays a major role.

When anyone receives positive feedback, dopamine fires off in the brain's reward areas, providing a rush of pleasure. But in a narcissist's brain, this reaction is amplified. Their brains light up more intensely with praise, making them crave it almost like an addiction.

This heightened response wires narcissists to chase attention and admiration, as if they need it to feel complete. It's not just a personality quirk; it's a deep-seated drive for approval. At the same time, this sensitivity cuts both ways. While they react strongly to praise, criticism hits just as hard.

One moment, they feel invincible from admiration, and the next, a small criticism can trigger defensiveness or even rage. This constant need for positive reinforcement often makes their relationships tense, and more often than not, unstable.

Additionally, narcissists tend to view the world in a way that protects their ego.

They're quick to claim credit for anything positive in their lives, but when things go wrong, they place the blame elsewhere. This mindset makes it difficult for them to admit their faults or recognise any room for growth. Instead, they double down on their self-image, reinforcing their sense of superiority. So even when they do reflect on themselves, it doesn't lead to humility or change; it simply fuels their need to preserve their inflated self-image.

Narcissism can lead to chronic stress, anxiety, and emotional instability in narcissists. Beneath their grandiose exterior, they often struggle with deep feelings of inadequacy. This internal conflict can trigger a range of mental health issues, including depression and intense rage, especially when their self-image is threatened.

For victims of narcissistic behaviour, the psychological toll is often even more severe. Narcissistic abuse can cause long-lasting damage, leading to anxiety, depression, Complex PTSD (C-PTSD), and other psychological issues. The constant cycle of idealisation, devaluation, and discard erodes self-worth, leaving the victim emotionally shattered.

Understanding these mental health effects is crucial in recognising the damage caused by narcissism and taking the necessary steps toward healing.

Therapeutic Approaches for Narcissists

- ### Cognitive Behavioural Therapy (CBT):

CBT helps narcissists confront their distorted beliefs by focusing on improving emotional regulation and reshaping their self-perception.

It aims to replace harmful thought patterns with healthier, more constructive ones.

- **Schema Therapy:**

Schema Therapy delves into the core beliefs formed in childhood. By addressing these ingrained issues, narcissists can heal and adopt healthier behaviours, leading to significant improvements in their relationships and overall life.

- **Psychodynamic Therapy:**

This approach uncovers unconscious conflicts and explores how early life experiences shape current behaviour. By gaining insight into these roots, narcissists can begin to make meaningful changes in their lives.

For Those Affected by Narcissism

- **Supportive Counselling:**

For victims of narcissistic abuse, supportive counselling provides a safe space for emotional validation, coping techniques, and resilience-building, helping them regain strength and confidence.

- **CBT Techniques:**

CBT can also benefit victims dealing with the aftermath of narcissistic abuse. It equips them with tools to manage stress, navigate emotional turmoil, and regain control over their mental well-being.

- **Self-Care and Resilience:**

Practising self-care, setting clear boundaries, and building supportive networks are essential for maintaining mental health and overall well-being when dealing with a narcissist.

Couples and Family Therapy

- **Couples Therapy:**

Couples therapy helps partners address relationship issues tied to narcissism, encouraging better communication while maintaining individual identities.

- **Family Therapy:**

Family therapy supports families in managing narcissistic behaviours and fostering healthier dynamics, creating a space where everyone can thrive rather than being caught in manipulation and conflict.

Practical Strategies for Managing Narcissism

- **Boundaries:**

Setting and enforcing boundaries is crucial for protecting your emotional health. Clearly define where you end, and the other person begins.

- **Support Networks:**

A strong personal and professional support network helps you navigate the complex patterns of narcissism.

- **Healthy Communication:**

Use clear, assertive language to express your needs and feelings. While it's wise to avoid conflict triggers, when possible, don't hesitate to speak your truth and establish how you want to be treated.

Conclusion

In this chapter, we've examined the complexities of narcissism, focusing on its profound impact on both the narcissist and the people they affect.

Narcissism isn't just about self-absorption; it's an ingrained condition rooted in insecurities, emotional regulation issues, and distorted self-perception. This condition creates a cycle of internal conflict for the narcissist and significant emotional toll for people involved with them.

Therapeutic approaches such as Cognitive Behavioural Therapy (CBT), Schema Therapy, and family therapy have been highlighted as powerful tools for addressing the narcissist's underlying issues and the damage inflicted on their victims.

We've also explored the deeper psychological aspects of narcissism, particularly its connection to self-esteem and emotional regulation. Understanding that narcissism is often a result of emotional vulnerabilities rather than just a desire for admiration can help promote greater empathy and clarity, allowing us to navigate it with more compassion.

By gaining insight into these patterns and the brain's role in shaping narcissistic behaviour, we can begin to heal and rebuild. Whether through therapy or by applying practical tools in everyday life, it's possible to reclaim a sense of self-worth and create healthier, more fulfilling relationships. Narcissistic behaviour doesn't define the people affected by it; healing and growth are always possible with the right support and strategies.

Chapter 24

Shifting Walls of the Labyrinth

Echoes of the Digital Abyss: Narcissism in the Digital Age

The influence of social media on narcissistic behaviour and self-protection

Social media has become a breeding ground for narcissism, offering endless opportunities for validation, attention-seeking, and curated personas. The digital age has amplified narcissistic behaviours, allowing people to project a false image to the world while hiding behind the screen. The instant gratification of likes, shares, and comments feeds ego, reinforcing behaviours that place emphasis on external recognition rather than internal satisfaction. This culture of performance breeds an environment where people feel compelled to chase perfection, creating a version of themselves that laughs in the face of authenticity.

Behind this facade, however, is a deeper, insidious emptiness — one masked by the volume of digital engagement.

The lines between reality and online personas become blurred, leading some people to measure their own worth by the engagement they get in a virtual world, regardless of whether it's positive or negative, and not by who they really are.

In this chapter, I'll explore how narcissism manifests in various environments, focusing on the rise of cyber-narcissism and how social media fuels narcissistic behaviour.

I'll also offer strategies for protecting yourself online. By understanding how narcissists adapt to different contexts, you'll be better equipped to identify and navigate these shifting dynamics.

Take social media influencers as an example. These people build idealised versions of their lives for the world to see. In an age where likes, shares, and followers become a measure of success, it's no wonder that so many people start to base their self-worth on the approval they get online. As they compare themselves to the curated images they see, the pressure to fit into a narcissistic mould grows.

This endless chase for validation takes a toll, as people begin to care more about external recognition than about real connections. Despite the promise of social media as a tool for connection, a lot of them are still left feeling alone and unfulfilled.

I've seen people completely consumed by their online personas. They pour hours into crafting their posts, checking obsessively to see how many likes and comments they've received.

If their content doesn't perform well, it's crushing. It becomes an endless race for approval. But when the attention fades, so does their sense of worth, leaving them more alone and emptier than before.

The need for constant validation can lead to serious mental health issues like anxiety, depression and much more. Instead of building real connections, they get caught in a cycle of comparison, constantly chasing after ideals they can never reach.

Social media dictates that these people measure their worth based on this false image, valuing outside approval over their own core values.

This obsession distorts their identity, making them more concerned with how they appear than with who they really are.

Personal Reflection:

Media and Celebrity Culture:

Some people treat social media like their personal playground, where rules, reality, and even basic decency don't apply, as long as they're the centre of attention. Their lives become a performance — a carefully manufactured fiction designed to impress strangers while trampling over boundaries, ignoring consequences, and rewriting their own rules.

Laws and accountability are inconveniences for these people, who are too busy chasing likes, sharing half-truths, and pretending their chaos is glamorous. But the cracks in the facade are glaring. Behind the filters and grandiosity lies a storm of instability — a mind consumed by narcissism, driven by impulsivity, and trapped in delusions.

The erratic highs and crushing lows, hallmarks of bipolar disorder, bleed into their daily lives, while borderline personality tendencies leave a trail of fractured relationships and burned bridges. Paranoia and erratic thought patterns expose deeper struggles, like schizophrenia, while unchecked anxiety and depression swirl beneath the surface.

Add substance abuse to the mix, and you're left with a volatile cocktail of dysfunction that no amount of likes or filters can hide. For some people, social media isn't just an escape; it's an enabler. The constant cycle of validation amplifies narcissistic tendencies, reinforcing a warped self-image and fuelling a relentless need for attention.

But no matter how carefully they curate their lives online, the hollowness behind the scenes is impossible to ignore. Fame, self-promotion, and superficiality become poor substitutes for genuine happiness and meaningful connections. In their pursuit of validation, they're not just losing sight of reality — they're losing themselves entirely.

I've met narcissists in all walks of life. Whilst each time, their tactics were different, it's all about undermining confidence. But no matter the setting, the outcome was always the same: they take what they want, and you're left feeling drained. You just have to be thankful that in the long run, you were sharp enough to dodge the bullet.

How Society Shapes and Is Shaped by Narcissism

To understand narcissism better, it's helpful to zoom out and consider the broader picture of how culture and society influence it. Narcissism isn't just a personality trait — it's shaped by the norms we live by.

Our social environment, the media, and our expectations of success all push people towards self-centred behaviours. At the same time, narcissism impacts these very same systems, reinforcing the values of individualism and self-promotion. It becomes a cycle where society reflects and amplifies narcissistic traits, making them harder to escape.

Cultural Values and Their Impact

The culture we live in deeply shapes how narcissism manifests in people. In cultures where individual achievement and self-promotion are prioritised, narcissistic behaviours are sometimes seen as normal, or even admirable. On the other hand, in places that emphasise collective effort and cooperation, the same behaviours are less accepted. Context matters a lot; what one culture might view as self-assurance, another might view as selfishness. It's all about how our values shape the way we see narcissism in other people.

Looking at these people who are so consumed by this need for recognition and approval makes me wonder — how do we stay true to ourselves in a world that celebrates the shallow and the superficial?

When seeking acceptance only leaves people feeling lost and disconnected, how can we break free from the pressure to conform?

The Role of Socialisation and Media

How we're raised and what we're exposed to in the media also have a big impact on narcissism. From a young age, we're shaped by what we see in the world around us.

When success, fame, and self-promotion are constantly celebrated, it's easy for narcissistic behaviours to seep into how people interact with the real world. If society continually glorifies these traits, it's not surprising that more people will start to adopt them.

Socialisation is a fundamental process through which we learn and internalise norms, values, and behaviours. In today's digital age, social media has become a primary platform for this socialisation, influencing how we perceive ourselves and other people.

Social media platforms create environments where these idealised lives of influencers and peers are on constant display, blurring the lines between reality and fantasy.

As we scroll through our feeds, we're bombarded with images and perspectives that promote a particular version of success, beauty, and happiness.

This barrage can create a skewed sense of what's normal or desirable, leading a lot of people to measure their worth against these unrealistic standards.

Social media cultivates a culture of comparison, where people evaluate their lives based on the filtered experiences of other people.

This cycle creates feelings of inadequacy and self-doubt, as users chase after approval that always seems perpetually out of reach.

Moreover, social media can act as an echo chamber, reinforcing these narcissistic behaviours and values. Users who engage with content that emphasises self-promotion and superficiality are more likely to adopt similar behaviours, craving validation through their own likes, shares, and comments.

This pattern not only shifts the focus from genuine connection to self-interest but also discourages empathy and vulnerability in relationships.

The need to curate an online persona often takes precedence over authentic interactions, still leaving people feeling isolated despite their digital connections.

The Echo Chamber Effect

Social media doesn't just reflect narcissistic values; it amplifies them. The platforms themselves become echo chambers where specific traits — often self-serving — are rewarded with visibility and engagement. This positive reinforcement loop creates an environment where even well-meaning users can adopt narcissistic traits, not from innate tendencies but as a response to the metrics of success.

The more users are rewarded for narcissistic behaviour, the more likely they are to prioritise image over substance, leaving genuine connections by the wayside.

The Weight of Cultural Trends on Narcissism's Rise

Societal trends, especially in the age of digital self-promotion, have fuelled the glorification of certain traits commonly associated with narcissism. This widespread hustle culture which idolises relentless self-promotion and career ambition, has subtly shifted focus away from community values toward individual achievement. As a result, the cultural portrayal can sideline empathy and collaboration. This shift can leave people feeling they have to adopt more self-centred behaviours just to stay relevant, thus creating a fertile ground for narcissistic tendencies to flourish.

Strategies for Dealing with Social, Cultural, and Professional Relationships

- **Notice the Patterns:**

Pay close attention to how narcissists behave in different situations. Are they constantly seeking validation or trying to elevate themselves at the expense of other people? Do their behaviours shift based on the audience, always aimed at impressing and securing approval?

- **Check in with Your Feelings:**

Reflect on how interactions with narcissists make you feel.

Are you drained, belittled, or made to feel inferior after spending time with them?

Do you feel like you're constantly walking on eggshells, unsure of where you stand?

- **Set Boundaries:**

Setting clear, firm boundaries is essential for protecting your mental and emotional well-being. Don't be afraid to communicate your limits and be consistent in enforcing them. Narcissists thrive when they can push boundaries without consequences, so maintaining your space is critical.

- **Be Assertive:**

Narcissists may try to undermine your contributions or dismiss your feelings. It's essential to assert yourself in these situations, expressing how their behaviour affects you. Use "I" statements to communicate your thoughts and feelings without sounding accusatory.

- **Limit Engagement:**

Sometimes, the best strategy is to limit your exposure to narcissistic people. If their behaviour consistently leaves you feeling drained, dismissed, or diminished, stepping back may be the healthiest choice for your well-being.

Reflecting on a Need for Balance

Recognising the patterns of narcissistic behaviour in society is crucial for understanding how they shape our interactions and relationships. If we continue to prioritise self-promotion and external validation over qualities like empathy and connection, we risk losing touch with what truly matters.

As individuals, we need to strike a balance — finding success while still honouring the values of humility, compassion, and community.

If we can create a culture that values these qualities, we can begin to heal the divisions that narcissism creates and build a world where real relationships thrive.

Conclusion

In a world that seems to prioritise personal brand over personal growth, it's easy to chalk up narcissism as just a sign of the times. But there's more at play here. If we look closer, it's clear these behaviours are wrapped up in what our culture often praises: success, self-promotion, and the endless quest for validation.

Shifting away from this means we might need to put more weight on things like empathy, respect, and genuine connection.

Finding this balance doesn't mean letting go of our ambitions or individuality; it's about blending them with values that strengthen our communities as much as they do ourselves.

The more we recognise these patterns in our daily interactions, the easier it becomes to find ways to connect meaningfully, without getting caught up in the surface-level. And in doing so, we can start to create spaces where authentic relationships thrive, moving past the walls that narcissism puts up and finding the common ground that brings us together.

Chapter 25

Finding the Way Out

Treatment and Management of NPD
Therapeutic Interventions

Overview of therapeutic interventions for narcissism

Narcissistic Personality Disorder (NPD) is a deeply ingrained condition that can be extremely difficult to treat, especially given the nature of the disorder. The people affected by narcissism — whether they are the narcissist themselves, or the people close to them — often experience profound emotional struggles, and their relationships can be strained or even toxic. While overcoming NPD is undoubtedly challenging, there are therapeutic interventions that can help these people with NPD learn to understand themselves better, build healthier relationships, and manage their emotions in more constructive ways.

For people who've suffered from the impact of narcissism, understanding available treatment options and self-help strategies is essential for healing. Treatment doesn't guarantee a "cure," but it offers ways to manage and mitigate the negative consequences of NPD in daily life, both for the narcissist and those around them.

In this chapter, I'll explore not only how to manage co-occurring conditions but also how various therapeutic approaches — such as psychodynamic therapy, cognitive behavioural therapy (CBT), and schema therapy — can be used to address the symptoms of NPD. Additionally,

I'll offer self-help strategies aimed at those recovering from narcissistic abuse, providing practical advice for people who are still healing from these toxic relationships. I'll also look at newer and emerging treatments that specifically target the conditions that often accompany NPD, such as depression and anxiety.

The goal is to equip people with NPD and their victims with tools that can help them improve their daily functioning, manage emotional dysregulation, and build healthier relationships.

Personal Reflection:

During the relationship, she began therapy, hoping to find clarity and reclaim her sense of self. However, after just one session, she was unwilling to acknowledge her role in the chaos and decided to abandon the therapy, choosing instead to listen to the advice of her 19-year-old son, with his unqualified insights, claiming he would help her navigate her struggles. In her view, his perspective was clearly far more valid than any qualified therapist's insights.

After our relationship ended, I couldn't shake the feeling that I'd lost myself along the way. Training in psychology became a pivotal turning point for me — learning about boundaries, understanding what had happened, and beginning the slow process of rebuilding my self-esteem. Through this journey, I gradually uncovered the layers of manipulation I'd endured and rediscovered the inner strength to reclaim my identity.

Dealing with NPD isn't straightforward. People with NPD often exhibit grandiosity, a lack of empathy, and a range of difficulties in their relationships. They can react defensively, struggle with acknowledging flaws, or become defensive when their behaviour is questioned. This makes therapeutic work extremely challenging.

Challenges of Addressing Narcissism

Understanding narcissism in theory is one thing; addressing it in practice, particularly within a therapeutic setting, presents unique challenges.

To truly help someone with narcissistic traits, therapists have to navigate tricky terrain, carefully balancing their self-perception, defences, and deep-seated emotional issues.

Resistance to Change

One of the most significant obstacles in treating NPD is the narcissist's inherent resistance to change. Narcissists tend to view themselves as superior to other people, and because of this, they often fail to recognise the need for personal growth or development.

When faced with criticism, they often perceive it as a personal attack rather than an opportunity for self-improvement or introspection.

This resistance isn't passive; it's an active defence mechanism that stems from underlying insecurities and fears of vulnerability. At the heart of these defences is a deep-seated fear that acknowledging their flaws or imperfections will cause them to lose their sense of superiority. Therefore, their desire to avoid feelings of inferiority leads them to fiercely reject anything that might challenge their self-image.

This is why creating a safe and non-threatening environment is essential when working with narcissists. Therapists have to be patient and strategic in introducing new perspectives. It's critical for them to show that self-reflection and vulnerability are not signs of weakness but tools to strengthen their sense of self-worth.

In this context, it's crucial to build rapport slowly and establish trust. Over time, as the therapist presents challenges to the narcissist's self-perception, it becomes possible to shift their viewpoint, encouraging them to see self-examination as a means of growth, rather than a threat to their self-esteem.

Struggles with Empathy

Another profound challenge in treating NPD is the difficulty people with narcissism face when it comes to understanding and empathising with other people's emotions. It's not that narcissists are incapable of feeling emotions; they're capable of experiencing strong emotions, but they often struggle to recognise or value the emotional experiences of other people.

This lack of empathy manifests itself in many ways, including misunderstandings, arguments, and more destructive behaviours, such as manipulation or emotional abuse. This creates a significant barrier to building and maintaining healthy relationships.

Therapists have to work with narcissists in helping them acknowledge and recognise the impact of their behaviours on the people around them. This often involves working on emotional regulation, as people with NPD can have intense and disproportionate emotional reactions when their ego is threatened. For example, a seemingly minor disagreement might lead to an outburst of anger, defensiveness, or withdrawal. Part of the therapeutic process for someone with NPD is teaching them how to manage these emotional responses.

Emotional regulation techniques, such as mindfulness practices, cognitive restructuring, or relaxation exercises; can help narcissists to become more aware of their emotions and reduce their tendency to react impulsively.

By developing these skills, they can also start to see the emotional effects of their actions on other people, improving their ability to relate to other people with greater empathy.

Managing Expectations in Therapy

Working with narcissistic clients requires not only technical expertise but also patience. Progress tends to be slow, and it's important to remain realistic about what can be achieved in a relatively short amount of time. Narcissists can experience periods of breakthrough, followed by setbacks, and often, the therapy process can feel like two steps forward and one step back. This requires a steady, consistent approach. The key is to celebrate small victories along the way, such as moments of self-reflection or improvements in emotional regulation. For someone with NPD, these moments, albeit small, are significant signs of progress.

Overview of Therapeutic Treatments for Narcissistic Personality Disorder

Narcissistic Personality Disorder is complex, and treatment typically requires a long-term, multifaceted approach. Although there's no "cure" for NPD, the right therapeutic interventions can help people with the disorder manage their symptoms, improve emotional regulation, and build healthier, more fulfilling relationships.

Therapeutic treatments for NPD often focus on helping people increase self-awareness, develop greater empathy, and address underlying emotional wounds. Treatment isn't about eliminating narcissistic traits, but helping people learn how to manage them. This typically involves a combination of psychotherapy, self-help strategies, and the support of loved ones.

The goal isn't only to alleviate symptoms but also to foster a deeper understanding of the self and healthier ways of relating to other people.

Therapies for NPD address maladaptive coping mechanisms, such as the need for constant validation or external admiration and aim to replace these patterns with healthier ways of interacting with other people. Over time, therapy helps people address the deeper issues of insecurity and emotional vulnerability that fuel narcissistic behaviours, encouraging more balanced and realistic self-concepts.

Psychodynamic Therapy: Exploring Early Life Experiences

Psychodynamic therapy is one of the most commonly used therapeutic approaches for treating NPD. This form of therapy explores someone's early life experiences, particularly attachment relationships, to understand how these early interactions shaped their current personality traits. Often, the grandiosity associated with NPD is rooted in childhood experiences of emotional neglect, trauma, or rejection, which leads people to develop defence mechanisms like denial and projection. These defence mechanisms are designed to protect them from feelings of inadequacy and shame.

Through psychodynamic therapy, people can start to uncover these buried emotions and confront the deep-seated beliefs that drive their narcissistic behaviours. It's not uncommon for people with NPD to have an intense fear of being seen as weak, vulnerable, or unworthy.

However, by revisiting and processing these early experiences, therapy can help these people challenge the belief that they need to protect themselves through inflated self-importance or entitlement.

Psychodynamic therapy also delves into patterns of emotional dysregulation learned early in life, helping these people begin to "unlearn" the harmful patterns and develop healthier emotional responses.

Cognitive behavioural Therapy (CBT): Reshaping Thought Patterns

Cognitive behavioural Therapy (CBT) is another effective approach for treating narcissistic traits. Unlike psychodynamic therapy, which focuses more on the past, CBT targets the present thoughts, beliefs, and behaviours that contribute to narcissistic patterns. This approach is particularly helpful for addressing the distorted thinking that regularly underpins NPD. Narcissists tend to hold unrealistic beliefs about their superiority and entitlement, and struggle with negative self-perceptions when these beliefs are challenged. In CBT, people with NPD work to identify these harmful thought patterns and replace them with more balanced, reality-based thinking.

One of the core goals of CBT is to increase self-awareness and challenge cognitive distortions such as "all-or-nothing" thinking, overgeneralization, or catastrophizing. For example, if a narcissist feels slighted by a minor criticism, they can interpret it as evidence that they're worthless or unworthy. Through CBT, they can learn to reframe these thoughts and assess situations more objectively. By consistently challenging distorted thoughts, people can reduce their need for external validation and start to develop healthier self-esteem based on a more realistic sense of self-worth.

Additionally, CBT can help narcissists with emotional regulation. Since so many narcissists react impulsively or defensively when they feel criticised or rejected, CBT can teach them healthier coping strategies. This includes recognising emotional triggers, practising mindfulness, and implementing strategies like deep breathing or self-soothing techniques.

Over time, these skills can help reduce the intensity of emotional reactions, allowing them to interact more constructively with other people and navigate challenges with greater calm and perspective.

Schema Therapy: Addressing Deep-Rooted Emotional Wounds

Schema Therapy is an integrative approach that combines elements of CBT with psychodynamic therapy and experiential techniques. This therapy is especially useful for people with complex personality disorders like NPD because it addresses deep-rooted emotional issues that have been developed over a lifetime.

Schema Therapy focuses on identifying and changing these maladaptive core beliefs or patterns that influence how people perceive and react to themselves, other people, and the world.

For someone with NPD, these schemas often stem from early childhood experiences of neglect, criticism, or overvaluation. For instance, a person with NPD might have developed a schema of "defectiveness" or "unlovability," which drives their need for constant admiration and external validation. In therapy they can work to identify these schemas and learn how they contribute to their narcissistic behaviours. They also learn to explore the emotional pain behind these schemas, like feelings of worthlessness or inadequacy.

In Schema Therapy, the therapeutic relationship is central, because the therapist becomes a "corrective emotional experience" for the client.

Through a supportive, empathetic relationship, a therapist can help the narcissist start to understand the impact of their behaviours on other people and develop healthier ways of thinking and interacting.

For example, they could learn to replace self-criticism and shame with a more compassionate and balanced self-reflection.

Confronting ingrained emotional wounds, can help people with NPD start to heal and adopt healthier ways of relating to themselves and the world.

Dialectical Behaviour Therapy (DBT): Improving Emotional Regulation

Dialectical Behaviour Therapy (DBT) is another form of treatment that can be beneficial for people with NPD, particularly those who struggle with emotional dysregulation and impulsivity. Originally developed to treat borderline personality disorder, DBT has been adapted to help people with a variety of personality disorders, including NPD. This approach is based on the idea that people with emotional difficulties need to learn how to accept themselves while simultaneously striving for change.

DBT combines individual therapy with group skills training; it focuses on four core areas: mindfulness, distress tolerance, emotional regulation, and interpersonal effectiveness. For people with NPD, DBT can help by teaching them how to manage intense emotional reactions, like anger or shame, without resorting to destructive behaviours like narcissistic rage or withdrawal. It also helps these people develop healthier coping mechanisms for dealing with stress, criticism, and interpersonal conflicts.

Mindfulness is a central practice in DBT, helping people with NPD become more aware of their thoughts, emotions, and sensations. By increasing mindfulness, they can learn to pause and reflect before reacting impulsively. Distress tolerance techniques, such as self-soothing or distraction strategies, provide immediate relief when emotions become overwhelming.

These skills are crucial for narcissists who struggle with emotional impulsivity and find it difficult to manage feelings of vulnerability, rejection, or failure.

Medication for Co-Occurring Symptoms

While there's no medication specifically designed to treat NPD, some people with the disorder might benefit from medication to address co-occurring conditions, such as anxiety, depression, or mood swings. Medications, like antidepressants or mood stabilisers, can help manage these symptoms and make it easier for people to engage in therapy. Selective serotonin reuptake inhibitors (SSRIs), commonly used to treat depression and anxiety, can help alleviate some of the emotional distress that may fuel narcissistic behaviours.

However, medication should never be seen as a substitute for therapy. It's actually most effective when used in combination with psychotherapy. By addressing the underlying emotional issues that fuel NPD, therapy provides the tools necessary to make lasting changes, while medication helps to manage co-occurring symptoms that can hinder the healing process. It's also important for people to work closely with their healthcare providers to ensure that any medication prescribed is appropriate for their specific needs and is closely monitored for side effects.

Self-Help Strategies for Those Affected by Narcissistic Abuse

While therapeutic interventions for individuals with NPD are essential, it's equally important to provide support and practical strategies for people who have been affected by narcissistic abuse. Healing from narcissistic abuse can be a long and painful journey, but with the right tools and support, recovery is possible.

One of the first steps in recovering from narcissistic abuse is recognising the impact of the abuse and understanding the manipulative tactics used by narcissists. Narcissistic abuse often involves gaslighting, emotional manipulation, and control, which can leave the victim feeling confused, isolated, and unsure of themselves. For victims, the process of rebuilding self-esteem and gaining clarity about their experiences is vital.

This can involve keeping a journal to document thoughts and feelings, seeking therapy to process the trauma, and finding support groups or communities of people who understand the experience of narcissistic abuse.

Setting and maintaining boundaries is another key aspect of recovery. Victims of narcissistic abuse regularly struggle with boundaries, as narcissists routinely push them or disregard them altogether. Learning to set clear, firm boundaries is crucial for regaining control over your life and emotions.

This involves saying "no" when necessary, being clear about personal limits, and recognising that it's okay to distance yourself from toxic people.

Additionally, victims should focus on self-care practices to restore emotional balance.

This includes engaging in activities that bring joy, practising mindfulness or meditation to reduce anxiety, and surrounding oneself with supportive, empathetic people. Building a solid support network is essential in healing from narcissistic abuse. A strong support system provides validation, encouragement, and a reminder that the survivor is not alone in their struggles.

Conclusion

To wrap things up, I've taken a close look at the various challenges and therapeutic approaches when working with NPD.

The treatment of NPD is complex, and while no one-size-fits-all approach guarantees success, a combination of therapy and self-help strategies can significantly improve the quality of life for people with NPD, and the people around them affected by their behaviours.

Whether through psychodynamic therapy, CBT, Schema Therapy, or DBT, therapeutic interventions offer tools to manage narcissistic behaviours and address underlying emotional wounds.

For victims of narcissistic abuse, recovery is possible with the right support, self-care strategies, and a commitment to rebuilding self-worth and establishing healthy boundaries.

The path to healing may well be a long road, but with patience, perseverance, and the right interventions, it's possible to break free from the cycle of narcissism and regain control over your life. Whether you 're the one struggling with narcissism or you've been impacted by the actions of someone else with NPD, remember that change is possible, and you are not alone on the journey.

Chapter 26

Guarding the Entrance

Red Flags, Prevention, and Awareness of Narcissistic Traits

Raising awareness to foster healthy relationships

Raising awareness and prevention is the strongest defence against narcissism. It's crucial for spotting narcissistic traits early, before they can inflict lasting harm.

Personal Reflection:

If I'd noticed the red flags earlier, I could have saved myself years of heartache. Now, I make it a point to educate other people — friends, family, and clients — about the signs of narcissism. I've learned that awareness is power. The more people that understand these traits, the less likely they are to fall into the same traps I did.

In this section, I'll focus on the importance of awareness, education, and prevention, offering practical advice on recognising narcissistic traits early and avoiding narcissists altogether. My aim is to help you become more skilled at identifying these behaviours and protecting yourself from their damaging effects.

In a world where relationships play such a key role in our happiness and mental health, understanding the traits linked to narcissism is vital for emotional well-being.

Whether it's in your personal life or professional interactions, chances are you'll come across people who display narcissistic tendencies at some stage. These behaviours can often seem subtle at first but recognising them early allows you to set firm boundaries and shield yourself from emotional harm. By becoming more aware, you can avoid unnecessary pain and take charge of your emotions, safeguarding your mental health in the process.

This section highlights why raising awareness of narcissistic traits and focusing on prevention is so important. It'll give you the tools to protect your emotional well-being and build healthier, more balanced relationships where narcissistic behaviours aren't given the space to take root. With the right knowledge, you'll be able to recognise these traits before they cause harm, ensuring you stay one step ahead and avoid falling into the traps narcissists often set.

The Importance of Early Recognition

Spotting narcissistic behaviours early is one of the best ways to protect yourself from their long-term effects. The earlier you recognise these traits, the easier it is to respond in a way that keeps you safe. Early awareness lets you act before emotional ties deepen, saving yourself the heartbreak and pain that often come with relationships involving narcissistic people. By recognising the signs early, you can avoid becoming trapped in patterns of manipulation and emotional abuse, giving you the ability to safeguard your emotional health and well-being.

Red Flags: The Warning Signs You Can't Ignore

Spotting the signs of narcissistic personality disorder can be challenging, especially in the early stages of a relationship.

Narcissists often come across as charming, persuasive, and seemingly empathetic, making it hard to see through their polished exterior.

However, beneath this facade lies a consistent pattern of behaviour that reveals the true traits of NPD. Recognising the red flags early is crucial, as it helps protect you from manipulation, emotional exhaustion, and long-term harm.

The sooner you identify these warning signs, the better prepared you'll be to set boundaries and avoid getting caught in a toxic dynamic.

One of the first signs to look out for is someone constantly seeking your approval or validation.

At first, it might seem harmless or even flattering, but when this need becomes excessive and relentless, it's a clear warning. Narcissists crave admiration, and when they don't get it, they can become irritable or dismissive.

This isn't just about wanting praise — it's an insatiable demand that can quickly overwhelm the relationship. Over time, their constant need for attention creates emotional strain, chips away at your self-worth, and breeds resentment.

Another major red flag is their expectation that everything revolves around their needs and desires. If you find yourself constantly rearranging your plans, behaviour, or even your thoughts to suit them, it's a sign to step back and reassess. Narcissists rarely acknowledge or care about the needs of other people. They demand to be the centre of attention and expect everyone around them to fit into their narrative. This disregard for other people leaves you feeling drained, frustrated, and invisible, as though your feelings and needs don't matter.

Pay close attention if someone routinely dismisses your emotions or brushes off your concerns. This isn't a minor oversight — it's part of a larger pattern that shows a lack of empathy. Narcissists are incapable of genuinely understanding or relating to the feelings of other people. When they consistently invalidate your emotions or trivialise your worries, it's not a small character flaw — it's a clear indicator of how they operate. This behaviour leaves you feeling unheard, hurt, and devalued.

You might also notice that they take advantage of you, often in subtle ways at first. Narcissists are experts at turning relationships into one-sided arrangements, always seeking something to gain.

If they only reach out when they need something or exploit your kindness and generosity, it's a sign the relationship is centred on their needs rather than mutual care. This self-serving attitude can leave you feeling used and unappreciated, like you're always giving while they're always taking.

A recurring red flag with narcissists is their sense of superiority. They carry an air of arrogance, belittle other people, and act as though they're above rules or standards. This isn't just the occasional boast — it's a deeply ingrained belief that they're more important and deserving than everyone else. This superiority complex affects how they treat other people and their relationships, often leaving those around them feeling inferior or undervalued.

Be wary if you start doubting your own thoughts and feelings because of them.

Narcissists are skilled at making you question yourself, subtly twisting situations to shift the blame onto you. They'll manipulate events and make you feel responsible for their problems. If someone regularly uses guilt-tripping tactics or distorts the truth to make you feel at fault, it's a serious red flag. This kind of manipulation is one of the most damaging tools they use to maintain control and keep you emotionally tethered. Recognising it early is vital to protect your sense of self and avoid being ensnared in their games.

While the earlier section explored the broader red flags of narcissistic behaviour, these examples highlight specific warning signs to watch for. By understanding these subtle, everyday behaviours, you can spot the patterns of manipulation and control more clearly and protect yourself from their harm.

Some Warning Signs to Look Out For:

• **Overemphasis on Personal Achievements:**

If someone constantly boasts about their accomplishments and never acknowledges the contributions of other people, it's a clear sign of narcissistic traits. They make everything about themselves, constantly seeking praise and admiration.

These people often fail to recognise the value other people bring to the table and act as though they're the sole reason for any success. This self-centred approach can be draining for people around them.

- **Excessive Flattery and Charm:**

Narcissists are masters at using charm to draw people in. They shower you with compliments and affection, often making you feel special. While compliments can be genuinely appreciated, be cautious when someone is excessively flattering or overly charming early on. Their excessive attention can feel overwhelming and, more often than not, it's used to manipulate and control you. It's not about you — it's about them, and what they can gain from you.

- **Inability to Accept Criticism:**

A person with narcissistic traits typically reacts defensively when faced with criticism. They see any feedback as a personal attack and struggle to accept any kind of negative evaluation. Instead of seeing criticism as a way to improve, they get angry or dismiss it altogether. They refuse to take responsibility for their actions and will deflect blame onto other people, making it impossible to have constructive discussions or help them grow.

- **Lack of Genuine Interest in Other People:**

When someone is consistently more interested in talking about themselves than in listening to you, it points to a lack of empathy and self-absorption. These people often fail to notice or care about how other people feel, making the conversation all about their own experiences. They're so caught up in their own world that they rarely ask questions or show interest in other people's lives. Their need to be the centre of attention can leave you feeling unheard and unimportant.

You'll also notice a narcissist belittling the achievements of other people, sabotaging colleagues to make themselves look better, or subtly undermining your successes. This competitive behaviour isn't limited to the workplace — it extends into personal relationships as well. Instead of celebrating your progress, they resent it or try to make you feel small to elevate themselves. They thrive on feeling superior and will stop at nothing to make sure they dominate any situation.

When they can't elevate themselves to your level, they'll try to drag you down to theirs.

By staying vigilant and recognising these behaviours early on, you can assess whether the relationship is healthy or if it's time to stand clear, firm boundaries. Trust your instincts and take action before these toxic traits have the chance to cause lasting harm.

The Narcissist's Masks: Lessons in Deception

Narcissists don't show their true colours all at once. They wear masks tailored to the occasion, often reflecting the desires and vulnerabilities of those they wish to ensnare. In the beginning, they're everything you've ever wanted — attentive, kind, and seemingly devoted. It's only later, when the mask slips, that their true nature emerges.

Mask of The Charmer:

This is perhaps the most common guise. The narcissist showers you with attention, affection, and praise, creating a whirlwind romance that feels almost too good to be true. And it is. Their charm is a calculated tool, designed to make you lower your guard and invite them into your life.

Mask of The Victim:

Sometimes, a narcissist will present themselves as someone who's been wronged by the world. They share stories of betrayal and hardship, drawing you in with their vulnerability. It's a ploy to exploit your empathy, making you feel responsible for their well-being.

Mask of The Hero:

In some cases, they position themselves as the saviour, offering help, guidance, or solutions to problems you didn't even know you had. Their goal is to create a sense of dependency, making sure you feel like you owe them something in return.

Personal Reflection:

For years, I ignored the nagging feelings that told me something wasn't quite right. I kept wondering if maybe I was overthinking, being overly sensitive, or misjudging the situation. I convinced myself that perhaps I just didn't understand or was being unfair. But, in reality, the inner voice that seemed to whisper to me when I was alone was trying to warn me.

Breaking the Illusion: Trusting Your Intuition

Recognising a narcissist is a challenge in itself, but one of the hardest aspects is learning to trust your intuition again. Narcissists excel at creating cognitive dissonance — where their words and actions don't align. It's easy to get lost in their contradictions, where the chaos they generate makes you question your own perceptions. They might apologise for one thing, only to commit another offence moments later. This mental confusion is precisely their aim — to make you doubt yourself.

Narcissists breed doubt, making it incredibly hard to trust your own judgment. Their behaviour, such as sudden emotional shifts or contradictory statements, chips away at your ability to rely on your instincts. One moment they might tell you how much they care, and the next, they'll be cold, dismissive, or even hostile. This creates a mental fog, making you question reality.

Reclaiming your intuition is a personal journey, one that involves recognising that your instincts — no matter how faint they may seem — are valuable.

This can be the toughest part because you've spent so long doubting yourself. But when you begin to listen to your inner voice, whether it's the uneasy feeling in your gut or the thought that something doesn't feel right, you're starting to reclaim your sense of self.

Trusting your intuition takes practice and patience. Listen to that voice, even if it's quiet or you're uncertain. Acknowledge that your emotions and instincts are valid, even if they contradict what someone else is telling you. They're a part of you, and in the face of a narcissist, they might be your only reliable defence.

Ask yourself:

Does this person's behaviour match their words?

Do I feel safe, respected, and valued around them?

If the answer is no, don't ignore it. Trust the feeling of unease; it's a reflection of a reality you might not be ready to face yet.

The more you practice listening to and trusting your intuition, the more powerful it becomes. Eventually, it'll become your greatest ally, helping you keep narcissists at arm's length.

Learning to trust yourself again is an act of self-preservation. It's a major step towards breaking free from the manipulation and regaining your independence.

Challenging the Misconceptions

One of the biggest obstacles to recognising narcissistic abuse is how society romanticises toxic behaviours. The belief that jealousy signals love, that persistence means care, or that possessiveness is devotion fosters the illusion that narcissistic traits are just part of a passionate relationship.

These misconceptions create fertile ground for narcissists to thrive, as their behaviours are mistaken for love or commitment. They use these false beliefs to manipulate and control.

When a narcissist is possessive, jealous, or controlling, they'll disguise it as love or concern. They'll insist they care so much that they want to protect you, or that their extreme emotional reactions are signs of deep feelings. But these behaviours aren't love — they're tools of control.

Breaking these misconceptions begins with recognising the truth: Love isn't about control, and respect isn't earned through fear or submission. Narcissists might disguise their need for control as love,

336

presenting jealousy and possessiveness as signs of deep affection. But real love creates trust, respect, and freedom, not fear and manipulation.

Healthy relationships are built on mutual trust, open communication, support, and equality — not power games.

Genuine love empowers both people to grow independently and together, while narcissism thrives on control and emotional manipulation.

We need to challenge the idea that narcissistic abuse or manipulation means love. By redefining what love should look like, we can empower people to make better choices in their relationships.

This shift won't happen overnight, but every conversation, every book, and every shared story brings us closer to a world where narcissists have fewer places to hide.

The Cost of Ignoring the Signs

What happens when we overlook or dismiss these red flags?

The result is narcissistic abuse — a whispering war — a quiet, underhanded battle waged against your mind; a slow, creeping shadow that poisons everything in its path, systematically eroding your soul and leaving devastation in its wake.

Personal reflection:

I speak from experience. By the time I realised what was happening, I was a shadow of my former self. My confidence was shattered, and my trust in other people was destroyed. It took a long time to rebuild what she'd stolen from me. But I consider myself one of the lucky ones. Too many people stay trapped in these toxic dynamics, unable to find a way out.

This is why prevention is crucial. The sooner you recognise the signs, the easier it is to escape.

Education for Prevention

Knowledge is power. The more you understand narcissistic behaviours and tactics, the better equipped you are to recognise and respond to them. One of my greatest tools in escaping the maze of narcissistic abuse was knowledge. I studied psychology.

Studying psychology and reflecting on my relationship with someone who had comorbid narcissistic personality disorder, as well as studying the psychology of abuse, gave me the language to describe what I'd been through.

But education wasn't just about gaining intellectual insight — it was about recognising the patterns, manipulations, and warning signs I'd ignored for far too long. Narcissism isn't just about grandiose behaviour or obvious selfishness. It's subtle, insidious, and hard to identify, especially when you're emotionally invested.

Recognising this difference was pivotal in helping me separate my emotions from the reality of the situation.

For me, it was like switching on a light in the darkness. Suddenly, the patterns were clear, and I could see the labyrinth for what it was.

Education isn't just about academic knowledge; it's about experiencing abuse. It's about setting healthy boundaries, emotional intelligence, and self-respect. It's also about connecting with other people who've walked the same path, and that combination is a powerful tool for healing.

Prevention begins early, and its ripple effects can change lives. Teaching other people about emotional intelligence, self-respect, and recognising unhealthy behaviours has become life changing.

Building Resilience: A Shield Against Narcissism

- ### Practice Self-Reflection

Regular self-reflection helps you understand your thoughts, emotions, and reactions. By recognising what triggers your emotional responses, you can develop greater awareness and respond more effectively to challenging situations with narcissistic people. Self-awareness allows you to respond with strength and clarity, helping you stay in control and avoid manipulation.

- ### Cultivate Emotional Intelligence

Emotional intelligence helps you recognise, understand, and manage your own emotions, while also empathising with the feelings of other people. This awareness makes it easier to spot red flags early in relationships, allowing you to respond to narcissistic behaviour with confidence. Strengthening your emotional intelligence equips you to navigate complex interactions and create healthier, more balanced connections.

- ### Embrace Change and Adaptability

Life is unpredictable, and we all face challenges. Adaptability is crucial to resilience, as it helps you adjust to new situation.

It helps you keep moving forward despite adversity. Embracing change strengthens your capacity to recognise and cope with difficult situations, helping you stay grounded and maintain your emotional well-being.

- ### Healthy Relationships

The people you surround yourself with impact your emotional resilience. By nurturing positive, supportive relationships, you build a foundation of strength that helps you weather the emotional storms caused by narcissists. These relationships act as a buffer, providing emotional support and helping you maintain balance.

Awareness is just part of the equation. To protect yourself fully, you need to cultivate emotional resilience. This means developing the strength to set boundaries, say no, and walk away when necessary.

- **Strengthen Your Self-Worth**

Narcissists prey on insecurity. By building a strong sense of self, you become less vulnerable to their manipulation. This might involve therapy, self-help books, or simply surrounding yourself with supportive people.

- **Practice Assertiveness**

Learning to assert your needs and enforce boundaries is essential. Narcissists thrive on control, but when you take that control away, their power diminishes.

- **Develop a Support Network**

Isolation is a narcissist's ally. By staying connected to friends, family, and support groups, you create a buffer against their influence.

Resilience doesn't mean you won't encounter narcissists — it means you'll be better equipped to handle them when you do.

A Journey Worth Taking

Reflecting on my journey, I realised that escaping narcissistic abuse isn't just about escaping pain — it's about moving toward something better. It's about opening the door to healthier, more fulfilling relationships, embracing joy, freedom, and reclaiming your life.

When you learn to recognise red flags and trust your instincts, you open the door to stronger, more authentic connections. Escaping the emotional grip of a narcissist isn't easy, but it's a journey worth taking.

With each step forward, you 'll move closer to the person you were always meant to be. There will be challenges, moments of doubt, fear, and guilt. But every time you stand your ground and resist manipulation; you grow closer to your true self.

The rewards are immeasurable.

In the aftermath, you'll rediscover parts of yourself that were hidden — perhaps buried under lies, guilt, or exhaustion. Once free, you'll begin to trust your own voice again, make decisions aligned with your values, and set goals that reflect who you truly are.

You'll find your strength, rebuild your confidence, and remember who you are — outside of the toxic grip of someone who never deserved your love.

Take this knowledge with you. Use it to protect yourself and the people you care about. The labyrinth may be dark, but you hold the key to staying out of its grasp.

Trust yourself — you're stronger than you realise.

Conclusion

Narcissistic Personality Disorder can manifest in both subtle and extreme ways, but certain behaviours consistently stand out.

Recognising these warning signs early is essential for protecting yourself from the emotional chaos of narcissistic relationships.

Whether it's the manipulative tactics, the constant need for admiration, or the cycle of idealisation and devaluation, understanding these red flags equips you to set healthy boundaries and avoid the narcissist's web.

Safeguarding your emotional well-being requires awareness, resilience, and self-worth. By recognising narcissistic traits and arming yourself with knowledge, you empower yourself to create healthier relationships and strengthen your emotional defences.

This chapter is my way of handing you a torch to illuminate your path, helping you spot the dangers ahead before they consume your peace of mind.

Chapter 27

Escaping the Labyrinth

Recovery, Healing, and Self-Care After Narcissistic Abuse

Strategies for overcoming narcissistic abuse and rebuilding self-esteem

In this chapter, I'll break down what it really takes to recover from narcissistic abuse and share self-care strategies that support long-term healing.

I'll also focus on practical steps you can take — like setting firm boundaries and rebuilding your self-esteem — to help you regain control and start moving forward.

Understanding Narcissistic Abuse

Before we get into recovery, it's important to understand what narcissistic abuse actually is. It's not like physical abuse where the damage is visible. Narcissistic abuse is subtle, creeping in through emotional manipulation, gaslighting, and controlling behaviour. Over time, it chips away at your confidence and sense of reality, leaving deep psychological scars.

Recovery isn't just about physically walking away. Recovering from narcissistic abuse is a long and challenging journey — the emotional damage runs deep, and it doesn't simply disappear once the relationship ends. The manipulation can leave you doubting your self-worth and your decisions for years.

Personal Reflection:

The hardest part of my recovery wasn't cutting ties with her — it was learning how to rebuild my sense of self after years of emotional abuse. I'd internalised so many of her criticisms and doubts, that I no longer trusted my own judgement. Journaling and support from family and close friends helped me slowly piece myself back together. But it wasn't an easy process. Healing from narcissistic abuse isn't linear — it's a winding road, much like the labyrinth itself.

Healing the Narcissist — Is It Possible?

When you're caught in a relationship with a narcissist, it's easy to hope they might change. You might even believe that if you love them enough, or support them enough, they'll eventually heal. But the reality is far more complicated. Healing for a narcissist is a difficult process because it demands something they struggle with the most — self-awareness. Without the ability to reflect on their own behaviour and recognise the harm they cause; meaningful change is almost impossible. Their deep-rooted resistance to facing their own pain stops them from even acknowledging that they need help.

The idea of healing a narcissist can be tempting, especially if you've invested a lot into the relationship. But their transformation, if it ever happens, depends entirely on their willingness to change — and that's usually lacking. Even when therapy is involved, like cognitive behavioural therapy, it's just the first step. Real healing demands humility and vulnerability — two things' narcissists find almost unbearable. They would need to confront the pain they've spent their entire lives avoiding, and that's no easy task.

It's important to recognise that their healing isn't your responsibility. You can't force someone to change, no matter how much you want to.

Recovery and Healing Yourself

For people in relationships with narcissists, their recovery and healing journey can be frustrating. Narcissists' emotional wounds cause them to behave in toxic ways, leaving their partners feeling emotionally drained.

However, understanding where these behaviours come from, without excusing or enabling them can be a key part of protecting yourself. Maintaining strong boundaries while offering empathy is a difficult but important balance to strike.

Recovery and Healing — The Difference

Recovery:

Recovery is the immediate phase of restoring some sense of stability and safety following the trauma of narcissistic abuse.

During this stage, you start the difficult process of rebuilding your self-esteem, recognising the manipulative tactics the narcissist used, and beginning to break free from the toxic patterns of the relationship. It's about learning to protect yourself emotionally and physically, setting boundaries, and gradually regaining normality in your daily life.

At its core, recovery is about survival — getting through each day while you rebuild your self-esteem and break free from toxic patterns. It's also about learning how to stand up for yourself and start the process of reclaiming your voice.

This will involve distancing yourself not only from the narcissist but also from the enablers or "flying monkeys" that they might have used to maintain control.

This can be one of the hardest aspects to face — letting go of the false hope that the narcissist will change or provide the closure you desperately wanted. Recovery isn't about waiting for a shift in their behaviour — it's about recognising the truth and learning how to navigate the aftermath.

Throughout recovery, you'll experience moments of confusion and emotional chaos while you struggle to regain a sense of safety and control. This emotional toll is heavy, but it gradually becomes more empowering. It's about learning how to protect yourself, finding emotional independence, and ultimately, building a foundation that will allow you to start growing again.

Recovery marks the moment when you start to regain stability and focus on the future.

Healing:

Healing, on the other hand, is a much deeper process. It goes beyond just feeling better or getting through each day. Healing is about facing and processing the emotional and psychological scars left by narcissistic abuse. It's a long-term journey of reclaiming your sense of self-worth, rediscovering who you are, and finding a way to move forward without the constant weight of guilt, shame, and anger that often follow this kind of trauma.

Healing requires confronting emotions that were suppressed during the abuse. It's about learning how to feel and express those feelings safely, so they no longer control you. The narcissist's manipulations might have made you doubt your own perception of reality, but healing is the process of regaining trust in yourself and, over time, in other people. It's about addressing the emotional wounds caused by the abuse and learning how to love and trust yourself again, without the narcissist's toxic influence clouding your judgement.

As you move through healing, you'll start to rebuild the broken pieces of your identity. This stage is about transforming your emotional pain into strength, resilience, and peace. Healing doesn't happen overnight, and it isn't linear — it's about gradually learning to live without the constant emotional manipulation and re-establishing a healthier connection with your own worth. It's a process of moving from mere survival into true emotional resilience.

Where recovery is about regaining function, healing is about creating a new, healthier version of yourself. It's the emotional work that restores your sense of identity, enables you to build new, positive relationships, and prepares you for a fulfilling life that's free from the narcissist's toxic influence.

Letting Go of the Narcissist's Control

One of the hardest challenges after a narcissistic relationship is accepting that the narcissist won't take accountability for their actions. Narcissists rarely admit fault because they need to maintain control and superiority. Even if they do reach out, it's usually for their own benefit — seeking validation or attention — not to make amends or offer closure.

Holding onto the hope that they'll change keeps you emotionally trapped. The longer you wait for them to take responsibility, the more power you give them over your emotional state — even if they're no longer physically in your life. Focusing on your own healing and growth is far healthier than waiting for an apology, that to be blunt, won't ever come.

Shifting Focus to Your Healing

Letting go of the narcissist's control is hard, but it's crucial for your recovery.

If you find yourself repeatedly going over the same feelings of betrayal, it's normal to feel stuck. Narcissists have a way of manipulating your emotions, making you long for validation that might never arrive. But here's the truth: healing starts when you focus on yourself, not on the narcissist's behaviour.

You might have spent a lot of emotional energy hoping they would change or take responsibility. That hope can keep you tied to the past. Instead, focus on practical steps you can take to regain control of your life. Seek support from friends, a therapist, or other people who understand what it's like to survive narcissistic abuse.

You deserve to heal, and the first step is to stop waiting for the narcissist to change.

Reclaiming Your Dreams

It's natural to feel like the narcissist stole your heart, and your dreams, when the relationship ended. You likely invested a great deal emotionally, and now it might feel like your future has been taken away. But here's an important truth: those dreams were real because they belonged to you, not the narcissist. They don't vanish just because the narcissist isn't in your life anymore.

Reclaiming your dreams is an essential part of healing. You've got the power to create a future that's not defined by the narcissist's actions or how they made you feel. It might be difficult to imagine new dreams right now, but the act of reclaiming — or even reshaping them — will help you move forward.

The road to recovery can be long and fraught with difficulties, but it can lead to transformative change. Establishing a supportive therapeutic relationship, setting realistic expectations, and maintaining ongoing support are crucial for successful treatment.

Focusing on a Future Without the Narcissist

When you've been deeply hurt, it's tempting to look for someone new who can reignite the same dreams you once had. You might feel that these hopes and desires are tied to the person who caused the pain. But the truth is, what you're really looking for is the emotional connection and sense of security you envisioned. Those dreams can still exist without the narcissist; they're a part of you.

The key is realising that new dreams can take shape, even if they look different from before. Your next relationship won't be a repeat of the past; it'll be something entirely new. Focus on finding someone who shares your values and wants to build a future with you based on mutual respect and shared goals. Look for qualities that create the healthy relationship you deserve, instead of falling back into the patterns of your past.

Healing from Narcissist Induced Guilt

One of the most damaging effects of narcissistic abuse is the guilt they force upon you. Even when you gave everything you had to the relationship, the narcissist likely twisted things to make you feel entirely responsible for their behaviour and the relationship's failures.

Narcissists are masters at projecting their insecurities onto you, leaving you doubting your own thoughts and feelings.

They shift the blame onto you, making you question your worth and your ability to trust your own judgement. Over time, this emotional manipulation causes you to carry guilt that was never yours to bear and letting go of this false responsibility is a vital step in healing.

But remember this: your efforts were genuine, and they mattered. You did your best, and the relationship's failure wasn't a reflection of your value, but of the narcissist's inability to appreciate what you brought to the table. Narcissists make you feel like nothing you do is ever good enough, but that's their manipulation, not your reality.

Releasing this guilt takes time, but it can be done. Start by acknowledging all the things you did right. Reflect on how much you gave and cared and remind yourself that you deserved a relationship where your efforts were met with the same level of commitment.

Writing these thoughts down or sharing them with someone supportive, whether it's a therapist or a trusted friend, can help you start letting go of the narcissist-imposed guilt and reclaiming your sense of self.

Conclusion

Taking Back Your Power:

Recovery from narcissistic abuse is a personal and challenging journey, filled with ups and downs, moments of doubt, and gradual steps forward. The effects of emotional manipulation, trauma, and identity loss can leave lasting scars, but with each small step forward, you begin to regain the control the narcissist tried to steal from you.

The key is giving yourself the space to heal. By acknowledging your pain, setting boundaries, and rebuilding your identity, you start to reclaim your sense of self-worth. Healing isn't an event; it's a process. You don't need to have all the answers right now, and there's no rush to figure everything out. Be patient with yourself, knowing that every small step brings you closer to freedom and peace.

Your value was never determined by how someone else treated you, or how they made you feel.

You're worthy of love, respect, and happiness. By taking control of your healing journey, focusing on self-care, and rebuilding your life, you can create a future no longer defined by abuse.

Narcissistic abuse may have taken a toll on you, but it doesn't define your future. Employing practical strategies for healing, building self-worth, and creating healthy boundaries allows you to regain control of your life and emerge stronger than ever. It's time to let go of the past and focus on the future you can build for yourself — one filled with the peace and happiness you deserve.

Chapter 28

Journeys Through the Labyrinth

Case Studies of Narcissistic Behaviour

Case studies highlighting the complexities of narcissistic behaviour and recovery

This chapter delves into the experiences of victims, survivors, and even narcissists trying to find their way toward recovery, it shares diverse stories from people who've navigated their way through narcissistic relationships, offering valuable lessons on resilience, healing, and hope.

Narcissistic behaviour is elusive, complex, and often hard to grasp, especially for people who've experienced it firsthand. Real-life case studies help us understand the different ways narcissism shows itself and the impact it has on people's lives.

These case studies reveal the harsh realities faced by people caught in the grip of narcissistic behaviour. They highlight important lessons learned and offer a sense of hope to anyone still navigating the labyrinth of narcissism.

Personal Reflection:

While my own story might seem extreme, it's not unique. Since training in psychology I've spoken with countless people whose lives have been upended by narcissistic partners, parents, or friends. The common factor in all these stories is the feeling of being trapped, whether by love, obligation, or manipulation. But what these stories also have in common is hope. Recovery is possible, and these real-life accounts show that no matter how dark the labyrinth seems, there is always a positive way out.

Case Studies and Personal Stories to Highlight the Dynamics

Case Study: John's Narcissistic Friend

John had been friends with David for ten years. In the beginning, David's outgoing and confident personality drew John in. David was always the centre of attention, and John admired his ability to command a room. Over time, however, John realised that David only reached out when he needed something; whether it was a favour, validation, or company when he felt lonely. When John tried to set boundaries, David became distant and critical. The friendship ended when John realised, he'd been giving more than he was receiving and that David saw him as disposable.

Lessons Learned:

- ### Recognising Self-Worth:

John's experience highlights the importance of recognising and valuing your own needs in a relationship. Understanding that friendships should be reciprocal helps prevent situations where one person is giving significantly more than they're receiving.

- ### Boundaries as Protection:

Setting and maintaining boundaries is essential, especially when dealing with people who take advantage of other people. John's attempt to set boundaries revealed the true nature of his friend's intentions, emphasising that boundaries can serve as a crucial tool for self-preservation.

- ### The Value of Healthy Relationships:

This case demonstrates the necessity of looking for friendships that are balanced and nurturing. John's realisation that his friend saw him as disposable underscores the need to choose relationships that offer genuine support and mutual respect.

Case Study: Emma's Romantic Relationship with a Narcissist

Emma, a 29-year-old marketing executive, met Mark, a charismatic and successful man. At the beginning of their relationship, Mark showered Emma with gifts, attention, and love, making her feel like she'd found the perfect partner. However, after a few months, Mark's behaviour began to shift. He criticised Emma's appearance, made her feel inadequate, and began to withdraw emotionally whenever she expressed her own needs. When she tried to leave, Mark convinced her to stay by promising to change, only to repeat the same patterns of emotional manipulation. After years of emotional abuse, Emma finally left the relationship, but it took her time to rebuild her self-esteem and trust in future relationships.

Lessons Learned:

- ### The Power of Red Flags:

Emma's relationship shows how important it is to notice early signs of manipulation and control. Recognising red flags like criticism, emotional withdrawal, and conditional affection can help people identify unhealthy relationships before they deepen.

- ### Breaking the Cycle:

Emma's experience underscores the difficulty of leaving a manipulative relationship, particularly when promises of change are repeatedly broken. This case highlights the courage required to break free from an abusive cycle and prioritise your own well-being.

- ### Reclaiming Self-Worth:

After her relationship ended, Emma needed time to rebuild her self-esteem and trust in other people. Her story illustrates the impact that narcissistic abuse can have on self-worth and the importance of focusing on self-care and healing after leaving such a relationship

Case Study: Laura's Struggle: The Emotional Rollercoaster

Laura was in a relationship with a man who, at first, seemed perfect. Charming, attentive, and full of promises, he showered her with affection during the early stages. However, the relationship soon began to take a darker turn.

Laura's partner would alternate between extreme affection and harsh criticism, leaving her feeling confused and unstable. This cycle of idealisation, devaluation, and discard; a hallmark of narcissistic relationships, left Laura questioning her own worth. She became hyper-vigilant, constantly trying to keep him happy, but nothing she did ever seemed to satisfy him.

Lessons Learned:

- #### The Narcissistic Cycle:

Laura's experience is a prime example of the narcissistic cycle, where a person is idealised, then devalued, and finally discarded when they no longer serve the narcissist's needs.

- #### The Power of Manipulation:

Narcissists use emotional manipulation, like guilt-tripping, gaslighting, and passive aggression, to control their victims.

- #### Recognising the Signs:

Laura's story underscores the importance of recognising these patterns early on. Identifying the red flags; like inconsistent behaviour, lack of empathy, and controlling tendencies; can help people protect themselves before getting too deeply entangled.

Case Study: Mark's Reflection: From Narcissist to Awareness

Mark, in his 40s, had always been the life of the party. Confident, outgoing, and constantly looking for validation, he struggled with deeper emotions.

For much of his life, he'd been unaware that his behaviour was rooted in narcissism, he'd belittle other people to make himself feel superior and had a hard time forming meaningful connections because he was only interested in relationships that would feed his ego.

Eventually, Mark hit rock bottom. His personal and professional relationships began to fall apart. Friends stopped inviting him out, his romantic relationships ended, and he faced mounting conflicts at work. At this low point, Mark decided to seek help. Through therapy, he began to understand how his narcissistic traits; like a lack of empathy, the need for admiration, and an inability to handle criticism; were hurting the people around him and isolating him from the people who cared about him.

Lessons Learned:

- ### Self-Awareness is Key to Change:

Mark's journey emphasises that while narcissism can be entrenched, recovery is possible with self-awareness and a willingness to change. Narcissists might not initially recognise their behaviour as harmful, but with the right support, they can begin to understand its impact.

- ### The Role of Therapy:

Therapy plays a crucial role in helping narcissists reflect on their behaviour and its consequences. Cognitive Behavioural Therapy (CBT) and Schema Therapy are commonly used approaches for addressing narcissistic traits.

- ### Empathy as a Catalyst for Change:

Learning to develop empathy is one of the most important steps for narcissists seeking recovery. By recognising and understanding the emotions of other people, they can start to build deeper, more genuine relationships.

Case Study: Rebecca's Rebirth: Life After Narcissistic Abuse

Rebecca had been in an abusive relationship with a covert narcissist for five years. Unlike overt narcissists, her ex-partner was more subtle in his manipulation. He didn't openly demand attention or admiration but instead used passive-aggressive tactics to undermine Rebecca's confidence, he'd dismiss her emotions, criticise her ideas, and subtly accuse her of being overly sensitive. The emotional abuse left Rebecca feeling anxious and emotionally drained.

It wasn't until she confided in a friend who had also been in a similar relationship that Rebecca realised the pattern she'd been living in. With support, Rebecca made the difficult decision to leave her partner, but the journey to recovery was just beginning. For months, she experienced intense emotional turmoil, guilt, shame, and sadness. However, with time, therapy, and self-care practices, Rebecca began to rebuild her life.

Lessons Learned:

- **Covert Narcissism is Just as Harmful:**

Rebecca's case illustrates that covert narcissism can be just as damaging as overt narcissism. The subtlety of the manipulation can make it harder for the victim to recognise the abuse, but it's still abuse.

- **Healing Takes Time:**

Recovery from narcissistic abuse isn't linear. Rebecca's story shows that healing is a process filled with setbacks and breakthroughs. It's important to be patient and not rush the journey.

- **Support Networks Are Essential:**

Having a strong support system of friends, family, or a therapist who understands the patterns of narcissistic abuse is vital for healing. Rebecca found solace in sharing her experience with other people who had been through similar situations.

Case Study: Nina's New Beginning: Healthy Boundaries After Narcissistic Abuse

Nina had been in a toxic friendship with a woman who displayed narcissistic tendencies for years. Initially, their friendship seemed fun and exciting, but over time, Nina began to feel used. Her friend would turn conversations back to herself, never acknowledging Nina's struggles, and consistently demanded her attention without ever offering support in return.

Nina's breaking point came when her friend manipulated a group of mutual friends to turn against her, causing her to lose several important relationships. After taking time to reflect, Nina realised that her friend's behaviour was emblematic of narcissism and that she needed to distance herself to protect her mental health. She began setting stronger boundaries, limiting her exposure to toxic people, and rebuilding her sense of self.

Lessons Learned:

- **Toxic Friendships are Real:**

Narcissistic behaviour can occur in any kind of relationship, not just romantic ones. Nina's experience highlights how narcissistic friendships can be just as harmful as abusive romantic relationships

- **Setting Boundaries is Crucial:**

After cutting ties with her narcissistic friend, Nina focused on learning how to set healthy boundaries in her relationships. She realised that maintaining her mental and emotional health meant protecting herself from toxic influences, even if that meant losing people along the way.

- **Rebuilding Trust:**

While Nina had lost some friends during the conflict, she began to rebuild stronger, more supportive relationships with other people who shared her values. This helped her trust people again and realise that not everyone had the same narcissistic tendencies.

How These Journeys Provide Hope, Insight, and Understanding

These case studies all provide valuable insights into the complex patterns of narcissistic behaviour. Each journey offers a different perspective on how narcissism affects lives, whether through emotional manipulation, a lack of empathy, or the abuse of power in personal relationships.

The most important lesson we can take from these case studies is that recovery is possible.

Whether you're a victim, a survivor, or someone who recognises narcissistic traits in themselves, there's always hope for change.

Understanding the signs of narcissism and taking the necessary steps to protect yourself — whether through therapy, setting boundaries, or seeking support — can make a world of difference.

Ultimately, these stories remind us that while narcissistic behaviour can cause significant pain and disruption, it doesn't define us. With self-awareness, support, and a commitment to healing, it's possible to navigate the labyrinth of narcissism and emerge stronger on the other side.

Conclusion

In conclusion, let's reflect on what we've learned about narcissism: It's a multifaceted concept with deep historical, psychological roots.

The key characteristics we've discussed — grandiosity, the need for admiration, lack of empathy, and entitlement — demonstrate just how complex this issue is.

Understanding narcissism and its effects on relationships is vital. It provides an insight into how these traits develop, manifest, and impact people's lives.

Chapter 29

Reflections from the Labyrinth

Personal Reflections from My Own Journey Through the Abyss

Final personal reflections on narcissism's complexities, its impact, and my personal journey to understanding and healing.

Escaping from the labyrinth of narcissistic abuse was far from straightforward. It was full of twists and turns, forcing me to confront painful truths while rediscovering who I was. As I reflect on my maze of experiences, I find myself revisiting the dark corridors, the hidden traps, and the brief glimpses of light that shaped my escape.

These reflections aren't just about understanding the impact of narcissism; they're about recognising the strength I uncovered and the potential for healing.

Reflection:

In the beginning, it felt like I was trapped in a maze with no way out. But now, looking back, I can see how much strength I found during the dark moments. Each reflection brings me closer to understanding not just the relationship, but also the person I became because of it. A stronger and wiser version of me emerged from the labyrinth.

The Complexity of the Narcissism

The narcissism I faced wasn't obvious; it took on many forms — masquerading as humility, self-pity, victimhood, and even narcissistic altruism, all while she hid a deeply rooted need for control and validation.

Her weapon was ambiguity. She didn't always attack me directly but instead created a web of confusion and manipulation that left me constantly off-balance.

Reflection:

At the time, I couldn't see her manipulation for what it was. She seemed so kind, and so self-sacrificing, but there was always something beneath the surface — a dark side, like a shadow just out of reach. It was a slow, poisonous process, and it took me years to realise that I wasn't in a relationship; I was caught in a snare.

She wasn't outwardly cruel or demanding; instead, she excelled at playing the victim. She made me feel responsible for her well-being and emotional state. Her needs always seemed urgent and legitimate, while mine were dismissed as trivial and unimportant. She manipulated me, drawing me into an emotional cycle where I gave endlessly and received almost nothing in return.

Reflection:

I'd internalised her needs believing they were my responsibility. She had a way of making me feel as though I was the only one who could fix things. The more I gave, the more she needed, and the more exhausted I became. Looking back, I realise now how much I sacrificed just to keep her from withdrawing or becoming angry. But nothing was ever enough.

Understanding this complexity has been a double-edged sword. On one hand, it allowed me to recognise the patterns and tactics of her narcissism.

On the other hand, it forced me to confront difficult truths about my own vulnerabilities.

Why had I allowed this to continue?

What part of me had ignored the red flags, and rationalised her behaviour?

These questions weren't easy to face, but they were essential to my recovery.

Reflection:

I had to face the uncomfortable truth that part of me had enabled the abuse. I'd ignored warning signs, believed the lies, and justified her behaviour just to avoid conflict. It wasn't about weakness — it was about a need for her love and acceptance, and left unchecked, it blinded me to the manipulation I was living with.

She knew how to pull me close just enough to keep me invested, but never really enough to fulfil me. This push-me-pull-you dynamic created an addictive cycle of hope and despair, leaving me perpetually striving for a connection that stayed just out of reach and never truly materialised.

Looking back, I can see how this cycle eroded my self-worth, leaving me trapped in a relationship that was emotionally and psychologically unsustainable.

Reflection:

As I reflected on our time together, I began to recognise a pattern. The moments of closeness were always fleeting, leaving me chasing them like searching for water in the desert. The pain of never being enough was exhausting and drained me, but I couldn't stop, hoping that the next time would be different.

The complexity of narcissism has the ability to shape-shift. Narcissists wear so many different masks; One moment they're caring and attentive, the next, they're distant and cruel. This unpredictability hooked me in, leaving me trying to figure out who she'd be today, and what she'd expect from me.

The longer it persisted, her lack of consistency bred confusion and insecurity, making it harder to distinguish where the manipulation ended, and reality began.

I was left questioning my judgment, and the uncertainty became a heavy weight, pressing down on my mind, clouding my thoughts and feelings.

Reflection:

This shape-shifting unpredictable behaviour was one of the most damaging aspects of the relationship. I spent so much energy trying to anticipate her moods, and meet her needs, that I lost sight of myself in the process. I was so entangled in her web that I couldn't hear my own voice anymore. I couldn't distinguish it from the distorted version she created for me.

The Journey's Impact

The emotional toll of narcissistic abuse on me was profound, its effects rippled through every aspect of my life.

For me, the impact was both immediate and long-lasting. At the height of the abuse, I felt like a shadow of myself — exhausted, confused, and constantly on edge. I doubted my perceptions, questioned my instincts, and began to lose sight of who I was.

Reflection:

I had no idea how much I'd lost until I started to reconnect with who I really was. I'd become so entangled in her version of me that I couldn't remember the person I used to be. It took time, but with each step away from the relationship, I started to remember that I wasn't just a reflection of her needs; I had my own needs, my own desires, and my own worth.

One of the most damaging aspects of her narcissistic abuse was the erosion of my self-trust. I knew something was wrong, but after a few words from her, I was often left wondering whether I'd imagined it all.

Over time, this constant self-doubt became debilitating. I found myself second-guessing every thought, every action, and every emotion. What used to be a simple act of self-assurance became a complex web of doubts and contradictions.

Reflection:

It felt like living in a constant haze, where my thoughts and instincts seemed to betray me. I'd been so deeply conditioned to doubt myself that when I began to rebuild my confidence, it was like navigating uncharted territory. Trusting myself again wasn't easy — it was a battle to reclaim what had been stolen.

The gaslighting wasn't just about distorting facts; it went much deeper, warping my very sense of identity. She manipulated my words, intentions, and character so thoroughly that I barely recognised myself. I felt like a puppet, with every action dictated by her wants and demands.

The constant tension of waiting for the next emotional ambush kept me in a state of high alert. It was exhausting — mentally, emotionally, and physically. I couldn't trust my reactions anymore, let alone the motives of someone who was supposed to be my partner.

In those darker moments, it felt like I was losing fragments of who I was. The weight wasn't just emotional — it was the disorienting inability to separate reality from the twisted games she played.

Reclaiming my sense of self felt like piecing together a shattered mirror, one shard at a time.

The psychological toll of the abuse only deepened as she constructed her version of events. In her narrative, she was always the hero or the victim, and I was the perpetual villain.

This version of reality was reinforced through subtle comments, manipulative conversations, and carefully orchestrated scenarios designed to shift the blame onto me.

Over time, I began to internalise her story, convinced that I was the root of the relationship's dysfunction. Guilt and shame became constant companions, eroding my sense of self-worth piece by piece.

Reflection:

The guilt was suffocating. I was always trying to prove my worth and fix the unfixable, trying to make things right. Her imposed sense of guilt was overwhelming. I couldn't see how much she was warping reality, until I stepped back and realised that everything was simply her fabricated version of events, not the truth.

The damage was incessant. The physical toll became undeniable. My body was reflecting abuse I hadn't even fully recognised. When I began to heal, it wasn't just my emotional state that improved, but my health as well. It was a reminder that narcissistic abuse doesn't just break you emotionally; it can destroy you physically.

Reflection:

The abuse affected both my mental, and my physical health, my relationships with other people, and even my professional life. I became withdrawn, unable to focus, and constantly anxious. The stress took a toll on my body, manifesting in major health consequences; fatigue, frustration, depression, headaches, and even a heart attack, along with other symptoms that I didn't initially connect to the emotional strain I was under.

It wasn't until I began the process of healing that I realised just how deeply the abuse had infiltrated my life. The exhaustion wasn't just a result of my sleepless nights — it was a reflection of the energy that I expended trying to navigate an impossible relationship; one that drained me of everything I had to give.

The Journey to Understanding

Understanding the dynamics of narcissistic abuse didn't happen overnight. It was a gradual process, one that took patience, introspection, and a willingness to confront uncomfortable truths. For years, I lived in a fog of confusion, unable to explain what was happening to me. It wasn't until I began educating myself and training in psychology that the pieces of the puzzle began to fall into place.

Reflection:

It took years for me to understand that her love wasn't actually love at all. It was control, manipulation, and validation-seeking, disguised as affection. Once I realised this, I could finally start to break free from the hold she had on me.

I devoured information about narcissistic behaviour, learning about tactics like gaslighting, triangulation, and projection. These terms gave me the language to describe my experiences and helped me recognise the patterns I'd been so blind to.

Knowledge became my armour, protecting me from falling back into the same traps. But understanding narcissism wasn't just about identifying her abusive behaviour; it was also about understanding myself.

Why had I stayed in the relationship for so long?

Why had I ignored the warning signs?

These questions weren't easy to answer, but they were paramount for my growth.

Reflection:

I began to realise that it wasn't just her behaviour I had to confront; it was my own beliefs, fears, and insecurities. The questions I asked myself weren't about blaming myself but about understanding what kept me in that toxic cycle for so long.

I started to explore the deeper wounds that had made me susceptible to manipulation. I examined my own need for validation, my fear of conflict, and my tendency to prioritise other people's needs over my own.

This painful process of self-discovery was liberating. It forced me to confront aspects of myself that I'd ignored for a long time, but it also gave me the tools to break free from the patterns that had kept me trapped. I started to see the relationship wasn't a failure on my part, but a painful chapter that taught me invaluable lessons about my own worth and resilience.

Reflection:

I realised that this wasn't just about surviving the abuse, it was about healing the parts of me that had been wounded since I met her. Studying psychology didn't just help me understand her behaviour — it helped me understand the ways I'd let myself be damaged.

Understanding narcissistic abuse also allowed me to detach from the emotional weight that she'd placed on me. Her behaviour reflected her own dysfunction, not a statement of my inadequacy. This realisation was a powerful turning point in my healing. For the first time, I saw myself as a survivor, not a victim. I'd been subjected to manipulation and abuse, but that didn't define me. I could now see that I had the strength to rebuild my life and that I deserved to live authentically, free from the constraints of someone else's toxicity.

Reflection:

I stopped seeing myself as someone who'd been broken by the relationship, and started seeing myself as someone who had learned, grown, and emerged stronger. My identity wasn't tied to the abuse anymore — it was defined by my ability to reclaim my life.

My Path to Healing

Healing from her narcissistic abuse wasn't easy. It was a long and winding road, filled with speed bumps, roadblocks, moments of clarity, and breakthroughs. For me, the journey began with an eventual single terrifying decision: to stop pursuing the relationship.

Making that choice, even though it was difficult, marked the first step, not just physically, but mentally too. It meant letting go of the hope she'd change, the need for her approval, and the guilt that she'd instilled in me.

Letting go wasn't just about cutting ties — it was about breaking free from the emotional and mental chains that had kept me captive. Each day without her now feels like a victory.

Reflection:

Healing wasn't about erasing the past or forgetting what happened. Instead, it meant learning to carry the experiences with strength and transforming them into wisdom that would shape my future.

Training in psychology gave me a space where I could process my emotions, challenge the distorted beliefs I'd developed, and start rebuilding my self-esteem.

I learned to set boundaries — not just with her, but with myself. I stopped blaming myself for the abuse and accepted the truth for what it was — a toxic relationship that I had the power and strength inside me to leave behind.

Reflection:

Psychology didn't just help me understand the complexity of my feelings; it gave me the tools to create the emotional distance I needed to heal.

Self-care was another cornerstone of my recovery. For years, I'd neglected my own needs, pouring all my energy into keeping the relationship afloat.

Rediscovering the importance of self-care was a revelation. It wasn't just about taking care of my physical health; it was also about nurturing my emotional, and mental well-being. I started writing, meditating, and reconnecting with things that made me happy.

Reflection:

Self-care wasn't just about external changes; it was about finding peace within myself. It was about learning to be kind to myself again and give myself permission to heal.

Rediscovering My Identity

One of the most profound parts of my journey was rediscovering who I am. Narcissistic abuse eats away at your identity, leaving you feeling like an empty shell.

Reclaiming my identity after the abuse was a gradual process of reconnecting with my passions, values, and aspirations.

I had to rebuild myself from the ground up, rediscovering who I was outside of her influence.

Reflection:

I had to relearn who I was; not based on her expectations but based on what made me happy and fulfilled. The more I rediscovered myself, the more I realised that I wasn't just surviving her — I was thriving without her.

Rebuilding my identity meant I had to learn how to set boundaries, communicate my needs, and prioritise my well-being. It wasn't easy, especially after years of being conditioned to put her needs first. But it was a necessary step, redefining these habits allowed me to create a healthier, more fulfilling life.

Reflection:

Redefining relationships wasn't just about other people — it was about redefining my relationship with myself. Once I learned to prioritise my own needs again, healthier interactions naturally followed, and I attracted connections that reflected self-respect.

I also had to confront the fear of vulnerability. For a long time, I saw vulnerability with weakness, convinced it was the reason I was targeted by a narcissist. Through my journey, I've now learned to see vulnerability as a strength. It's what allows us to connect with other people, to love, and to heal. Embracing vulnerability has been one of the most empowering aspects of my recovery.

Reflection:

Embracing vulnerability wasn't just about being open with other people — it was about being honest with myself. That honesty proved I had the strength to heal.

I then started by reflecting on who I was before the relationship.

What made me?

What were my dreams?

These questions helped me with the parts of me that I'd lost, suppressed, or forgotten. I also explored new interests and experiences, giving myself permission to grow and evolve.

Reflection:

Rediscovering my dreams was like reclaiming lost pieces of myself. Every new interest and every experience were a piece of me coming back to life.

Lessons from the Labyrinth

Looking back on my journey, a number of important lessons stand out.

Firstly, healing isn't about erasing the past; it's about finding its meaning. The pain I experienced was real, but it also taught me valuable lessons about resilience, self-worth, and the power of choice. The pain wasn't something that had to be erased — it was just something that needed to be understood.

Every painful moment gave me strength, and they all became part of my growth.

Secondly, healing isn't a destination; it's a journey. There's no magic formula or timeline for healing. Healing takes patience, compassion, and a willingness to face your pain.

Reflection:

Healing isn't linear, and it doesn't have a set time frame. I had to stop rushing it and accept the process for what it was — a personal journey with no clear end.

I eventually realised I'm not defined by the abuse I went through. It's a part of my story, but it doesn't define the whole story, nor does it define who I am.

Reflection:

I'm more than my pain, my past, or the scars I carry. Those scars are just reminders of the strength I've gained along the way.

One of the key lessons I learned was how to respect my feelings without guilt. For so long, I'd buried my emotions to avoid conflict. Now, I let myself feel anger, sadness, resentment, and fear. I understand that these emotions aren't just valid; they're vital for my healing.

Reflection:

Respecting my emotions marked a turning point. I realised they weren't a weakness, but a testament to my resilience and recovery.

A New Chapter

The future will still come with challenges. This journey has been one of the toughest experiences of my life, but it's also been one of the most transformative. I'm not the same person I was when I entered the labyrinth. What once felt like an endless struggle has become a source of growth.

Even through the pain, I've grown and changed. I've learned to trust myself again, to listen to my instincts, and to embrace who I've become. That trust is the foundation of my freedom.

While the road ahead won't always be easy, I've gained the strength to face it. I'm proud of who I am now, and for that, I'm deeply grateful. For the first time in a long time, I can say with confidence that I'm free.

Closing this chapter brings me hope and gratitude. The labyrinth may have shaped me, but it hasn't defined me. No matter how lost you feel or how deep the abyss seems, there's always a way out.

Healing won't happen overnight, and the road may be long, but it'll be full of opportunities to grow, and it'll be worth it.

Reflection:

My journey out of the narcissists' labyrinth wasn't just about me escaping; I want my story to show that anyone can escape too.

Escaping the labyrinth is more than a journey.

It's a compass to freedom !

This concludes:

"The Labyrinth of Narcissism"

"Journey Through a Toxic Kaleidoscope"

"Remember"

"Recovery gets you on your feet. Healing brings you peace."

"Stay strong and keep moving forward."

"Some of the worst journey's lead to the best places" !

THE END

About the Author:

Gary Woods is dedicated to understanding the human mind and behaviour. Holding international advanced diplomas in Psychology and Advanced Cognitive Behavioural Therapy (CBT), he has cultivated a deep understanding of cognitive processes and emotional patterns. His studies have expanded to include areas like Advanced Cognitive Therapy, Psychiatry, Depression, and the Science of Brain Disorders, along with a focused expertise in narcissistic personality disorder.

Through further exploration, Gary has developed a keen interest in Neurophysiology and Neuro-instrumentation, connecting the intricate workings of the brain to the challenges faced by individuals navigating mental health struggles. As an accredited and certified Professional Life Coach and Mentor, he brings both academic insight and practical tools to help others on their journey of healing and self-discovery.

Gary's approach combines rigorous study with compassion and real-world personal experience, offering readers a bridge between complex psychological concepts and their real-world application, particularly in the realm of narcissistic abuse recovery and personal growth.

Having personally navigated the effects of narcissistic abuse, Gary's insights are grounded not only in academic study but also in firsthand experience, offering a deeply compassionate perspective on healing and growth.

Connect with Gary Woods:

Website: **PsychPositivity.Com**
Email: **info@psychpositivity.com**
Social media: **https://linktr.ee/psychpositivity**

Other Works by Gary Woods:

Escape from the Labyrinth

Available Formats for:

The Labyrinth of Narcissism
"Journey Through a Toxic Kaleidoscope"

Hardback	(Matte 6 x 9)	**ISBN:** 978–1–0683446–0-2
Hardback	(Glossy 6 x 9)	**ISBN:** 978–1–0683446–5-7
Paperback	(Matte 6 x 9)	**ISBN:** 978–1–0683446–4-0
Paperback	(Glossy 6 x 9)	**ISBN:** 978–1–0683446–1-9
Special Edition (Personalised)		**Special order only**

Please contact Vanguard Publishing House directly at:

info@VanguardPublishingHouse.com quoting reference **TLONSE** to order your preferred personalised edition.

(Please also be sure to include your preferred message or dedication in the email)

www.ingramcontent.com/pod-product-compliance
Lightning Source LLC
Chambersburg PA
CBHW051242020426
42333CB00025B/3021